# The Marriage Motive: A Price Theory of Marriage

Shoshana Grossbard

# The Marriage Motive: A Price Theory of Marriage

## How Marriage Markets Affect Employment, Consumption, and Savings

Springer

Shoshana Grossbard
San Diego
California
USA

ISBN 978-1-4939-4250-3 ISBN 978-1-4614-1623-4 (eBook)
DOI 10.1007/978-1-4614-1623-4
Springer New York Heidelberg Dordrecht London



Printed on acid-free paper

Springer is part of Springer Science+Business Media (www.springer.com)

*This book is dedicated to Gary Becker, my mentor, who unexpectedly died while I was writing this book.*

# Acknowledgments

I am grateful to all those who helped me with this book: the extraordinary economics teachers who inspired me early on and helped me develop my ideas on marriage: Gary Becker, Milton Friedman, Jacob Mincer, H. Gregg Lewis, Edward Lazear, James Heckman, and T.W. Schultz; Ronald Cohen, the anthropologist who served in my dissertation committee and opened my eyes to the realities of marriage among the Kanuris; my coauthors J. Ignacio Gimenez, Jose Alberto Molina, Alfredo M. Pereira, and Victoria Vernon for allowing me to use materials that we wrote jointly; earlier coauthors with whom I published articles mentioned in this book: Catalina Amuedo-Dorantes, Shoshana Neuman, and Xuanning Fu; Joni Hersch and Victoria Vernon for providing me with specific computations; Glenda Sachs Jaffe and Oana Tocoian for helpful comments on most of the book; Marina Adshade, George Davis, Leta Hong Fincher, Andrew Francis, Joni Hersch, Nacho Gimenez, Charles Horioka, Bertrand Lemennicier, Jose Alberto Molina, Sonia Oreffice, Michal Shechtman, and Elena Stancanelli for helpful comments on selected chapters; Hazem Alshaikhmubarak for helpful research assistance; Lorraine Klimowich and Jon Gurstelle at Springer for their encouragement and assistance; Brian Halm, Anoop Kumar, and Puja Kumari at Springer for their help with copy editing and preparation for production; and the Department of Economics and the College of Arts and Letters at San Diego State University for supporting my research.

I also thank my children, Michal Hannah, Zev Mordechai, Chaim Yehoshua, and Esther Chava, and the many generations of students who studied economics of marriage with me at San Diego State University and elsewhere, for motivating me to write this book. I hope my ideas will help them find success and happiness. Finally, I thank my husband Robert Yaronne for his encouragement and support, for doing much of the WiHo in our home while I was writing, and for his helpful comments on the manuscript.

# Contents

## Part III Consumption and Savings

# Chapter 1
# Introduction

## Introduction

Price theory is a founding block of economic theory, especially according to the Chicago school of economics in which I was trained. In this book, price theory is used to analyze how economic outcomes—employment, other time uses, consumption, and savings—are related to marriage markets. Marriage is defined as a couple with at least one person who engages in household production. Couples could cohabit without being married. Unless otherwise assumed, couples could differ in their sexual orientation.

## Marriage Markets and a Price Mechanism: A Chicago Approach

My approach is Chicagoan in two ways. First, it heavily relies on price theory. According to Milton Friedman (1976), winner of the 1976 Nobel prize in economics, there are only two organizing principles for organizing an economy: the market principle and the command principle. The market principle needs prices to operate; hence the central importance of prices and price theory.

Second, my approach is Chicagoan as it was influenced by Gary Becker's expansionist view of economics. Becker started the *New Home Economics* (NHE) with Jacob Mincer while they both taught at Columbia University in the 1960s (see Becker 1960, 1965; Mincer 1962, 1963). Some call the NHE the Chicago–Columbia approach to household economics.[1] According to the NHE, marriages are

[1] Becker studied at Chicago and taught there most of his life (before and after moving to Columbia). Mincer received the postdoctoral degree at Chicago and was a Visiting Professor there in the 1970s.



S. Grossbard, *The Marriage Motive: A Price Theory of Marriage*,
DOI 10.1007/978-1-4614-1623-4_1

nonprofit firms that organize household production. Becker published his theory of allocation of time while still at Columbia and his economic theory of marriage soon after moving to Chicago in 1969.

How do marriages organize production and distribution? What explains allocation of individual men and women into marriages? Friedman had an unambiguous answer to the first question. As stated in his textbook, *Price Theory,* "The principle of organization operating in the household is similar to that employed in a collectivistic society—central authority. The major difference is that participation in the household is voluntary for adults. But even this difference does not exist for children." (Friedman 1976, p. 4). Since Friedman's textbook first appeared, in 1962, USA and other Western countries underwent fundamental changes. How often do Westerners think of surrendering to a central authority when marrying in the second decade of the twenty-first century? If Friedman is right and there are only two ways of organizing production—market or command—and we limit the role of the command principle, then we have to give more room to the market principle.

This book examines how competitive marriage markets and implicit or explicit price mechanisms possibly affect (1) matters of production, allocation, and distribution related to marriage, and (2) economic behavior—related to employment, consumption, and savings—that responds to such prices.

Explicit prices related to marriage go back to ancient times. Jacob had to pay Laban for Rachel and Leah according to Genesis. What Jacob and other men from times immemorial have paid for a bride is now called a bride-price. Sometimes the money goes in the other direction and women or their parents pay a dowry prior to marriage. Dowries and bride-prices can still be found in many parts of the world, and their coexistence in India led Martin Bronfenbrenner (1971) to write the first economic analysis of marriage.[2] Soon after, Becker (1973) published the first price theory of marriage, introducing competitive marriage markets with implicit prices. Consequently, price theory of marriage is applicable anywhere, even when there are no explicit prices for brides, grooms, or the work they do for each other.

## The Impact of Gary Becker, Pioneer in the Economics of Marriage

Gary Becker's theories of the family were singled out as one of the reasons why he was awarded the Nobel Prize in economics in 1992. He passed away in May 2014 but his ideas live on. This book is heavily influenced by Becker's price theory of marriage, a theory that consists of two separate models: a macro and a micro demand and supply model. Both involve market equilibria, implying optimal implicit prices and quantities as well as allocative efficiency. Becker (1973) emphasizes how these models can also help to analyze intramarriage distribution problems by

[2] Bronfenbrenner had received the PhD degree in economics at Chicago in 1939.

placing them in a section entitled "Division of Output Between Mates."[3] In particular, using his macromodel, he offers the first derivation of a sex ratio effect on personal consumption of wives and husbands (Becker 1973, 1981, Chap. 2). In this book, sex ratios play an important role: the relative number of men and women in a marriage market affects the price of marriage. Like Becker, I follow the traditional definition of sex ratio introduced by demographers: the number of men divided by the number of women.

In addition, (Becker 1973) Fig. 2 presents a micro-Marshallian partial equilibrium model for one particular type of man and one type of woman, with multiple types of men and women participating in separate but interrelated markets. In each market, there are homogeneous women and men.[4] I also follow Becker in the sense that I have separate macro and micro price-theoretical models. However, our models are different, as is explained below.

Becker's (1965) model of allocation of time also inspired me.[5] This model can be applied to single individuals (which is how it was presented in Becker 1981), to separate individuals in a two-person household who act independently and take the other's income into account in their budget constraints, or to a household blending the identities of two people. In the *Treatise on the Family* (Becker 1981) and in Becker's (1973) earlier article on marriage a couple's production function is joint and Becker does not elaborate on how households make decisions regarding the allocation of individual time to the household's production. I use Becker's allocation of time model as an independent individual model applicable to individuals in couples.[6]

Becker's opus in economics of the family contains many other models, but they have had little impact on my research. In addition to the two price-theoretical models already mentioned, Becker (1973, 1981) also presented sorting models of marriage based on Koopmans and Beckman (1957) and Gale and Shapley (1962).[7] In principle, Becker could have used his Marshallian model to analyze both allocation and distribution problems. Instead, Becker (1973) gives limited weight to the Marshallian partial equilibrium model by placing it after sorting models addressing the allocation problem and a macro demand and supply model. The Marshallian model fares even worse in the *Treatise*, from which it is removed altogether.[8] Furthermore,

---

[3] More on Becker's theories of marriage in a comparative perspective can be found in Grossbard (2010).

[4] In more recent terminology, this model can be labeled as "hedonic." Rao (1993) is possibly the first to use the "term hedonic" to describe this kind of multimarket Marshallian model. Hedonic markets were first introduced by Sherwin Rosen (1974).

[5] This model is closely related to Mincer (1963).

[6] An earlier model that can be characterized as is an independent individual model is Robbins' (1930) individual labor supply model. More on independent individual models of the household can be found in Grossbard (2011).

[7] Becker's last analytical publication on marriage is a chapter with Kevin Murphy in their book *Social Economics* (2000). It includes a sorting model of marriage and no Marshallian model.

[8] See Grossbard (2010) for possible reasons why Becker did not include his microlevel demand and supply model in the *Treatise*.

a reader of the *Treatise* could easily form the erroneous impression that the macro demand and supply model of marriage is only relevant in a polygamous society, for it is placed in a chapter on polygamy.

In addition to various economic analyses of marriage, Becker's *Treatise* also includes unitary household models in which households are modeled as collectivistic agents with a combined utility function, joint household production function, and/or joint budget constraint.[9] In the 1970s, Becker seemed comfortable having a variety of models of family decision making.[10] His nonunitary price theories of marriage—featuring private utility functions—(Becker 1973, 1974a) appeared in print about the same time as his most well-known unitary model, Becker (1974b), which includes the rotten kid theorem. His approach, and that of most other professors at Chicago in the 1970s, was pragmatic: if a model helps to develop interesting testable implications, it is worth keeping. Friedman's emphasis on positive economics ruled. All theoretical models are welcome, as long as they "work."

Younger generations of scholars may have obtained a different impression of Becker's approach to the family after he published his *Treatise* in 1981. Becker's *Treatise*, one of the most frequently cited books in economics according to Google Scholar, conveys the sense of a unified theory. As a result, those who learned about Becker's models of decision making in households after 1981 may perceive his unitary models as more central to his opus on the family than those of us who learned from him before the *Treatise's* publication. For many years, I presumed that researchers interested in the family would be familiar with both of Becker's price-theoretical models. After I discovered that some prominent economists studying marriage were unaware of Becker's (1973) microlevel Marshallian model of marriage, I started making a conscious effort to explain that in both Becker's and my own price theory of marriage there is a macro- and micromodel. This book's structure emphasizes that: Part A contains a chapter at the macrolevel (II) and microlevel (III). Part B on labor supply has a chapter at the macrolevel and two chapters at the microlevel. The chapters in Part C contain both levels, with subtitles to clarify whether the level is macro or micro.

## My Price-Theoretic Models of Marriage

My economic modeling of marriage diverges from Becker's in a number of ways.

First, my models of marriage are all price-theoretical models. Becker offers a wide selection of marriage models, including price-theoretical models. In displaying this preference for price theory I am not alone: most other economists of marriage exposed to Becker's ideas before the *Treatise* became popular; all have used price-theoretical models of marriage more than Becker did. (More on what other economists have written is found in the Appendix to this chapter.)

---

[9] The term "unitary" was coined by Browning et al. (1994).

[10] Woolley (1996) also recognizes that it is possible to separate Becker's various models and adopt some but not all.

Second, Becker's marriage markets are markets for brides and grooms whereas my marriage markets are markets for work-in-household (WiHo) defined as time in household production that benefits the spouse (see Chap. 2). These markets then establish implicit prices that influence reservation wages and labor supply decisions. I model spouses as employing each other and maintaining their separate identity as worker and employer of WiHo after marriage. Most of my models also have spouses acting as private consumers, so there is nothing joint in my basic models (but some of my models allow for joint consumption, see Chap. 8 for example). Modeling wives and husbands as participants in WiHo markets place me on the extreme individualistic side of the individualistic–collectivist continuum of theories of the household (see the Appendix for a brief review of some other theories).

Third, Becker's theories of marriage have focused on marriage-related outcomes (such as marriage rates, polygamy rates, divorce, or bride-price) while I have also emphasized outcomes other than marriage. This book is about the marriage motive when studying more conventional topics in economics: labor supply, consumption, savings, and household production time.[11]

## The Marriage Motive

The major theme of this book is that marriage motives underlie the main economic behaviors of workers and consumers. How much people work, how much they earn, what kind of work they engage in is partially motivated by their marriage goals and commitments. To the extent that they participate in marriage markets the prices in these markets are among the parameters influencing their employment and wages. The marriage motive also influences consumption and savings decisions, as pointed out by Horioka (1987, 1997) in the economic literature on savings.

There are diverse forms of marriage motives. Some motivate individuals considering marriage or divorce. For example, among the explanations that have been given for the marriage premium in men's wages is an argument rooted in traditional gender roles stating that men want to earn more so they can attract or keep a wife (see Grossbard-Shechtman 1993, Chap. 12; Ahituv and Lerman 2011). Assuming the same traditional gender roles, it has been argued that when anticipating divorce, married women may be more motivated to enter the labor force than if their marriage is expected to last (Johnson and Skinner 1986). Japanese women anticipating marriages are less likely to save than their counterparts with low marriage probability, according to Kureishi and Wa.

Other marriage motives apply to parents who want to marry their children in societies where premarital payments are relatively high. Japanese parents report saving to help find the right mate for their children once they reach marriageable age (Horioka 1997). They may also work longer hours to make their children more attractive in the marriage market.

[11] Most of my research on marriage outcomes is covered in *On the Economics of Marriage: A Theory of Marriage, Labor and Divorce* (Grossbard-Shechtman 1993).

For marriage motives to influence economic behaviors there must be prices. In a traditional society allowing divorce and remarriage, how much money does it take for a husband to make his wife happy so she will not leave him? That clearly varies across economies. In Maiduguri, Nigeria, in the 1970s, it did not take much to make a wife happy according to anthropologist Ronald Cohen (1967): a roof over her head, a few dresses, and getting her turn on a regular basis when the husband was polygamous and followed Muslim laws mandating equal treatment of all wives. The divorce rate was high and often initiated by women unhappy with their husband and knowing that in a polygamous society they had many marriage opportunities (until they reached a certain age…). Traditional couples in Western countries today, or in Japan, have other prices in mind. What lifestyle corresponds to a "fair price" for the women doing much of the home production in the world? It varies across cultures and across classes within the same country.

Many women today refuse any such price and are motivated by an egalitarian marriage motive. In turn, this leads them to typically work full time and enter well-paying jobs. But are egalitarian marriages beyond prices and marriage motives? It is possible that contemporary modern women in the West are paying a price in order to afford egalitarian marriage. For example, if a particular man has a choice between two women with exactly the same traits but one is willing to do his laundry and the other is not, it may cost the liberated woman a small price to attract this man. Maybe she needs to be prettier than her competition, or nicer, or maybe have a higher income. After all, according to the American Time Use Survey, in 2012 men aged 20–55 spent an average of 5.58 min a day on doing laundry, in contrast with 19.37 min for women. There seems to be widespread willingness to do their husbands' laundry among American women.

Whether we like it or not, prices—implicit or explicit—are set in the various marriage markets in which most of us participate and help to explain how much we work, buy, or save. The prices are mostly taken for granted and behind the scenes, but when sex ratios vary they become more obvious, especially if sex ratios change dramatically.

## Sex Ratios

Sex ratios, defined as the number of men divided by the number of women in a marriage market, have been studied by demographers at least since Glick et al. (1963) and Henry (1975). If sex ratios exceed 1, men are in oversupply; if they are smaller than 1, there is a surplus of women. Becker (1973) is the first economist to have used the concept. A recent use of sex ratios in economic analysis comes from macroeconomists studying savings. As discussed more at length in Chap. 11, using data from China and cross-country comparisons Du and Wei (2013) and Wei and Zhang (2011) have documented that when sex ratios are higher, that is, women are scarcer in marriage markets, savings go up. They interpret these sex ratio effects as evidence of a *competitive savings motive*: men (or their parents) competing in marriage markets may need to save to acquire the expensive items that will attract wives.

Thinking about the term "competitive savings motive" has helped me arrive at this book's title: the *marriage motive*. Their term does not point to the root cause of the competition, namely, the desire to marry among many individuals participating in the same competitive marriage markets. If sex ratios affect savings, it is a consequence of the underlying desire to marry that really motivates savings. When sex ratios exceed 1 competition among men in the same marriage market will be more intense relative to a situation of balanced sex ratios or sex ratios smaller than 1. The worse the imbalance the more men are likely to save.

Furthermore, for the marriage motive to affect savings it is necessary that some kind of implicit or explicit price mechanism operates in marriage markets: individuals belonging to the gender in oversupply (or their parents) compete by offering higher "prices" to members of the scarce gender. In other words, those in oversupply seem to "buy" access to spouses or partners.

The marriage motive is also based on the assumption of heterosexuality and on cultural definitions of gender roles. The more traditional these roles the more it is likely that men "pay" in various forms.

The marriage motive can also explain what people consume after they marry. If divorce and remarriage are feasible, the competition does not end once marriage is entered. Men in oversupply need not only to save to entice women to marry them; they also need to do things to keep their wives when competitors may be interested in marrying their wives in case of divorce. Another aspect of the implicit price of marriage that men may pay in traditional cultures is the one that was mentioned in Becker (1973): allowing wives to access their personal income so their wives' personal consumption can exceed their own earnings.

Sex ratio effects on personal consumption of men and women can be tested to the extent that consumption is assignable to individuals. Certain consumer goods are known to benefit one gender more than the other (this varies cross culturally). For example, previous research has established that men tend to smoke more tobacco and to consume more alcohol than women do (see Chap. 10). It follows that the higher the sex ratios and the more men have to compete for scarce women, the more they may do things to keep the wives they have. Consequently, men will make more of an effort to smoke less and drink less alcohol. In Chap. 10, I also report some evidence from China obtained by Maria Porter (forthcoming, 2015): when sex ratios are higher and women are scarcer in marriage markets men consume less tobacco and alcohol.

Both the research by Wei and Zhang (2011) on savings and that by Porter (forthcoming, 2015) on consumption is based on recent dramatic increases in sex ratio due to China's one-child policy. According to a price-theoretical approach to marriage markets, both consequences indicate that the market value of women's time in marriage has increased. Men (or their families) need to pay higher prices to obtain wives and to keep them.

In contrast, the research reported in this book that documents sex ratio effects on labor supply was originally inspired by observing the consequences of very low sex ratios in the USA at the time when women born at the end of the World War II entered marriage markets.[12] Higher sex ratios raise the implicit market price of women's WiHo that benefits men, what I call WiHo (see Chap. 2). Therefore, when sex ratios are higher women will have a higher disposable personal income and will have less of a need to get their own income from employment in the labor force. Higher sex ratios are also likely to influence men's labor supply: if they have to pay more to get and keep a wife they will be more motivated to work, to choose careers that pay better, and to invest in their earnings potential. They may also earn higher wages. More on sex ratios and labor supply is found in Chaps. 4 and 6. There and in the Appendix of Chap. 7, I also report evidence from the USA showing that when sex ratios are higher and women are scarcer in marriage markets, women are less likely to participate in the labor force. They may also be employed for fewer hours. In contrast, labor supply by men may increase when sex ratios are higher. Chapter 8 suggests how sex ratio effects can be integrated into a graphical analysis of labor supply.

It is striking that these results for three different outcomes and two different countries are all consistent with the same story: (1) individual economic behavior is driven by a marriage motive (differently for men and women given that both societies have traditional gender roles, albeit in different ways); (2) individuals participate in competitive marriage markets affected by sex ratio imbalances, and (3) some kind of price mechanism operates in these marriage markets so that when sex ratios are more imbalanced in favor of women individual men (or their relatives) get signals that they should save more (especially before marriage), consume less (especially after marriage), and earn more in the labor market, while women get signals to work less in the labor market.

Another major application of my approach is the analysis of effects of compensating differentials in marriage on employment, consumption, and savings.

## Compensating Differentials

Compensating differentials are rooted in the Marshallian microversion of the theory presented in Chap. 3. When applied to labor markets a compensating differentials analysis leads to testable implications such as "garbage collectors earn more than drivers because there is a more limited supply of people willing to collect garbage." Applying a similar logic to marriage markets in Chap. 5, I present the following testable prediction involving compensating differentials in marriage: *women who are young relative to their husbands are likely to supply less labor to the labor force* (*Testable Implication TU12*).

[12] This idea first appeared in Heer and Grossbard-Shechtman (1981) and Grossbard-Shechtman (1984).

In the garbage collector example, the compensating differential is a difference in wage: the differential between the wage of a garbage collector and that of a driver. In the marriage market example, the compensating differential is the difference between two unobserved implicit prices of WiHo supplied by traditional women: that of identical young women, some married to old husbands and others to young husbands. The compensation in the labor market is for the undesirable aspects of garbage collection not experienced by drivers, while the compensation in the marriage market is for the undesirable aspects of an old husband relative to a husband of the same age. In the labor economics example, the testable outcome is the wage differential itself. In the marriage example, the testable outcome is a consequence of the difference in implicit price of WiHo: when married to a much older man a young woman can live the lifestyle of a trophy wife, and is likely to supply less labor to the labor force.

This implication was tested in Grossbard-Shechtman and Neuman (1988), using data on Jewish Israeli couples. Women were less likely to be employed when their husbands were substantially older: those older men may have paid compensating differentials relative to men who are younger. Grossbard-Shechtman and Fu (2002) documented compensating differentials in marriage in Hawaii by examining married women's labor force participation as a function of husband's ethnic group's status relative to that of the wife. It could be inferred that when married to a Hawaiian a Caucasian woman was getting a higher implicit price than when married endogamously to a Caucasian man, and therefore she was less likely to participate in the labor force. More on compensating differentials in marriage markets and labor supply can be found in Chap. 5.

In a recent study on compensating differentials in marriage, Chiappori et al. (2012) found that an additional unit of husband's body mass index (BMI) can be compensated by a 0.30 % rise in husband's average wage and an additional unit of wife's BMI can be compensated by a 0.15 % increase her average wage. The implication is that if individuals considered fat have a marriage motive they will need to earn more in the labor market in order to find a mate of given quality. According to the price theory of marriage presented in this book, behind these findings are people with a marriage motive, competition among potential mates in interrelated marriage markets, and a price mechanism that establishes prices for mates with differing physical appearances.

Compensating differentials are generated whenever those on the demand side in a particular market for WiHo have characteristics that only appeal to few people supplying their WiHo. Other characteristics that could be associated with compensating differentials in marriage and, therefore, with labor supply are mentioned in Chap. 5.

In addition to its testable implications for labor supply (employment) and wages the compensating differentials in marriage argument can also shed light on consumption, as explained in Chap. 10, and savings (see Chap. 11). To derive predictions regarding compensating differentials in any trait that matters and for any of the economic outcomes discussed above, we use the same three steps needed to obtain sex ratio effects: (1) a marriage motive that drives individuals to have a demand or a supply of WiHo; (2) competition in the marriage markets (i.e., markets for WiHo) in which they participate; and (3) some competition takes the form of price competition.

## Caveats

First, most of my models assume a traditional, gender-based division of labor according to which women are principally responsible for household production of type WiHo. This assumption is not based on my opinions or wishes but on the fact that in all countries collecting time use data on average women do more household production than men (Gimenez-Nadal and Sevilla-Sanz 2012). It can be assumed that if women do more household production they also do more WiHo (which existing data sets do not measure). So it is not far fetched to simplify and assume that on average, women perform WiHo for men but not vice versa. Nevertheless, the marriage motive does not need to always be about men paying women to perform household production on their behalf. More scenarios can be considered, depending on the problem being studied. For example, Cherry (1998) has modeled marriage among blacks with women paying men in marriage. Reversing the marriage motives could possibly help to explain some of the racial differences in the effect of Common-Law Marriage (CLM) reported in Chap. 7.

Second, by emphasizing economic consequences of implicit prices established in marriage markets; I am not denying that there are other very important consequences of couple formation, including (1) people in couples tend to be happier than their unpartnered and unmarried counterparts, and (2) on average children are better off being raised by a couple than by single parents. A recent study that followed a large number of USA respondents over time found that entering into a union (married or not) improved psychological well being and was associated with lower levels of depression (Musick and Bumpass 2012). Children raised by couples tend to be better off than those raised by single parents, e.g., in terms of better school performance (McLanahan and Sigle-Rushton 2004) and lower rates of depression and crime participation (Sigle-Rushton et al. 2005).

Third, the "marriage motive" as understood here is a motive that explains conventional economic behaviors. This book is not about what motivates marriage: biological drives, emotions of love and altruism, idealism, norms, etc.

## How This Book Is Organized

Part A presents the basic price-theoretical models of marriage. These are markets for WiHo and it is assumed that goods are privately consumed. Chapter 2 is a macromodel; Chap. 3 has multiple markets for WiHo.

Part B applies the models to the analysis of labor supply and other time uses. Time use (TU)-related predictions are derived. Chapter 4 includes a formal derivation of sex ratio effects, a major way by which marriage markets affect employment at the macrolevel. In addition, bringing in the marriage motive and marriage markets leads to new insights regarding income effects—including gender differences in such effects—wage effects and cross-wage effects on labor supply. Chapter 5 presents the first set of implications of a Marshallian partial equilibrium model of marriage markets: implications regarding the partial effects of age, education, race, ethnicity, and weight of individuals as well as implications regarding compensating differentials based on the age gap and weight gap between spouses, and differences in spouses' race, ethnicity, and education. The need for simultaneous estimations of couples' labor supply is emphasized.

Chapter 6 revisits the labor supply effects of sex ratios, income, and wage. This chapter presents the bulk of the available evidence regarding sex ratio effects on employment. It also includes new insights on how income and wage effects could be affected by marriage market conditions. The chapter concludes with a discussion of the effects that some marriage-related laws may have on labor supply. More on the last theme is found in Chap. 7, reporting on recent research with Victoria Vernon on labor supply and CLM.

Chapter 7 starts by adapting the price theory of marriage presented in this book to the analysis of how CLM laws would possibly affect labor supply, and why such effects would vary by race and college degree. Identification of CLM effects on labor supply and time in home production arises through cross-state variation and variation over time, as three states abolished CLM over the period examined in the CPS data (now only 11 states still have such laws). We find that for married women CLM availability leads to a reduction in weekly hours of work of 1–2 h. In addition, some CLM effects on married men's labor supply are positive. Consequently, the abolition of CLM in some states helps to explain the convergence of men and women's labor supply over time.

The last chapter on labor supply, Chap. 8, presents a simple graphic analysis of labor supply that integrates marriage market factors such as sex ratios.

Part B concludes with recent research with J. Ignacio Gimenez and J. Alberto Molina on household production and racial intermarriage in the USA. We analyzed time spent on chores by whites and blacks based on the American Time Use Survey data for the years 2003–2009. We found that white women married to black men devote 0.4 fewer hours per day to chores than their counterparts in all-white marriages, which is comparable to the effect of a child on their hours of chores. White men also work less at housework when in couple with black women than when in all-white couples. Conversely, blacks appear to do more chores if they are in couple with whites than when in all-black couples. We interpret these racial intermarriage differentials in hours of household work as evidence of racial discrimination by whites against blacks in marriage markets. The same differentials in the implicit price that white women "charge" for their WiHo are likely to account for effects of racial intermarriage on labor supply (as discussed in Chap. 5) and on time spent doing chores: the higher the price charged, the less women engage in chores and the less they work in the labor force.

Part C is about consumption and savings. A number of testable predictions are derived in Chaps. 10 and 11, numbered C1–C14. In Chap. 10, the concepts of WiHo and its compensation are integrated into a theory of individual consumer choice in which it is assumed that individuals demand WiHo to obtain home-produced private goods and that there are competitive markets for WiHo. One testable implication is that the elasticity of individual demand varies with ability to obtain a spouse's WiHo. Given traditional gender roles this implies that relative to women's demand, men's demand for consumer products replacing household production will be more price elastic. One testable implication derived in the chapter is that women are likely to be charged more for dry cleaning. Another testable implication is that sex ratios in marriage markets influence consumption. For example, it is predicted that in countries with more emigration of men than women, women will be expected to make higher contributions to newlyweds' costs of housing. The third major prediction is that compensating differentials in marriage will influence individual consumption. For instance, women married to men who are considerably older than they are will consume more compared to women married to men close to their own age. The model also leads to the well-established generalization that consumption in marriage depends on the individual income of each marriage partner rather than on a pooled household income. Implications of recognizing that some consumption is a public good to the couple are discussed.

Section 11.1 in Chap. 11, developed jointly with Alfredo M. Pereira, presents a macrolevel model of savings, marriage, and divorce. It is an intertemporal model of individual savings behavior that considers intramarriage financial transfers and assumes uncertainty about marriage and divorce. Some spouses are net recipients of intrahousehold transfers, implying that after marriage their personal unobservable disposable income exceeds their (observable) personal observed income. Others are net contributors of such transfers. Depending on their stage in life (before or after marriage), individuals will save more or less depending on whether they are net recipients or contributors of intramarriage transfers. This chapter's Sect. 11.2 links these intramarriage transfers to the concepts of WiHo, WiHo price, and WiHo market models presented in Chaps. 2 and 3. The primary predictions found in this section deal with the savings effects of sex ratios, WiHo-related productivity indicators, older age, and age differences. The discussion of sex ratio effects includes recent findings on how high sex ratios in China are affecting household savings.

Throughout the book, whenever there is a marriage motive and marriage market conditions affect economic outcomes, the analysis is first at a macrolevel and at a microlevel, allowing for the presence of multiple markets for different types of WiHo.

## Implications for Policy and Strategy

This book is only the tip of an iceberg. So much more can be accomplished with a price theory of marriage! The theoretical models I presented need more development. More empirical research is needed on how sex ratios affect economic behaviors and many more implications of compensating differentials in marriage could be tested in the context of consumption, savings, or employment.

A price-theoretical approach to marriage of the kind presented here carries enormous legal and policy implications as well as implications for firms and individuals.[13] Implications for policy include insights regarding taxes, government programs to alleviate poverty, national accounting methods, laws dealing with marriage and divorce, and macrolevel policies related to household savings. Firms also need to adapt to the roles that their employees play as WiHo workers or users of WiHo. There may be more possibilities for compensations that accommodate WiHo workers or those who "hire" them. Depending on the type of worker this can lead to new ways for attracting good workers. WiHo workers will respond more to firms who introduce flexible schedules. WiHo users will respond more to higher pay checks even if they are asked to live a less balanced life.

A price-theoretical approach to marriage can help individuals when they design life strategies. It can help all of us be less judgmental of people who use strategies different from our own. I may like gender equality and prefer an egalitarian relationship in my own marriage. However, that does not put me in a position to impose my norms on others and to look down at housewives who are happy with their lifestyle and pay all their bills with money earned by their husbands. Thinking of the large and varied markets for WiHo out there makes one more accepting of different lifestyles, including different marriage motives.

Explicit prices for marriage can be degrading. It is particularly sad that some people sell access to their bodies or their children's bodies, opening the way to extreme levels of physical and mental abuse. Abuse is pervasive even in situations where marriages are mutually agreed to. In contrast, increased awareness of implicit prices in the marriage markets in which we participate is not only not likely to contribute to any such abuse but it may protect against such abuse by helping us realize that our market value in marriage markets often exceeds the value that our spouses and relatives allow us to perceive.

Thinking more clearly about our own marriage motives and those of the people with whom we interact can help us be more successful at reaching our individual goals. At society's level we may also want to reexamine some of the institutions that we inherited from past generations and use a price theory of marriage to help us reboot some unnecessary laws and customs.

## Appendix: Other Models of Marriage and Decision Making in Marriage

While his Marshallian partial equilibrium model of marriage was underemphasized by Becker himself, it is precisely that model that attracted most Chicago-linked scholars entering the economics of marriage around the time that Becker pioneered the field, in the 1970s and 1980s. All three Chicago students who wrote dissertations on the economics of marriage under Becker's supervision at that time principally relied on Becker's micro price-theoretical model: Alan

[13] More practical recommendations can be found at the end of my introduction to *Marriage and the Economy*, an edited book (Grossbard-Shechtman 2003).

Freiden, Michael Keeley, and I, then known as Amyra Grossbard. Freiden (1972, 1974) estimated an empirical model of marriage rates using data for US states, explaining allocation into marriages as a function of factors that shift the demand for or supply of brides. Keeley (1974, 1977, 1979) developed a search theory based on the concept of "marital wage" defined as the equilibrium value of a spouse in his or her marriage market. Keeley (1977) and Becker et al. (1977) were published in the same year. Both apply search theory to the analysis of marriage. Keeley studies age at marriage, whereas Becker et al. study divorce. The analysis by the student relies more on an explicit price mechanism than that by the professor and his coauthors.

Becker's Marshallian model of marriage is also the preferred model of the following scholars who had a direct connection to Becker and entered the field of economics of marriage and: (in chronological order of entry into the field of economics of marriage) Lisa Landes, Ivy Papps, Bertrand Lemennicier, Elizabeth Peters, and Aloysius Siow. Landes had been Becker's student at Columbia in the 1960s and worked with him and Robert T. Michael on an analysis of divorce (Becker et al. 1977). Her empirical piece on alimony, another explicit price related to marriage and divorce, is based on the Marshallian model (Landes 1978).[14] So is a study of bride-price by Ivy Papps (1983), a student at Chicago in the 1970s. Bertrand Lemennicier, who visited Chicago in 1977, relies on price theory of marriage in Lemennicier (1979) and in his book on marriage markets (especially in a chapter on the price of women in contemporary societies (Lemennicier 1988)). Elizabeth Peters (1986), a student at Chicago in the 1980s, used price theory in her analysis of the impact of no-fault divorce laws, and so did Aloysius Siow, who entered Chicago in the late 1970s and had taken Becker's class on economics of the family. Siow entered the economics of marriage later, using price-theoretical models of marriage to study dowry (Botticini and Siow 2003) and marriage formation (Choo and Siow 2006). I share that preference for Marshallian models over optimal sorting models of marriage.

Furthermore, in the 1970s a number of influential applications of the time allocation model adopted a nonunitary approach. First, Michael Grossman, who studied with Becker and Mincer when they were both at Columbia, published a model of health production in couples (Grossman 1976) in which he tested how resources of husband and wife—including each partner's education levels—affected both his health and her health. He made no assumptions as to the distribution of health produced within the couple or whether men and women play any cooperative or noncooperative games when investing in the human capital that helps them fight illness. He found that marriage to a more educated spouse is associated with higher individual health. I would classify Grossman's model as an independent individual model of the production of health at home.

Another early example of research modeling wife and husband that is consistent with the assumption of independent individual decision making is found in labor economics. Glen G. Cain (1966), a Chicago PhD, separated between

[14] On the topic of alimony also see Ira Ellman (1989).

the effect of husband's income on wife's labor supply and the effect of nonlabor income on that supply. He thereby recognized implicitly that who earned the income mattered, that is, income effects were not what Apps and Rees (2009) call "anonymous," perhaps because after marriage individuals continue to make some of their own decisions.

In contrast to the relatively large number of Becker-connected scholars who in the 1970s and 1980s adopted his Marshallian marriage models or adapted his allocation of time model to the case of independent decision making by individual members of a couple, I am not aware of any students or visitors at Chicago in this period who used Becker's optimal sorting models.

The major contributors to the economics of marriage in more recent decades have come from outside Chicago and adopted multiple approaches. They have been critical of unitary models of the household and have proposed to replace them with models assuming that in multiperson households decisions are made by individuals who have their own preferences and their own constraints, as is the case with bargaining models assuming that households play games of a cooperative (e.g., McElroy and Horney 1981) or a noncooperative (e.g., Konrad and Lommerud 1995) nature. Other critics, including Chiappori (1988) and Apps and Rees (1988), have proposed to follow Samuelson's (1956) consensual approach and assume that households have a social welfare function. Their conclusions cannot always be distinguished from those of Becker's nonunitarian models, such as his marriage market analyses and interpretations of his allocation of time model assuming independent individual decision makers. Furthermore, given the large degree of heterogeneity in the population Del Boca and Flinn (2012) concluded that in most cases it is not possible to empirically distinguish between models based on assumptions of Pareto efficiency from noncooperative models.[15]

Most models of how decisions are made in a couple are on a continuum between two extremes: totally individualistic and totally unitary. The former view every dimension—consumption, resources, including time—at the individual level; the latter consider every measurable dimension as joint to the household. Jointness can take the form of playing a game with your partner or spouse (more so if the game is cooperative than if it is noncooperative) or of having a joint welfare function or a joint production function (as in the case of Becker's price theory of marriage).[16] Becker's (1965) allocation of time model applied to independent individual decision makers who are married to each other is a model with individualistic elements but a joint production function and implicit prices at the household level. The separate sphere model of Lundberg and Pollak (1993) has household members as joint decision makers regarding some outcomes while they maintain separate spheres regarding other outcomes.

[15] Del Boca and Flinn (2012) also develop a model within which households choose between behaving cooperatively or not, and their estimates indicate that about 25 % of households are noncooperative.

[16] For a similar categorization of models of decision-making in households, see Apps and Rees (2009).

## References


Ahituv, Avner, and Robert I. Lerman. 2011. Job turnover, wage rates, and marital stability: How are they related? *Review of Economics of the Household* 9 (2): 221–249.

Apps, Patricia, and Ray Rees. 1988. Taxation and the household. *Journal of Public Economics* 35:355–369.

Apps, Patricia, and Ray Rees. 2009. *Public economics and the household.* Cambridge: Cambridge University Press.

Becker, Gary S. 1960. An economic analysis of fertility. In *Demographic and economic change in developed countries,* ed. A Conference of the Universities—National Bureau Committee for Economic Research. Princeton: Princeton University Press.

Becker, Gary S. 1965. A theory of the allocation of time. *Economic Journal* 75:493–515.

Becker, Gary S. 1973. A theory of marriage: Part I. *Journal of Political Economy* 81:813–846.

Becker, Gary S. 1974a. A theory of marriage: Part II. *Journal of Political Economy* 82:511–526.

Becker, Gary S. 1974b. A theory of social interactions. *Journal of Political Economy* 70:1–13.

Becker, Gary S. 1981. *A treatise on the family*. Cambridge: Harvard University Press.

Becker, Gary S., Elizabeth Landes, and Robert Michael. 1977. An economic analysis of marital instability. *Journal of Political Economy* 85:1141–1188.

Becker, Gary S. and Kevin M. Murphy. 2000. Social economics. *Market behavior in a social environment.* Cambridge: Belknap/Harvard University Press.

Botticini, Maristella, and Aloysius. Siow. 2003. Why dowries? *American Economic Review* 93:1385–1398.

Bronfenbrenner, Martin. 1971. A note on the economics of the marriage market. *Journal of Political Economy* 79:1424–1425.

Browning, Martin, Francois Bourguignon, Pierre-Andre Chiappori, and Valerie Lechene. 1994. Incomes and outcomes: A structural model of intra-household allocation. *Journal of Political Economy* 102 (6): 1067–1096.

Cain, Glen C. 1966. *Married women in the labor force*. Chicago: University of Chicago Press.

Cherry, Robert. 1998. Rational choice and the price of marriage. *Feminist Economics* 4:27–49.

Chiappori, Pierre-Andre. 1988. Rational household labor supply. *Econometrica* 56:63–90.

Chiappori, Pierre-Andre, Sonia Oreffice, and Climent Quintana-Domeque. 2012. Fatter attraction: Anthropometric and socioeconomic characteristics in the marriage market. *Journal of Political Economy* 120 (4): 659–695.

Choo, E., and A. Siow. 2006. Who marries whom and why. *Journal of Political Economy* 114 (1): 175–201.

Cohen, Ronald. 1967. *The Kanuri of Bornu*. New York: Holt, Rinehart, and Winston.

Del Boca, Daniela, and Christopher Flinn. 2012. Endogenous household interaction. *Journal of Econometrics* 166:49–65.

Du, Qingyuan, and Shang-Jin Wei. 2013. A theory of competitive saving motive. *Journal of International Economics* 91:275–289.

Ellman, Ira M. 1989. The theory of alimony. *California Law Review* 77:3–81.

Freiden, Alan. 1972. A model of marriage and fertility. PhD Diss., University of Chicago.

Freiden, Alan. 1974. The U.S. marriage market. In *Economics of the family,* ed. T. W. Schultz. Chicago: University of Chicago Press.

Friedman, Milton. 1976. *Price theory*. New York: Aldine de Gruyter.

Gale, David, and Lloyd S. Shapley. 1962. College admissions and the stability of marriage. *American Mathematical Monthly* 69:9–15.

Gimenez-Nadal, J. I., and A. Sevilla-Sanz. 2012. Trends in time allocation: A cross-country analysis. *European Economic Review* 56 (6): 1338–1359.

Glick, Paul C., John C. Beresford, and David M. Heer. 1963. Family formation and family composition: Trends and prospects. In *Sourcebook in marriage and the family*, ed. Marvin. B. Sussman. Boston: Houghton Mifflin.

Grossbard, Shoshana Amyra. 2010. How 'Chicagoan' are Gary Becker's economic models of marriage? *Journal of the History of Economic Thought* 32 (3): 377–395.

Grossbard, Shoshana A. 2011. Independent individual decision-makers in household models and the new home economics. In *Household economic behaviors,* ed. J. Alberto Molina. New York: Springer.

Grossbard-Shechtman, Amyra. 1984. A theory of allocation of time in markets for labor and marriage. *Economic Journal* 94:863–882.

Grossbard-Shechtman, Shoshana. 1993. *On the economics of marriage*. Boulder: Westview Press.

Grossbard-Shechtman, Shoshana. 2003. Marriage and the economy. In *Marriage and the economy: Theory and evidence from advanced industrial societies,* ed. S Grossbard-Shechtman. New York: Cambridge University Press.

Grossbard-Shechtman, S. A., and Xuanning Fu. 2002. Women's labor force participation and status exchange in intermarriage: An empirical study in Hawaii. *Journal of Bioeconomics* 4 (3): 241–268.

Grossbard-Shechtman, A. S., and S. Neuman. 1988. Women's labor supply and marital choice. *Journal of Political Economy* 96:1294–1302.

Grossman, Michael. 1976. The correlation between health and schooling. In *Household production and consumption,* ed. N. Terleckyj. New York: Columbia University Press.

Heer, David M., and Amyra. Grossbard-Shechtman. 1981. The impact of the female marriage squeeze and the contraceptive revolution on sex roles and the women's liberation movement in the United States, 1960 to 1975. *Journal of Marriage and the Family* 43:49–65.

Henry, Louis. 1975. Schema d'Evolution des Marriages apres de Grandes Variations des Naissances. *Population* 30:759–779.

Horioka, Charles Yuji. 1987. The cost of marriages and marriage-related saving in Japan. *Kyoto University Economic Review* 57 (1): 47–58.

Horioka, Charles Yuji. 1997. A cointegration analysis of the impact of the age structure of the population on the household saving rate in Japan. *Review of Economics and Statistics* 79 (3): 511–516.

Johnson, W. R., and J. Skinner. 1986. Labor supply and marital separation. *American Economic Review* 76:455–469.

Keeley, Michael C. 1974. A model of marital information: The determinants of the optimal age at first marriage and differences in age at marriage. PhD Diss., University of Chicago.

Keeley, Michael C. 1977. The economics of family formation. *Economic Inquiry* 15:238–250.

Keeley, Michael C. 1979. An analysis of the age pattern of first marriage. *International Economic Review* 20:527–544.

Konrad, Kai A., and K. Erik Lommerud. 1995. Family policy with non-cooperative families. *Scandinavian Journal of Economics* 97:581–601.

Koopmans, Tjalling C., and Martin. Beckman. 1957. Assignment problems and the location of economic activities. *Econometrica* 25:53–76.

Landes, Elizabeth. 1978. The economics of alimony. *Journal of Legal Studies* 1:35–63.

Lemennicier, Bertrand. 1979. The economics of conjugal roles. In *Sociological economics,* ed. L. Lévy-Garboua. London: Sage.

Lemennicier, Bertrand. 1988. *Le Marche du Mariage et de la Famille*. Paris: Presses Universitaires de France.

Lundberg, Shelly., and Robert. A. Pollak. 1993. Separate sphere bargaining and the marriage market. *Journal of Political Economy* 101:988–1010.

McElroy, Marjorie B., and M. J. Horney. 1981. Nash bargained household decisions: Toward a generalization of the theory of demand. *International Economic Review* 22:333–349.

McLanahan, Sara, and Wendy Sigle-Rushton. 2004. Father absence and child wellbeing: A critical review. In *The future of the family,* ed. D. Moynihan, L. Rainwater and T. Smeeding, 116–155. New York: Russell Sage Foundation.

Mincer, Jacob. 1962. Labor force participation of married women: A study of labor supply. In *Aspects of labor economics,* ed. H. Gregg Lewis. Princeton: Princeton University Press.

Mincer, Jacob. 1963. Market prices, opportunity costs, and income effects. In *Measurement in economics,* ed. C. Christ. Stanford: Stanford University Press.

Musick, Kelly, and Larry Bumpass. 2012. Reexamining the case for marriage: Union formation and changes in well-being. *Journal of Marriage and Family* 74 (1): 1–18.

Papps, Ivy. 1983. The role and determinants of bride price: the case of a Palestinian village. *Current Anthropology* 24:203.

Peters, Elizabeth. H. 1986. Marriage and divorce: Informational constraints and private contracting. *American Economic Review* 76:437–454.

Porter, Maria. 2015. How do sex ratios in China influence marriage decisions and intrahousehold resource allocation? *Review of Economics of the Household.* http://link.springer.com/article/10.1007/s11150-014-9262-9, forthcoming.

Rao, V. 1993. The rising price of husbands: A hedonic analysis of dowry increases in rural India. *Journal of Political Economy* 101 (4): 666–677.

Robbins, Lionel. 1930. On the elasticity of demand for income in terms of efforts. *Economica* 10:123–129.

Rosen, Sherwin. 1974. Hedonic prices and implicit markets: Product differentiation in pure competition. *Journal of Political Economy* 82 (1): 34–55.

Samuelson, Paul. A. 1956. Social indifference curves. *Quarterly Journal of Economics* 70:1–22.

Sigle-Rushton, Wendy, John Hobcraft, and Kathleen Kiernan. 2005. Parental disruption and adult well-being, a cross cohort comparison. *Demography* 423:427–446.

Wei, Shan-Jin, and Xiaobo Zhang. 2011. The competitive savings motive: Evidence from rising sex ratios and savings rates in China. *Journal of Political Economy* 119 (3): 511–564.

Woolley, Frances. 1996. Getting the better of Becker. *Feminist Economics* 2:114–120.

# Part I
# A Model of Work-In-Household and Labor Supply with Privately Consumed Household Goods

# Chapter 2
# A Theory of Allocation of Time in Markets for Labor and Marriage: Macromodel

*This chapter and the following are adapted from "A Theory of Allocation of Time in Markets for Labor and Marriage," Economic Journal, Vol. 94, pp. 863–882, December 1984. While writing it I benefited from helpful comments from Gary Becker, Jerry Green (from Harvard University), colleagues at Tel-Aviv University, Bar-Ilan University, and San Diego State University, and from anonymous referees.*

In this chapter, a macroanalysis of labor and marriage markets is presented assuming just two types of representative individuals: a man and a woman, both heterosexual, an assumption relaxed in Chap. 3. This macroanalysis is based on microfoundations. It is assumed that individuals can supply labor to firms or work-in-household (WiHo) to a partner.

## Work-In-Household (WiHo)

Central to this theory is the concept of WiHo—defined as an activity that benefits another household member who could potentially compensate the individual for these efforts. That other individual is usually an adult such as a spouse or partner.[1] In addition to what is commonly called "chores," such as cleaning, shopping for food, meal preparation, or gardening, WiHo could also include caring psychologically or physically for the spouse.[2] Having sex is only WiHo for people who would enjoy doing something else instead.

Household production also plays a central role in the writings of the mentors who inspired me when I first came up with this concept. The founders of the New Home Economics, Gary Becker (1965) and Jacob Mincer (1963), were my professors in

[1] I do not consider the very long run. After they grow up, children could possibly pay their parents back for the time they devoted to them when they were young and such time could possibly be defined as WiHo.

[2] There are some parallels with the concept of domestic labor in Himmelweit and Mohun (1977) and the concept of caring labor in Folbre (1994).



S. Grossbard, *The Marriage Motive: A Price Theory of Marriage*,
DOI 10.1007/978-1-4614-1623-4_2

graduate school and their writings on household production had a big influence on me. However, not all time spent in household production is what I call WiHo: Becker, Mincer, and most other economists studying couples' economic decisions do not distinguish between household activities that benefit a spouse and those that do not. Most people do not make that distinction either, which is why English, French, Spanish, Dutch, or Hebrew do not have a word that captures what I mean with WiHo. Does any language have a good term for this?

The idea of WiHo came about in 1974 and was inspired by what I learned about African marriage. I had majored in economics, sociology, and social anthropology at Hebrew University and did a special field in anthropology while a doctoral student at Chicago. When I started to work on my dissertation on the economics of polygamy in Nigeria I plunged into learning more about the Kanuris as most of the respondents in my data belonged to that tribe. A specialist on the Kanuris, Ronald Cohen, conveniently taught at Northwestern University, also in Chicago, and agreed to serve on my dissertation committee (see Cohen 1967, 1971). The women in my samples were the poorest of the poor, working long hours in food preparation, and owning none of the wealth (as I now know men tend to be the only wealth owners in sub-Saharan Africa). I applied price theory using the following equivalents: households == firms; husbands == employers of WiHo; and wives == workers in WiHo. It then became easy to apply the market principle of organization: my marriage markets were markets for WiHo labor with implicit prices![3] I assumed that there are markets for different types of men and women and that an equilibrium "price of WiHo" is set in each submarket, in line with Becker's second Marshallian marriage market model (Grossbard 1976). The analysis led to untestable predictions regarding the effects of various characteristics of men and women on the unmeasurable price of women's WiHo and to testable predictions on the measurable number of wives in the household.

Not only do household members not necessarily cooperate, as is assumed in cooperative models of household decision making, but they may not behave according to noncooperative models of decision making either, in the sense that such models view a need to establish equilibrium allocations for the household. My approach allows for the cohabitation of family members who are independent decision-makers. This was a natural assumption in the context of the Muslim polygamist Kanuris who lived in compounds, with each wife having her own little house. Custody rights over children naturally belonged to fathers, so children were not really public goods. I was most chocked to learn that older wives would often be divorced unilaterally by their husbands and some would die on the streets for not having where to go and lacking ways to earn a living.

I realized that I needed a new term since my first publication (Grossbard 1976) analyzing data from Nigerian tribes who do not allow men to do any household production. In that context I used "wife services." "WiHo" has the advantage of being gender neutral. Also, including the term "work" in the expression WiHo helps emphasizing that this concept is about one spouse working for the benefit of the other, and that such work possibly entails an opportunity cost. That was not so clear from

[3] At the time I called those prices "wife wages" (Grossbard 1976).

other terms I have used such as "household labor" (Grossbard-Shechtman 1984) and "spousal labor" (Grossbard-Shechtman 1993).

Spouses "hire" each other to do WiHo that benefits them. In most cases, they could also have hired a third party, and therefore WiHo is included in the definition of "household production" introduced by Margaret Reid (1934). Reid distinguished between home production and leisure according to the third-party rule. An activity is called "home production" if a third party could be hired to do it. While WiHo is included in Reid's definition of home production, the opposite does not hold: not all work that can be done by hired hands is WiHo. The same activity can be leisure or WiHo depending on who benefits from it.

## Some Underlying Assumptions

The distinction between WiHo and other household production is related to further underlying assumptions. First is the assumption of individual decision making. Ever since the first incarnation of WiHo in the 1970s in my models *individuals*, not households, are the optimizing agents. There are two individuals involved in WiHo: one who works for the other and the other possibly paying back the first. This implies that all my models based on the concept of WiHo are "nonunitary".[4] Both individuals maintain their own individual utility functions and budget constraints even if they form couples. They can also transfer utility, money, and goods to each other. They can barter to the extent that they exchange WiHo for WiHo. Alternatively, they can exchange WiHo for money or in-kind transfers.

A second assumption is that goods are *private*. Depending on who benefits from it, the same household production activity can be either WiHo (if the spouse benefits) or leisure (if the spouse does not benefit). In both cases, there may be an opportunity cost to the extent that the activity is not the individual's preferred activity. For simplicity, in the model below, there are just two household production activities: WiHo and leisure. WiHo could possibly include activities contributing only to the well-being of the spouse (involving the production of private goods for the spouse) as well as activities of benefit to both spouses, such as caring for joint children who are usually considered to be household public goods. The model can be expanded to include such household public goods, as was done in Grossbard-Shechtman (2003) and in Chap. 10.

Third, it is assumed that there is an institutional framework facilitating exchanges of WiHo for WiHo or WiHo for money or in-kind gifts. Couples keep track of who does what and who gets what even if they have joint bank accounts or otherwise pool financial resources. Payments for WiHo need not be explicit money movements, even if they are modeled as such. For example, if the husband vacuums, a task worth $ 50, the wife will probably not hand him $ 50, but next time they go to the mall she may approve of him buying a $ 50 video game. The intuition behind

[4] The term "unitary household" was introduced by Browning et al. 1994 (check). More on the nonunitary nature of marriage market models can be found in Grossbard (2011).

the model carries through even in settings where the couple appears to be a unitary decision-maker.[5]

## Macro- and Micromodels of Marriage

The theory presented in this book was developed in the period 1975–1981, while I was a graduate student at Chicago and a fellow at Stanford's Center for Advanced Study in the behavioral sciences. Becker's (1973) pioneering theoretical paper on marriage, my major source of inspiration, had included both a macro and a micro demand and supply (D&S) model of marriage: in the macromodel, there was only one type of man and one type of woman. In the micromodel, there were many types of men and women. Similarly, my theory of "allocation of time in markets for labor and marriage" (Grossbard-Shechtman 1984) uses D&S analysis and includes a macromodel with one type of man and one type of woman and a micromodel with many types of people.

In this book, I assume that readers are unfamiliar with D&S models of marriage and explain my theory more systematically than I did in the past. I still follow Becker's (1973) order of presentation and start with a macrolevel model with microeconomic foundations.

## Two Steps to the Analysis

There are two steps to the analysis, as in Marshallian economic theory. Step 1 analyzes individual decision making assuming that market equilibrium prices prevail in all relevant markets, including implicit prices for WiHo. Individual supplies and demands are derived. Step 2 derives market equilibria in the relevant markets: familiar labor markets and markets for WiHo. This chapter presents a general equilibrium, macrolevel model in which there is only one type of woman and one type of man. The model is expanded to the case of many different types of men and women in Chap. 3.

### *Step 1: Individual Maximization*

There are two categories of people: $i$ and $j$, but no other types of people. A representative individual $i$ makes decisions regarding (1) supply of WiHo to a spouse (or partner) $j$ and (2) demand for the WiHo supplied by a representative person $j$. Parallelly, a representative individual $j$ makes decisions regarding (1) supply of WiHo to a spouse $i$ and (2) demand for the WiHo supplied by a representative person $i$. In addition, the following individual maximization leads to the derivation of

[5] I thank Oana Tocoian for pointing this out.

a conventional labor supply and demand for consumption goods. The decision to form a couple can also be derived from this maximization: at zero (or very low) levels of WiHo it is optimal not to form a couple. To the extent that each representative individual has a nonzero supply of own WiHo and nonzero demand for a spouse's WiHo these demands and supplies have to match as a person can only marry one person at a time: *i* and *j* have to be spouses to each other.

Three categories of time-use enter a representative individual *i*'s utility function: labor, WiHo, and leisure. Furthermore, individual *i* derives utility from WiHo performed by a spouse or partner *j* and from goods and commercial services *x*. Individual utility functions, thus, include five elements:

$$U_i = U_i(l_i, h_i, s_i, h_j, x_i), \tag{2.1}$$

*i, j* = *f, m* where *f* stands for woman and *m* stands for man*;* *l* denotes time allocated to labor, *h* is WiHo, *s* is leisure (self-oriented time), and *x* denotes commercial goods that are private and separable within the household: the goods consumed by individual *i* do not include those consumed by spouse *j*. If couples are heterosexual $i \neq j$. Monogamy implies that only a single $h_j$ appears in the utility function).[6] Labor and WiHo may affect individual utility positively or negatively, depending on whether the individual enjoys working. Given diminishing marginal utility, negative marginal utility is more likely after a person is already engaged in a substantial amount of labor. A person supplying either kind of labor in the range of negative or zero wages is performing volunteer work.

The planning horizon consists of one period. The individual is constrained by limited time and disposable income defined as personal income *plus* or *minus* any income transfers to or from the spouse. This is in contrast to most economic models of labor supply where it is assumed that a household income constraint affects all members of a household.[7] Decisions are made *ex ante* assuming given equilibrium market prices known to all participants. This includes prices of WiHo.

Formally, the individual maximizes the utility function 2.1 subject to a time constraint

$$T = l_i + h_i + s_i, \tag{2.2}$$

and a monetary disposable income constraint

$$w_i l_i + y_i h_i + V_i = p_i x_i + y_j h_j, \tag{2.3}$$

[6] However, the model could be expanded to include same-sex marriages, cohabitation, and polygamy.

[7] This was certainly the case when I first published this model in 1984.

where $T$ is the maximum time available (e.g., 24 h/day), $w$ is market wage for labor, $y$ is the price of WiHo,[8] $V$ is nonwage income, and $p$ is a vector of prices of commercial goods and services. The left-hand side of the budget constraint indicates the sources of individual income: labor, WiHo, and income sources unrelated to work. The right-hand side consists of the individual's expenditures on commercial goods $x$ and WiHo supplied by the spouse.[9] Both income and expenditures are a function of the price of WiHo $y$. Disposable income includes quasi-earnings $y_i h_i$ and expenditures include what is paid to the spouse working in WiHo, namely, $y_j h_j$. It is also possible to move the term $y_j h_j$ to the left-hand-side. In that case, disposable personal income includes a deduction for what is paid to the spouse.

Consider the traditional case of a housewife (not in the labor force (LF)) married to a husband employed in the LF who compensates her for her WiHo. Then, $y_i h_i$ is positive in the wife's budget constraint and zero in that of the husband, whereas $y_j h_j$ will be zero in the wife's budget constraint and positive in that of the husband. More generally, whenever one spouse engages in more WiHo than the other—and this is also likely to occur in dual-earner couples—exchanges of WiHo for money and internal monetary transfers are likely to occur inside the household.[10] Quasi-earnings from WiHo can be used to purchase private goods and services that the WiHo worker enjoys, allowing individuals with low earnings in the labor market to enjoy a nice lifestyle. If both husband and wife supply WiHo to each other in equivalent amounts, barter may occur and net income transfers may possibly cancel out.

From the first-order conditions, and assuming $p=1$, we obtain:

$$w_i = \frac{MU_{si}}{MU_{xi}} + \frac{-MU_{li}}{MU_{xi}}, \tag{2.4}$$

which indicates that in equilibrium the real wage per hour of work in the LF is equal to the sum of the monetary equivalent of the value of that hour in leisure (self-oriented activities) and of the absolute (monetary) value of the disutility of this kind of work, and

$$y_i = \frac{MU_{si}}{MU_{xi}} + \frac{-MU_{hi}}{MU_{xi}}, \tag{2.5}$$

[8] In the past, I have called this price "*quasi-wage*." In the original article and in the 1993 edition of this book, the symbol for price of WiHo was "*w**." Since that symbol is often used by labor economists to denote "shadow wage" (the value of time of individuals out of the labor force) I have switched to "*y*."

[9] The maximization problem could also be expressed using an adaptation of Becker's (1965) concept of full income to incorporate earnings from supplying WiHo, as I did in the original article (Grossbard-Shechtman 1984) that is the basis of this chapter.

[10] More on this can be found in Chap. 10 and Amuedo-Dorantes et al. (2011).

which is the equivalent of Eq. 2.4 but for WiHo supplied to a spouse instead of labor supplied to a firm; wage is replaced by price of WiHo. Combining 2.4 and 2.5 yields Eqs. 2.6 and 2.7 that express trade-offs between the two types of work:

$$y_i = w_i + \frac{MU_{li}}{MU_{xi}} - \frac{MU_{hi}}{MU_{xi}}, \tag{2.6}$$

which can also be written as

$$y_i + \frac{MU_{hi}}{MU_{xi}} = w_i + \frac{MU_{li}}{MU_{xi}}. \tag{2.7}$$

Equation 2.7 implies that when in equilibrium a rational individual spends time in the LF and doing WiHo for a spouse to the point where the total marginal benefit from work in the LF (the right-hand side of the equation) equals the total marginal benefit from working for a spouse (the left-hand side of the equation). The total marginal benefit from each type of work includes a monetary component and non-pecuniary benefits (or costs) that economists often call "psychic" benefits. Given that there are two forms of labor, the demand for leisure does not simply lead to the supply of labor, as is the case in standard analyses of labor supply. The approach taken here is that of an analysis of occupational choice in which two occupations—labor and WiHo—differs in the disutility they generate.

The individual sets the following minimum asking wage before deciding whether to enter into the LF:

$$w*_i = y_i + \frac{MU_{hi}}{MU_{xi}} - \frac{MU_{li}}{MU_{xi}}. \tag{2.8}$$

The more the individual enjoys WiHo relative to work in the LF the higher the asking wage. This individual's supply of WiHo (2.9), supply of labor (2.10), and demand for a spouse's WiHo (2.11) can be summarized as:

$$h_i^s = h_i(w_i, y_i, y_j, V_i) \tag{2.9}$$

$$l_i^s = l_i(w_i, y_i, y_j, V_i) \tag{2.10}$$

$$h_j^d = h_j(w_i, y_i, y_j, V_i). \tag{2.11}$$

These are reduced forms: the individual's choice of hours of work supplied ($h_i^s$ and $l_i^s$) and hours of WiHo demanded from the spouse ($h_j^d$) are solely dependent on exogenously determined parameters, including prices for WiHo $y_i$ and $y_j$ and wages $w_i$ and $w_j$. These are choices that individual *i* makes independently from other household members. What actual or potential partners are willing to do is taken into

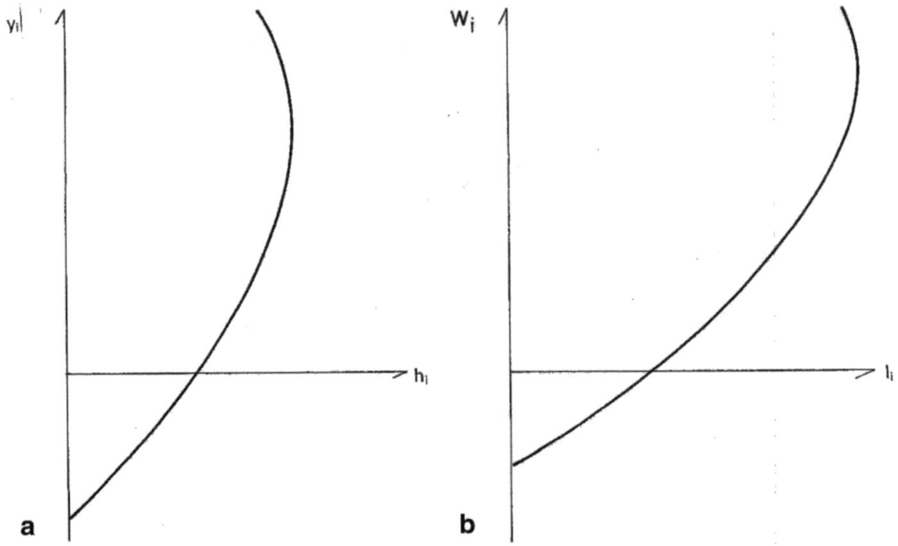


**Fig. 2.1** Individual supplies of WiHo labor (**a**) and labor (**b**).

account via prices $y$ for their WiHo in analogy with labor market analysis in which employers' calculations are integrated into equilibrium wages.

A graphic representation of supply functions 2.9 and 2.10 is found in Fig. 2.1. Panels *a* and *b* in Fig. 2.1 describe individual supplies of each kind of labor: WiHo (Panel *a*) and work in the LF (Panel *b*). It is assumed that initial hours of work produce positive marginal utility, causing the supply curves to start at negative wage levels. The individual depicted in Fig. 2.1 enjoys supplying the first hours of WiHo more than the first hours of labor.

The supply functions are upward sloping to the extent that the substitution effect caused by an increase in the real wage ($y_i$ in panel *a* and $w_i$ in panel *b*) initially dominates the income effect. The supplies could eventually become backward bending if the income effect comes to dominate the substitution effect.

The equivalent of nonleisure in conventional models is here the sum of labor and WiHo. Individual well-being is likely to be tied to total labor more than to total time at work and in household production, as is often calculated since time use surveys are widely available. The household production time benefiting the self only is likely to contribute more to happiness and well-being than household production time of the WiHo type.

Given that labor and WiHo are alternative occupations, it follows that the supply of WiHo $h$ is inversely related to wage in the labor market $w_i$, and that the supply of labor $l$ is inversely related to price of WiHo $y_i$. A substitution effect is likely to be reinforced by an income effect. Nonwage income $V$ is expected to discourage both kinds of labor supply.

The demand for spouse's WiHo $h_j$ is expected to be a downward-sloping function of price of WiHo $y_j$ for the usual reasons determining the slope of derived demands.

Assuming heterosexuality, individual women demand male WiHo whereas individual men demand female WiHo. Next, markets accomplish their function and establish equilibrium wages and prices of WiHo. To the extent that each representative individual has a nonzero supply of own WiHo and demand for the other's WiHo these demands and supplies have to match.

## *Step 2: Market Equilibrium*

All individuals *i* and *j* interested in supplying WiHo to a spouse will be included in an aggregate supply. All individuals interested in using WiHo by a spouse will be included in an aggregate demand in one of the two markets for WiHo. It is assumed that markets for WiHo suppliers are competitive. The first condition of competition—large numbers of participants—applies to the case of marriage: in most societies, large numbers of men and women could possibly compete for marriage partners. Competition is more likely when there are larger numbers of market participants, information is more easily accessible, and more protection is given to the rights of individual market participants (i.e., because marriage contracts are more binding). Since there is only one type of man and one type of woman WiHo is homogeneous. Individual *i's* are perfectly substitutable and so are individual *j's*. These assumptions follow Becker's (1973, 1981) first *D&S model of marriage* and are typical of macrolevel models.

Equilibrium wages and prices are established in the respective markets once all individual demands and supplies are aggregated and aggregate demands and supplies are juxtaposed in the appropriate markets. Aggregate D&S functions for women are presented in Eqs. 2.12–2.14, and for men in Eqs. 2.15–2.17. Superscripts *d* and *s* denote whether a function is a supply or a demand. Capital letters are used to denote aggregate hours of work.

$$H_f^s = H_f^s(y_f, w_f, y_m, p_f, V_f, \beta_f, N_f) \tag{2.12}$$

$$L_f^s = L_f^s(w_f, y_f, y_m, p_f, V_f, \beta_f, N_f) \tag{2.13}$$

$$H_m^d = H_m^d(y_m, w_f, y_f, p_f, V_f, \beta_f, N_f), \tag{2.14}$$

where $\beta$ is a factor describing tastes or productivity, and $N_f$ is the number of women married or eligible for marriage. The equations for men are analogous, subscripts *f* now being replaced by *m* and subscripts *m* by *f*:

$$H_m^s = H_m^s(y_m, w_m, y_f, p_m, V_m, \beta_m, N_m) \tag{2.15}$$

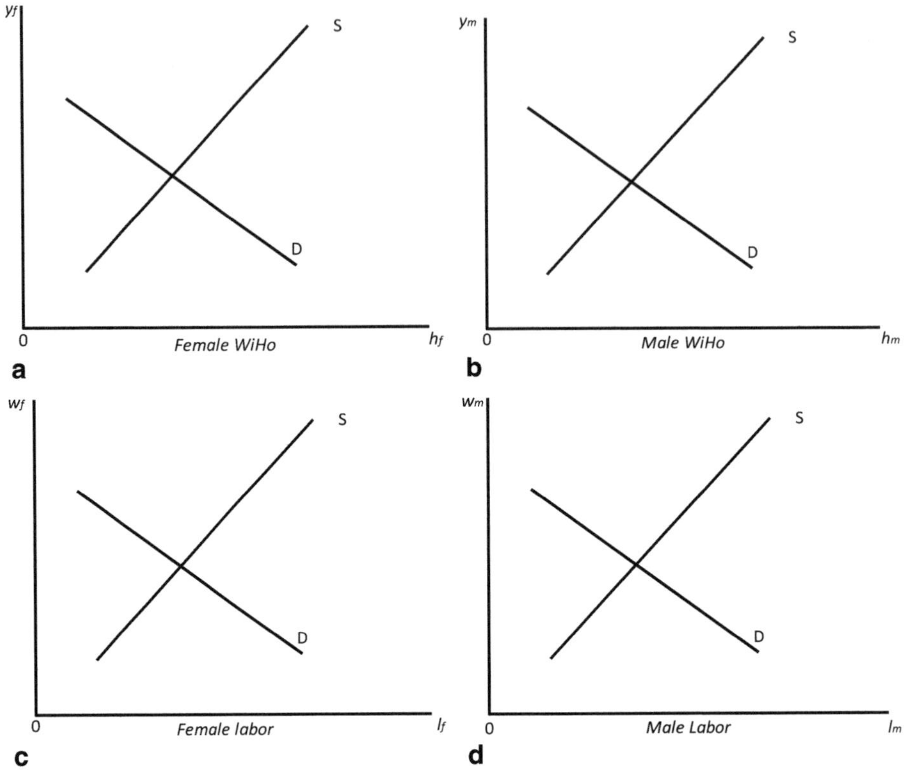


**Fig. 2.2** Markets for **a** female WiHo, **b** male WiHo, **c** female labor, and **d** male labor

$$L_m^s = L_m^s(w_m, y_m, y_f, p_m, V_m, \beta_m, N_m) \tag{2.16}$$

$$H_f^d = H_f^d(y_f, w_m, y_m, p_m, V_m, \beta_m, N_m). \tag{2.17}$$

Given that there is only one kind of woman and one kind of man the only mechanism that leads to upward-sloping supplies and downward-sloping demands is hourly variation in marginal individual (dis)utility (in the case of supply) and marginal utility and productivity (in the case of demand). In equilibrium, all marriages between identical men and identical women will be identical.

Four markets are interrelated in a general equilibrium: two markets for the WiHo supplied by men and women, and two markets for work in the LF supplied by men and women. Figure 2.2 presents the four markets that are, thus, obtained based on eight equations: the six Eqs. 2.12–2.17 and two equations of aggregate labor demand by employers. It is assumed that employers have separate demands for male and female workers.

Equilibrium wages, prices for WiHo, and employment levels are established in each of the four markets. Given demands *D* and supplies *S*, the equilibrium wages for women and men are, respectively, $\overline{w}_f$ and $\overline{w}_m$ (panels *c* and *d* in Fig. 2.2), and the equilibrium prices of WiHo for women and men are, respectively, $\overline{y}_f$ and $\overline{y}_m$ (panels *a* and *b*.) Equilibrium conditions in all four markets are interdependent. Wages in labor markets affect marital behavior and conditions in markets for WiHo influence labor supply.

Higher WiHo prices *y* mean that suppliers of WiHo obtain more "exit power," "threat power," or "bargaining power." In turn, higher bargaining power translates into more access to private consumption within a couple, more influence on decisions, etc. (see Chap. 10). Any behavioral outcome that is related to such price for WiHo can become a testing ground for this theory. Chapters 4–6 examine testable implications for labor supply. Chapter 10 presents testable implications related to consumption, and Chap. 11 examines savings.

Some of the testable implications that follow from this analysis also follow from other models analyzing determinants of bargaining power such as McElroy and Horney (1981) and Lundberg and Pollak (1993). One difference is that bargaining theories limit their analyses to two agents dealing with each other. In contrast, according to the market analysis presented here higher threat power does not necessarily result from bargaining between two agents. Hypothetical willingness to supply or to demand WiHo while one is single or married to someone else also has an impact on the price of WiHo and therefore on outcomes of interest such as access to consumption goods. Limitations that apply to labor market analyses also apply to markets for WiHo. For instance, in macromodels wage rigidity is a problem that has featured in many economic models. Likewise, there could be "wage" rigidity in markets for WiHo. Rigidity may even be worse in the case of prices of WiHo than in the case of regular wages, as the institutions regulating marriage and family life tend to change very slowly. An additional complication peculiar to markets for WiHo is the limitation to one-to-one matches when polygamy is prohibited. In a monogamous society, marriage will occur when at the equilibrium $\overline{y}_f$ and $\overline{y}_m$ the representative man has a demand for the amount of WiHo that the representative woman wants to supply and that woman demands the amount of WiHo that the man supplies. In this macromodel, one has to assume that representative individuals' hours of WiHo are given in order to obtain predictions regarding the number of individuals who are married in a society.

In equilibrium, the representative married couple experiences no excess demand for or excess supply of WiHo at the relevant *y*'s. This couple could be defined as egalitarian if the market value of her services $y_f h_f$ is identical to $y_m h_m$. Alternatively "egalitarian" could be defined in terms of equal amount of hours that each spouse works in WiHo. To the extent that $y_f h_f > y_m h_m$, a representative husband makes financial transfers (or purchases goods) to the representative wife. Net transfers from the wife to the husband will occur if $y_f h_f < y_m h_m$.

The next chapter expands the model to include many types of men and women.

## References

Amuedo-Dorantes, Catalina, Jens Bonke, and Shoshana Grossbard. 2011. Income pooling and household division of labor: Evidence from Danish couples. IZA Discussion Paper No. 5418, Jan 2011.

Becker, Gary S. 1965. A theory of the allocation of time. *Economic Journal* 75:493–515.

Becker, Gary S. 1973. A theory of marriage: Part I. *Journal of Political Economy* 81:813–846.

Becker, Gary S. 1981. *A treatise on the family*. Cambridge: Harvard University Press.

Browning, Martin, Francois Bourguignon, Chiappori Pierre-Andre, and Valerie Lechene. 1994. Incomes and outcomes: A structural model of intra-household allocation. *Journal of Political Economy* 102 (6): 1067–1096.

Cohen, Ronald. 1967. *The Kanuri of Bornu*. New York: Holt, Rinehart, and Winston.

Cohen, Ronald. 1971. *Dominance and defiance*. Washington, DC: American Anthropological Association.

Folbre, Nancy. 1994. *Who pays for the kids? Gender and the structures of constraint*. London: Routledge.

Grossbard, Amyra. 1976. An economic analysis of polygamy: The case of Maieri. *Current Anthropology* 17:701–707.

Grossbard, Shoshana A. 2011. Independent individual decision-makers in household models and the new home economics. In *Household economic behaviors,* ed. J. Alberto Molina. New York: Springer.

Grossbard-Shechtman, Amyra. 1984. A theory of allocation of time in markets for labor and marriage. *Economic Journal* 94:863–882.

Grossbard-Shechtman, Shoshana. 1993. *On the economics of marriage*. Boulder: Westview.

Grossbard-Shechtman, Shoshana. 2003. A consumer theory with competitive markets for work in marriage. *Journal of Socio-Economics* 31 (6): 609–645.

Himmelweit, S., and S. Mohun. 1977. Domestic labor and capital. *Cambridge Journal of Economics* 1:15–31.

Lundberg, Shelly, and Robert. A. Pollak. 1993. Separate sphere bargaining and the marriage market. *Journal of Political Economy* 101:988–1010.

McElroy, Marjorie B., and M. J. Horney. 1981. Nash bargained household decisions: Toward a generalization of the theory of demand. *International Economic Review* 22:333–349.

Mincer, Jacob. 1963. Market prices, opportunity costs, and income effects. In *Measurement in economics,* ed. C. Christ. Stanford: Stanford University Press.

Reid, Margaret. 1934. *The economics of household production*. London: Wiley.

# Chapter 3
# A Theory of Allocation of Time in Markets for Labor and Marriage: Multiple Markets for Work-in-Household

The macromodel presented in Chap. 2 assumed that there is only one type of woman and one type of man. In fact, men are not all identical to each other nor are women. They may differ in skills, appeal, education, ethnicity, religion, age, etc. The assumption that there is only one kind of man and one kind of woman made in Chap. 2 is now replaced with the assumption that there are many types of both. It is also assumed that men can easily substitute among women of different types and that women can easily substitute among men of different types and that there are competitive markets for each type. The separation among submarkets for particular types of WiHo suppliers is similar to the distinction between markets for skilled and unskilled workers often found in labor market analysis. The same assumptions also formed the basis of Grossbard-Shechtman's (1984) section on compensating differentials and group differences. If we assume no costs of matching and rematching these markets can be called "hedonic."[1]

As in the case of the macromodel in Chap. 2, the marriage markets analyzed here are markets for work-in-household (WiHo) that benefits a spouse. The analysis also follows the two steps of Marshallian price theory: derivation of (1) individual demands and supplies when prices are given; and (2) market prices in markets for WiHo based on aggregate demands and supplies in each market.[2]

*Step 1.* We first assume that prices are given and derive an individual supply of WiHo, demand for spouse's WiHo, and labor supply. In Chap. 2, an individual had one utility function 2.1 that was a function of WiHo supplied to a spouse $j$, $h_i$, and by a spouse $j$, $h_j$. Now, there are many types of spouses to which the individual can supply WiHo or who can supply WiHo to the individual. WiHo is denoted by $h_{ij}$, where $i$ stands for type of supplier and $j$ for type of WiHo beneficiary. If an individual of type $j$ also does WiHo for individual of type $i$ then $h_{ij}>0$ and also enters

[1] At the time Becker published his theory of marriage, the term "hedonic markets" had not yet been introduced by Sherwin Rosen (Rosen 1974). Since then Rao (1993) and Choo and Siow (2006) have used the term "hedonic" to describe multiple marriage markets of the kind found in Becker's second demand and supply model.

[2] There are parallels between step 1 here and the second step in models of household distribution with sharing rules such as Apps and Rees (1988) and Chiappori (1988).



S. Grossbard, *The Marriage Motive: A Price Theory of Marriage*,
DOI 10.1007/978-1-4614-1623-4_3

the utility function. For each type of potential spouse of type *j* an individual of type *i* has a utility function

$$U_{ij} = U(l_i, s_i, h_{ij}, h_{ji}, x_i) \tag{3.1}$$

If $j = 1, 2...m,.. R$ there are R such utility functions. In each case, the individual maximizes utility subject to time constraint 2.2 and a budget constraint based on given prices for $x$ and WiHo ($y_{ij}$ and $y_{ji}$):

$$w_i l_i + y_{ij} h_{ij} + V_i = p_i x_i + y_{ji} h_{ji}. \tag{3.2}$$

It follows from the first-order conditions that for every potential partner of type $j$ and $k$ ($j \neq k$):

$$w_{ij} + \frac{MU_{li}}{MU_{xi}} = y_{ij} + \frac{MU_{hij}}{MU_{xi}} = y_{ik} + \frac{MU_{hik}}{MU_{xi}}. \tag{3.3}$$

This condition states that the total—monetary and psychic—reward that individual of type *i* gains from engaging in any form of labor is the same regardless of whether the labor is in the labor force (*l*), WiHo benefiting a spouse of type *j* or WiHo benefiting a spouse of type *k*. However, the monetary share of the reward may differ from job to job and from spouse to spouse.

The individual supply of WiHo $h_i$ by one individual of type $i$ ($i = 1, 2...f,..K$) presented in Eq. 2.9 in Chap. 2 is now replaced with $R$ supplies $h^s_{ij}$ to each type of potential spouse $j$ with whom individual $i$ could match, such as:

$$h^s_{ij} = g'(\mathbf{y}_i, \mathbf{y}_j, w_i, V_i), \text{ where } j = 1, 2 \ldots m, .. R. \tag{3.4}$$

Given that all markets for WiHo by different types are interrelated, prices for WiHo $y_i$ and $y_j$ in Eq. 2.9 are now replaced by vectors of prices established in all the markets for WiHo in which the individual potentially participates, vectors $\mathbf{y}_i$ and $\mathbf{y}_j$, where each $y_{ij}$ in vector $\mathbf{y}_i$ is what an individual of type $i$ can earn if performing WiHo in a couple with a spouse of type $j$ and each $y_{ji}$ in vector $\mathbf{y}_j$ is the price that an individual of type $j$ can earn if performing WiHo for the benefit of a spouse of type $i$.

The same maximization by an individual of type *i* also determines labor supply (in the workforce). Instead of one labor supply (Eq. 2.10 in Chap. 2) there now are $R$ supplies of labor, each one corresponding to marriage to a different type of partner and a function of prices for WiHo established in all markets for $h_{ij}$ and $h_{ji}$.

$$l^s_{ij} = l'(\mathbf{y}_i, \mathbf{y}_j, w_i, V_i) \tag{3.5}$$

Furthermore, an individual of type *i* determines a demand for potential spouses' WiHo, one for each type of spouse *j*. Instead of one demand 2.11 in Chap. 2 there are $R$ demand functions 3.6:

$$h^{d}_{ji} = h'(y_i, y_j, w_i, V_i). \tag{3.6}$$

These choices are made by individuals of type *i* independently from other household members and possibly before they meet their partner or spouse. What actual or potential partners are willing to do is taken into account via prices *y* for their WiHo. Wages in the labor market help individuals to decide on their supply of labor in the labor force as well as their supplies and demands of WiHo. However, if monogamy prevails an individual can only provide WiHo to one spouse at a time, so that if WiHo supplied to a partner of a particular type *j* is positive, that is, $h^{s}_{ij} > 0$, supplies to the other types have to be zero.

At the same time, individuals of type *j* are also performing a similar optimization process, resulting in a vector of *K* demands by individuals of type *j* for the WiHo of spouses of type *i* ($h^{d}_{ij}$), where $i = 1, 2 \ldots f, . K$. Each demand $h^{d}_{ij}$ looks like this:

$$h^{d}_{ij} = h''(y_i, y_j, w_j, V_j) \tag{3.7}$$

Again, all relevant wages and WiHo prices that could affect demand appear on the right-hand side. Individuals of type *j* also derive their labor supply and supply of own WiHo, their supply functions being similar to 3.4 and 3.5 but with inverted *j* and *i*.

To the extent that they supply WiHo and use a spouse's WiHo as well, individuals participate simultaneously in markets for $h_{ij}$ and $h_{ji}$ on the supply or the demand side. Using the example of heterosexuals,[3] an individual marriage originates and will be maintained if at equilibrium values of WiHo prices and other parameters his type's demand for her type's WiHo is equal to her type's supply of WiHo to his type of man, that is, $h^{d}_{ij} = h^{s}_{ij}$, and her type's demand for his type's WiHo is equal to his type's supply of WiHo to her type of woman, that is, $h^{d}_{ji} = h^{s}_{ji}$.

*Step 2.* We add up the individual supplies such as Eq. 3.4 by all individuals of type *i* supplying their WiHo to the *R* types of spouse *j*. This generates *R* market supplies in *R* different $h_{ij}$ markets where there are individuals of type *i*. We also add up the individual demands such as Eq. 3.6 by all individuals of type *j* who have a demand for such work and generate *K* market demands for all the types *j*. Assuming no costs of matching and rematching in each hedonic market equilibrium prices of WiHo $y^{e}_{ij}$ and $y^{e}_{ji}$ (where *e* stands for *"equilibrium"*) are established at the intersection of aggregate demand and aggregate supply in each one of the $K \times R$ markets for $h_{ij}$ and $K \times R$ markets for $h_{ji}$, with a total of 2*KR* markets.[4]

The theory does not need to be embedded in gender-specific terms, but it is easier to proceed under the assumption that types *i* are women and types *j* are men. Then market prices $y^{e}_{ij}$ and $y^{e}_{ji}$ are a function of a vector of individual female

[3] The model can also be applied to same-sex marriages. For example, one of the *j* types could be someone of the same sex.

[4] There are parallels between the second step in this analysis and the first stage in models of household distribution with sharing rules: sharing rules are determined by some of the same factors that determine market prices of WiHo.

characteristics $Z_i$, a vector of male characteristics $Z_j$, and a vector of other factors $X$ (such as the macroeconomic conditions or existing laws) that are expected to affect demand or supply of $h_{ij}$ and $h_{ji}$ and therefore equilibrium prices. The following are gender-specific price determination functions labeled $F$ in the case of women and $G$ in the case of men:

$y^e_{ij} = F(Z_i, Z_j, X_{ij})$ and $y^e_{ji} = G(Z_i, Z_j, X_{ji})$ Any own desirable characteristic $Z_i$ of a supplier of $h_{ij}$ of type $i$ that is associated with higher demand by actual or potential spouses of type $j$ will lead to a higher market price $y^e_{ij}$ in the market for $h_{ij}$, implying a positive first derivative of $y^e_{ij}$ according to this characteristic: $\frac{\partial y^e_{ij}}{\partial Z_i} = \frac{dF}{dZ_i}|_j = \frac{\partial F(Z_i, Z_j, X_{ij})}{\partial Z_i} > 0$. Likewise, a desirable characteristic $Z_j$ of an individual of type $j$ supplying $h_{ji}$ to a type $i$ will be associated with a higher demand and thus higher price for $h_{ji}$: the first derivative of $y^e_{ji}$ according to own characteristic $Z_j$ will also be positive: $\frac{\partial y^e_{ji}}{\partial Z_j} = \frac{dG}{dZ_j}|_i = \frac{\partial G(Z_i, Z_j, X_{ji})}{\partial Z_j} > 0.$

Here are some examples of how $Z$ characteristics could affect demand and therefore prices of WiHo. Younger people may be more productive than older people. For instance, if people in their 50s are less productive than people in their 30s, demand and price of WiHo for people age 35 will be higher than that for people age 55. Education is also expected to affect productivity in WiHo. Market demand for a particular characteristic may also be affected by prejudice and statistical discrimination. For example, if colorism (see Burke 2008) prevails and there is a bias against dark skin demand and prices for the WiHo of dark-skinned men and women will be lower in equilibrium. Any factor $X$ that adds to the demand for WiHo, *ceteris paribus* will also lead to higher prices $y$ for WiHo and induce more WiHo.

*Compensating Differential in Marriage* In contrast to the predicted effect of own characteristics, desirable characteristics of partners are expected to have a negative effect on the price of an individual's WiHo. If the supplier of WiHo is of type $i$ the equilibrium price of $i$'s WiHo, $y^e_{ij}$, will be negatively related to partner $j$'s positive traits, namely $\frac{\partial y^e_{ij}}{\partial Z_j} = \frac{\partial F(Z_i, Z_j, X_{ij})}{\partial Z_j} < 0$. Similarly, $y^e_{ji}$ will be negatively related to partner $i$'s positive traits, that is, $\frac{\partial y^e_{ji}}{\partial Z_i} = \frac{\partial G(Z_i, Z_j, X_{ji})}{\partial Z_i} < 0$. For example, if $Z$ is light skin and colorism prevails, a partner with light skin is expected to pay a lower price to a WiHo supplier with light skin than a partner with dark skin. Then the difference between equilibrium price $y$ that a dark-colored partner needs to pay for the WiHo of a light-skinned individual and the price that a comparable light-colored individual needs to pay for such light-skinned person's WiHo is called a compensating differential in marriage.[5]

The model could possibly be extended by relaxing the assumption of perfect substitution. Monopolistic elements could lead to the need to distinguish between people in existing relationships and singles looking for a match: to the extent that

[5] A concept first presented in Grossbard-Shechtman (1983) and Grossbard-Shechtman (1984).

divorce and marriage are costly (e.g., due to search costs) current partners are not perfectly interchangeable with potential partners in the marriage market. The lower the divorce probability, the less it is likely that people participate in marriage markets after they marry and married people may not respond to changes in prices for WiHo as they would where there are no costs of divorce and remarriage. Also, if costs of divorce and recontracting are positive (possibly due to "on-the-job" training in WiHo occurring during marriage), there could be a discrepancy between a married person's actual $y$ and the $y$ that person could receive on the market.

**Testable Implications** Equilibrium prices for WiHo help individuals decide how much WiHo they want to supply and how much demand they have for a partner's WiHo. As shown in Part B of this book measurable outcomes related to employment and home production time can be explained in terms of a theory based on markets and prices for WiHo. In Part C, the theory is applied to consumption and savings.

## References

Apps, P., and R. Rees. 1988. Taxation and the household. *Journal of Public Economics* 35:355–369.
Burke, M. 2008. Colorism. In *International encyclopedia of the social sciences,* ed. W. Darity Jr., 2 vol. Detroit: Thomson Gale.
Chiappori, P.-A. 1988. Rational household labor supply. *Econometrica* 56:63–90.
Choo, E., and A. Siow. 2006. Who marries whom and why. *Journal of Political Economy* 114 (1): 175–201.
Grossbard-Shechtman, Amyra. 1983. A market approach to intermarriage. In *Papers in Jewish demography 1981,* eds. U. O. Schmelz, P. Gerson and S. DellaPergola. Jerusalem: Hebrew University Institute Contemporary Jewry.
Grossbard-Shechtman, Amyra. 1984. A theory of allocation of time in markets for labor and marriage. *Economic Journal* 94:863–882.
Rao, V. 1993. The rising price of husbands: A hedonic analysis of dowry increases in rural India. *Journal of Political Economy* 101 (4): 666–677.
Rosen, Sherwin. 1974. Hedonic prices and implicit markets: Product differentiation in pure competition. *Journal of Political Economy* 82 (1): 34–55.

# Part II
# Labor Supply and Other Time Uses

In this part the focus is on employment. Chapters 4 to 8 deal with labor supply. Chapter 9 addresses questions of household production. In addition, the marriage motive could also apply to wages. Many studies have shown that married men earn more than unmarried one (see Grossbard-Shechtman 1993, Chap. 12; Lerman and Ahituv 2011). When traditional gender roles prevail and the marriage motive drives men to earn more so they can obtain and keep wives, they can accomplish this by either working more or earning a higher wage.

# Chapter 4
# How Marriage Markets Affect Allocation and Valuation of Time Implications from a Macro Model

Both the macro model (Chap. 2) and the hedonic micro model (Chap. 3) presented unique concepts not found in other economic analyses of allocation of time: Work-In-Household (WiHo) and its price. This chapter and the following two chapters present implications for time allocation and valuation based on the concepts of WiHo and its price as determined in marriage markets. The effects on labor supply that are analyzed in this chapter are those of income (own and partner's), wage, and sex ratios and the model used to analyze those effects is the macro model presented in Chap. 2. The following two chapters apply the micro model of Chap. 3 to derive additional insights regarding marriage market effects on time allocation and valuation.

Some of the implications presented in these chapters on labor supply have independently been derived by others, but most are unique. The marriage market model I use is based on Becker (1973), where prices in marriage markets were first introduced. However, Becker did not write about how these prices may affect value of time, reservation wage, and time allocation to labor supply and household production.

I also report on some tests of the implications, even though some of the tests are old and could benefit from verification based on more recent data and research methods.

First, let us look at how labor economists have traditionally analyzed labor supply and typically continue to do so. Then I show how integrating competitive markets for WiHo into the analysis of labor supply outcomes modifies the analysis.

## Labor Supply, Reservation Wage, and Value of Time at Home

*Becker on Reservation Wage and Marriage* Consider the example of using Marshallian marriage market models to analyze allocation of time and valuation of time in household production. This is the first segment of Becker's (1973) theory of marriage regarding value of time:



S. Grossbard, *The Marriage Motive: A Price Theory of Marriage*,
DOI 10.1007/978-1-4614-1623-4_4

> …the "shadow" price of an hour of $t_f$ [female household production time] to a single M [male]—the price he would be willing to pay for $t_f$—would exceed $w_f$ [the female wage], and the "shadow" price of an hour of $t_m$ [male household production time] to a single F [female]—the price she would be willing to pay for $t_m$—would exceed $w_m$ [the male wage]. Both gain from marriage because M then, in effect, can buy an hour of $t_f$ at $w_f$ and F can buy an hour of $t_m$ at $w_m$, lower prices they then would be willing to pay. Of course this is also why married households use positive amounts of $t_f$ and $t_m$. (Becker 1973, p. 819)

The shadow price as defined here is the value of the marginal utility of a (potential) spouse's household production time to an individual decision-maker (what I call WiHo in Chap. 2). If an individual spouse is employed in the labor force the value of her time in household production is her wage in the labor force. This does not open the door to analyzing value of time as a function of factors influencing equilibrium prices of home production time, such as sex ratios. Becker's (1973) discussion of opportunity cost of home producers' time summarized above is disconnected from the Marshallian demand and supply models that he uses to explain intra-household distribution of income.

A few pages later, Becker (1973) discusses implicit prices of wives and husbands, using the Marshallian demand and supply models of marriage. He calls these implicit prices "unmeasurable shares of the gain from marriage received by men or women" and "equilibrium income [from marriage] that men and women obtain."[1] In Becker (1981) the opportunity costs of household production time in marriage and the implicit prices of wives and husbands appear in two different chapters.

When he introduces the concept of "salary," Becker seems to get closer to an explicit price mechanism linking production and distribution:

> Each marriage can be considered a two-person firm with either member being the "entrepreneur" who "hires" the other at the "salary" $m_{ij}$ or $f_{ij}$ and receives residual "profits" (…). Another interpretation of the optimal sorting is that only it enables each "entrepreneur" to maximize "profits" for given "salaries" of mates…(Becker 1973, p. 825) [quotation marks in the original].

However, Becker (1973) stops before using the concept of "salary" the way that prices are used in Marshallian models, and he drops the term "salary" altogether in the *Treatise*. In Becker (1973) these "salaries" do not indicate opportunity costs of time and therefore do not drive allocative decisions, such as choice of mate or investment in a mate's earning capacity.

In contrast, I linked the concept of opportunity cost of work in marital household production with the opportunity cost of marriage and modeled these wages as a function of marriage market conditions as is explained in more detail in this book.

*Gregg-Lewis' Model* All economists view decisions regarding labor supply—hours of work and labor force participation—as based on a comparison of the attractiveness of work and its alternative, staying home. When studying labor force participation, economists define a reservation wage as the minimum wage that workers

[1] In an email he sent me Becker (2004) uses the term "imputations."

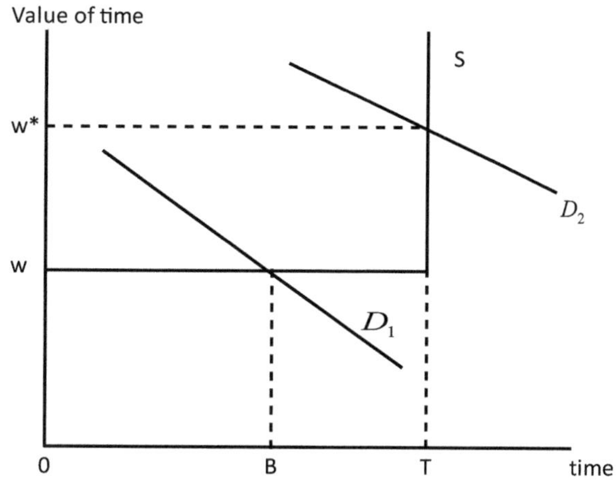


**Fig. 4.1** The value of time according to H. Gregg Lewis

need to earn in order to leave home for work. A rational person will participate in the labor force if $w > w^*$, where $w$ stands for wage and $w^*$ for reservation wage (see Killingsworth and Heckman 1986). Most labor economists following the tradition of the *New Home Economics* (*NHE,* see Chap. 1) have tied the reservation wage to home production, assuming a predetermined marital status: single or married, with no options to marry or divorce.

An early model in the NHE tradition by prominent economist H. Gregg-Lewis is particularly interesting because it considers three uses of time: labor, household production, and leisure.[2] He used the model to (1) analyze whether, in a traditional married couple in which the husband participates in the labor force, the wife will also participate in the labor force and (2) estimate the wife's value of time. The model is presented graphically in Fig. 4.1. It includes the *household's demand* for the person's home production and the *wife's supply* of time to home production. The demand is unitary (a term introduced in Chap. 1), with the entire *household* acting as a single decision-maker. Gregg-Lewis drew the wife's supply of time to home production in the form of a transposed $L$, horizontal at the wage level she would earn if working in the market sector and vertical after a time constraint (such as 18 h a day) is reached. A similar analysis that also separates leisure, labor, and home production can be found in Gronau (1977).

The assumption behind this transposed $L$ curve is that all of the wife's time is available to the household at the wage offered by employers. If her household needs her for only a few hours and $D$ crosses $S$ before the big $T$ is reached (the case of $D_1$ in Fig. 4.1) her opportunity cost of time equals the wage she could have earned in the labor force. Her supply of household work is OB. The difference between the total time she has available, OT and OB is BT, the amount of time she spends in the labor force. If her household needs her more, as in the case of demand $D_2$ that

[2] This section is based on my notes from a labor economics class taught by H. Gregg-Lewis at the University of Chicago in 1973–1974.

intersects individual supply in the vertical part of the supply, the wife will not work in the labor market and her reservation wage $w^*$ will be established at the intersection of demand $D_2$ and her supply. The reservation wage then exceeds the wage.

There are at least two problems with this traditional NHE analysis. First, the supply takes the wife (or any other household member working in household production) for granted in the sense that her own leisure is not defined based on her own preferences for leisure and home production. For example, she cannot prefer exercising over cooking. Second, since the model considers the household demand for her time, not the demand by her partner or husband, it does not allow for bargaining between them over how much of the production the wife will do and how she will be internally compensated for it. The partner cannot give her incentives to motivate her to do more of certain tasks. Gronau's (1977) model suffers from the same drawbacks.

*Introducing WiHo and its Price y* My model also views the labor supply decision as a function of a comparison between $w$ and $w^*$ and mostly applies to the spouse principally in charge of household production (more often the wife). However, in contrast to the models above it assumes that each member of the couple has an individual utility function that includes his or her leisure. The reservation wage is based on Eq. 4.1 (reproduced from Chap. 2) and is a function of the household worker's preferences for either type of work (labor supply or work in household production). It can also include a comparison between time in household production and leisure.

$$w^*_i = y_i + \frac{MU_{hi}}{MU_{xi}} - \frac{MU_{li}}{MU_{xi}} \tag{4.1}$$

Here, time in household production is restricted to WiHo, work in household production benefiting the spouse. This WiHo has a value based on marriage market conditions, $y$, and this price of WiHo affects the reservation wage. The equation states that the reservation wage equals the monetary compensation for WiHo paid by the spouse *plus* the difference between the monetary equivalent of the (dis)utility of WiHo and that of work (which could be positive or negative).

To facilitate comparison with the Lewis/Gronau model assume that the household worker is the wife. The term $MU_{hi}/MU_{xi}$ captures the wife's subjective value of own time supplied to WiHo, which depends on how much she enjoys the fruits of her home production labor and how much she likes doing that home production. In the example of food production, it is both about how much she enjoys home-cooked meals and about how much she likes cooking the meals. The more she likes home-cooked meals, the higher her reservation wage. The more she dislikes cooking the lower her reservation wage (she would rather be at work and buy ready-made food). In turn, she is more likely to enjoy the fruits of her labor if the goods produced for the spouse's benefit are of a (household) public good nature. For instance when WiHo is parenting children shared with a spouse the individual gets more benefits than if parenting the spouse's children from a previous relationship. Since the marginal disutility of producing goods in the household is likely to increase with hours of WiHo, the supply of WiHo is expected to be gradually upward-sloping rather than to take the form of a transposed *L*.

The reservation wage in 4.1 differs from that of previous labor economists—including Gregg-Lewis and Gronau—in that it includes prices *y* for WiHo. The higher *y* in a market for WiHo, the higher the reservation wage. In the case of traditional couples where wives are WiHo workers they can be incentivized to increase home production if their husbands are paying them a higher *y* for that work. Likewise, in nontraditional couples wives can give incentives to their husbands to motivate them to do more WiHo work benefiting them.

*Indivisibilities* If hours of work are not easily divisible, the representative individual may have to spend either too much or too little time at work relative to a situation of perfect divisibility. For instance, consider a case where the individual would like to spend 7 h in *h* and 1 h in *l*. If there are fixed costs of employment a solution involving 7 h of *h* and 1 h of *l* is not feasible. Instead, the individual may not work outside at all, i.e., *h* will be 8 and *l* will be zero. This implies that the value of time will be higher than the right-hand side of Eq. 4.1. If the individual spends "too much" time at work in comparison to an optimal allocation of time, then the actual value of time $w^*$ will be lower than the right-hand-side of the equation.

*Labor Supply of the Other Spouse* Labor supply of the other spouse, who is not the principal WiHo worker but is willing to pay for it, will also be influenced by the price of WiHo. The more this person needs to pay to the WiHo worker the more he or she needs income and this will influence labor supply.

My model based on the concept of WiHo and its price leads to new implications regarding income and wage effects on labor supply. It also implies that sex ratios will influence reservation wages and time use.

This chapter provides an analysis at the macro level, assuming there is only one representative woman and one representative man and they are heterosexual. This assumption is relaxed in Chaps. 5 and 6, presenting implications based on the micro model.

## Income Effects on Time Allocation and Value of Time

This chapter and the next one contain a number of testable implications regarding time use (TU) that have been numbered.

**Individual Versus Household Income** *Testable Implication TU1: The effect of each spouse's income on own and spouse's labor supply, other time uses and value of time are likely to differ. It is necessary to distinguish between household income and individual income.* The most common way to frame income effects on labor supply has been that of a unitary household considering leisure/goods trade-offs, as first introduced by Robbins (1930). It follows from my model that instead of

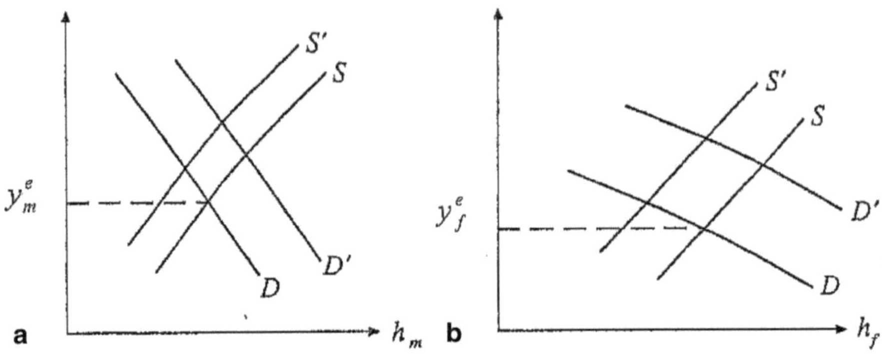


**Fig. 4.2** **a** and **b** Income effects on WiHo of men and women (3.4 in my 1993 book)

analyzing effects of household income on individual decisions such as labor supply, fertility, marriage, etc., or on value of time, one needs to analyze effects of *individual* income of each household member.This implication also follows, e.g., from McElroy and Horney (1981), Apps and Rees (1988), Chiappori (1988), McElroy (1990), and Lundberg and Pollak (1993).

What matters is personal disposable income defined as the share of the household income that an individual has access to. *Disposable personal income* will equal own income from labor, rent, and other traditional sources *plus* transfers from the spouse in the case of WiHo suppliers "earning" monetary (or in-kind) compensations from spouses who benefit from WiHo. In the case of spouses who benefit from WiHo and pay for it, personal disposable income equals personal income from outside sources *minus* transfers to the spouse supplying WiHo. Lack of data on WiHo and its price make it difficult to estimate such disposable personal income. Nevertheless, a WiHo-based analysis can help us better understand income effects. In standard labor supply analysis the effect of nonlabor income is to cause a shift in labor supply to the left. Likewise, changes in nonlabor income will affect WiHo supply.

Consider an increase in individual nonwork income *V*. It follows from Eq. 2.8 that such income increase is expected to cause an individual labor supply to shift to the left. At the same time, one also expects individual supply of own WiHo, Eq. 2.7, to shift to the left when *V* increases.

**Gender Differentials in Income Effect on Labor Supply** *Testable Implication TU2: If gender roles are traditional and all nonwage incomes change by the same proportion, these changes are likely to have different effects on men and women's labor supply.*

Figure 4.2a and b shows markets for WiHo denoted by *h*. In Fig. 4.2a men are the principal WiHo-workers, and demand is by women. In Fig. 4.2b women are the principal WiHo-workers, and demand is by men. The initial equilibrium prices in the two markets are $y_f^e$ and $y_m^e$. Assume that nonwage income increases at the macro level, and that this translates into income increases for all men and women.

Aggregate supply of men's WiHo shifts to $S'$ as a result of men's higher incomes. Women's supply of WiHo also shifts to the left when their income increases.

In addition, demands for spouse's WiHo are also expected to be positively related to own income. This follows from function 2.1 and is based on the assumption that the home-produced "goods" that the spouse consumes are normal goods. Higher incomes will then be associated with rightward shifts in demand for the other's WiHo. If all incomes rise both women's demand for men's WiHo and men's demand for women's WiHo are expected to increase, causing rightward shifts in both aggregate demands for WiHo in the two panels of Fig. 4.2. Men's supply of WiHo thus shifts to the left and women's demand for men's WiHo shifts to the right in the market for men's WiHo. If prices are flexible equilibrium price, $y_m^e$ , will rise. The amount of time spent in WiHo may stay the same, unless one curve shifts more than the other.

Likewise, in the market for women's WiHo demand increases and supply decreases. If prices are flexible equilibrium price $y_f^e$ is expected to rise. In case of flexible WiHo prices $y$ and unchanged hours of WiHo, the allocation of time by representative individuals will not change but there will be a redistribution of income: if $y$ increases more for one gender than for the other, the gender experiencing a relatively larger increase in WiHo price $y$ will get more consumption goods.

The size of income effects on equilibrium amounts of WiHo supplied (and therefore on equilibrium amounts of labor supplied) depends on factors influencing the slope of the aggregate demands and supplies. It follows from this model that these slopes are a function of a number of factors typically ignored in, conventional labor supply analyses. Two such factors are the availability of goods and services that can substitute for WiHo (see Grossbard-Shechtman 1993, Chap. 10) and the elasticity of substitution between labor and WiHo.

The effects of nonwork income on labor supplied also depend on how flexible WiHo prices are. If WiHo prices are rigid and do not rise sufficiently to eliminate excess demands caused by income increases, the representative individuals may further reduce their supply of labor in the labor force in order to accommodate extra demands for WiHo. Vice versa, if aggregate income drops and prices for WiHo are rigid, individuals will increase their labor supply to adjust to shrinking demand for WiHo. (However, in case of traditional gender roles, with men concentrating on labor$l$and women concentrating on WiHo $h$, men may have little room for further increases in labor supply in a downturn and women may have little room for further increases in supply of WiHo in an economic boom.)

I do not expect WiHo prices to be very flexible. Sticky wages is a problem that has been recognized in macroeconomic analyses of labor supply. It is rooted in institutional factors such as labor unions' refusal to allow wages to decrease. Sticky WiHo prices are at least as likely to be observed as sticky wages for labor: social norms regarding gender roles in the household influence WiHo prices and these norms tend to change slowly (see Sevilla-Sanz et al. 2010 on cross-country variation in such norms).

The more equilibrium WiHo prices adjust to shifts in demand or supply of WiHo, the less the amount of WiHo supplied will change and the less labor supply will change. Consequently, income effects on labor supply will depend on the degree of rigidity in WiHo price: the more rigid they are the more labor supply may need to adjust to fill excess demands or supplies of WiHo.

**Household Income and Individual Value of Time** *Testable Implication TU3: Effects of household income on individual value of time are not likely to vary much as a function of whether an individual is in the labor force or not.* As explained above it follows from Gregg-Lewis (1973) that married women's value of time depends on whether the woman is in the labor force or not: a wife's reservation wage equals the wage if she participates in the labor force (and household demand cuts the horizontal part of her supply in Fig. 4.1) and it equals the dollar amount corresponding to the intersection of individual supply if she does not participate in the labor force (and household demand cuts the vertical part of the supply). From here Gregg-Lewis inferred that an increase in husband's income will not affect a wife's value of time if she is employed in the labor force but will lead to a higher value of time if the woman does not participate in the labor force.

Similarly, in his economic theory of fertility Willis (1974) posits that if a wife participates in the labor force her time cost is her wage and does not vary with husband's income. But if she is NOT employed in the labor force her husband's income affects her time cost and therefore her value of time varies with his income. If the total effect of husband's income on a couple's fertility includes a pure positive income effect and a negative effect of that income on fertility due to the wife's higher time cost (ignoring husband's time cost) then Willis predicts the total effect of husband's income on the couple's fertility will be smaller if the wife is not employed than when she is in the labor force (and there is no effect of income on wife's time cost).

The Willis analysis is problematic according to my macro model because a representative wife's value of time is not likely to depend so much on whether she is employed in the labor force or not. Instead, the value of time (the reservation wage $w^*$ defined in Eq. 4.1 is based on equilibrium values of $y$ for women and men and these values are not expected to vary much with labor force participation. The general equilibrium model presented in Chap. 2 implies that employment levels, wages, and value of WiHo are all determined simultaneously in interrelated markets for labor and WiHo. When men's incomes rise their aggregate demand for women's WiHo rises (as long as demand for WiHo is "normal") and $y$, the price of women's WiHo rises. Consequently, the reservation wage of the representative woman rises even if she is in the labor force and her wage does not change. Representative individuals will be indifferent between being in or out of the labor force and between being in or out of marriage. An additional problem is that Willis only considers mothers' time cost of children.

If aggregate incomes change and prices for WiHo are rigid the determination of reservation wages and of how they vary with income is more complex. In the next chapter the strong macro assumption of only one kind of man and one kind of woman is relaxed and multiple types of men and women are considered. This implies, *inter alia*, coexistence of double-earner and single-earner couples.

## Wage Effects on Labor Supply

**Wage Elasticity and Elasticity of Substitution Between Work and WiHo** *Testable Implication TU4: The higher the elasticity of substitution between work and Work-In-Household (WiHo) the higher the wage elasticity.* An uncompensated wage ($w$) increase includes (1) an income effect (higher income leads people to work less in general and most likely less outside the home) and (2) a compensated wage effect leading to substitution of outside labor for WiHo and time for self, given that work in the labor force and WiHo are substitute ways of making a living (this encourages people to work more outside the home and less in WiHo). To understand wage effects on labor supply one therefore needs to pay attention to the connection between supply of labor and WiHo. We could derive further testable implications regarding the determinants of the wage elasticity of labor supply by adapting the consumption model presented in Chap. 10, which assumes more specific functions than those presented in Chap. 2.

*Testable Implication TU4': Own wage elasticity of labor supply is expected to be higher for women than for men.* If under traditional gender roles women engage in more WiHo than men, women's elasticity of substitution between the two forms of work will be higher than men's. Intuitively this can be shown by considering the extreme case where men only work in the labor market and not in WiHo, but women work in both types of work. Consequently, this form of substitution is only available for women and their labor supply will be more wage-elastic than men's. It can be shown that the higher the share of total time spent in WiHo the larger the possible effect of wage on hours worked in the labor force (this is based on an adaptation of Grossbard-Shechtman 2003a). A similar conclusion also follows from traditional labor theory.

*Evidence* A recent finding based on the estimation of a ten-equation simultaneous equation system for French husbands and wives confirms this prediction: own wage elasticity of hours of work was more than three times larger for mothers than for fathers (Bloemen and Stancanelli 2015).

**Backward-Bending Supply** *Testable Implication TU4": The higher the positive correlation between wage and price of WiHo the more likely it is that the observed labor supply curve bends backwards.* A backward-bending supply of labor has a negative slope instead of the normal direct association between wage and hours of work. The traditional explanation for such a negative slope is that at high wages a negative income effect dominates a positive substitution effect. Alternatively, according to my theory the supply of labor could bend backwards due to a positive correlation between wage $w$ and price of WiHo, $y$. Higher wage levels could cause leftward shifts in the supply of labor if $y$ and $w$ are positively correlated. This is explained with the help of Fig. 4.3 representing two supplies of labor, each associated with a different price of WiHo, $y_0$ and $y_1$, where $y_1 > y_0$.

If the wage in the labor market rises from $w_0$ and $w_1$ and the price of WiHo does not change, the representative individual will move along his or her supply of labor

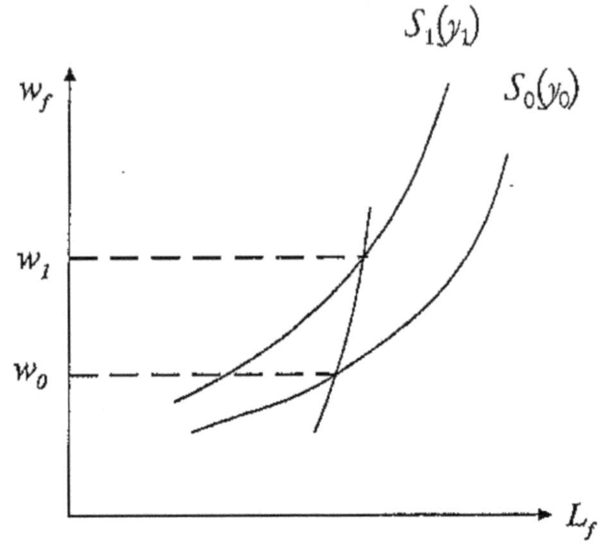


**Fig. 4.3** Observed and "true" labor supply elasticity (3.3 in my 1993 book)

(let's say along supply $S_0(y_0)$): she will work more hours at the higher wage. The supply $S_0(y_0)$ is upward-sloping (assuming the substitution effect of wages dominates the income effect). However, if changes in wage are positively correlated with changes in WiHo price $y$ (for example due to improvements in standards of living for the whole population) then as we move up the supply defined for a particular level of $y$ there will also be a shift to the left from $S_0(y_0)$ to $S_1(y_1)$ since $y$ also rises and this causes a decrease in labor supply (work in WiHo and in the labor force are substitute ways to make a living). The *observed* elasticity of labor supply is then based on a movement from a point corresponding to wage $w_0$ and WiHo price $y_0$ on supply $S_0$ to a point corresponding to wage $w_1$ and WiHo price $y_1$ on supply $S_1$. The observed elasticity—that of the "envelope supply" linking the relevant points on both supply curves—will then be lower than the true elasticity and can possibly be negative (as is the case in Fig. 4.3).

*Testable Implication TU4''': Backward-bending supplies are more likely to be observed for women than for men.* Since women are more likely to be paid for performing WiHo than men it follows that a backward-bending supply curve is more likely to be observed among women than among men. This could possibly explain why Link and Settle (1981) found a backward-bending supply of labor for a sample of female nurses in the USA. I am not aware of examples of backward-bending labor supplies for workers in a predominantly male profession.

The traditional explanation for a backward-bending supply of labor is limited to high wage ranges at which the income effect is likely to exceed the substitution effect. The explanation given here is not limited to high wage ranges. It is also possible that labor–supply curves have a negative slope at low wages due to the existence of a minimum subsistence level of income (see Dessing 2002 for a study based on data from a country with a large population close to subsistence levels).

## Cross-wage Elasticity of Labor Supply

The potential effect of the spouse's wage on own labor supply is not as straightforward in this theory as it is in the labor economics models that view the household as the decision-making unit. Here, the individuals are decision makers and the wage of the spouse only affects the individual's labor supply via its effect on the price of WiHo.

*Testable Implication TU5: Cross-wage elasticities on labor supply are likely to be negative.* First, the wage earned by the representative man can influence women's WiHo market conditions due to an income effect that shifts men's demand for women's WiHo. The income effect will be positive, assuming normality. There may also be substitution between his time and her time: the higher his wage the more he may have a demand for her WiHo as a substitute for his own time in household production. Due to both of these reasons higher wages for the representative man will cause a higher market demand for the WiHo of the representative woman. With no change in women's supply of WiHo this will lead to an increase in the price of women's WiHo, an increase in their reservation wage, and lower labor supply by women. It could also lead to an increase in time women spend in WiHo at the new equilibrium in the WiHo market, to the extent that the shift in demand occurs in an upward-sloping portion of women's supply of WiHo.

A similar analysis can be applied to men as suppliers of WiHo, with women on the demand side. If women's wage increases their demand for men's WiHo will increase due to an income and a substitution effect, leading to higher reservation wages for men and consequently reduced men's labor supply and increased hours of WiHo supplied by men in equilibrium.

Given that the cross-wage effects occur via a shift in demand for spouse's WiHo, one expects the magnitude of the changes in hours of WiHo and hours of regular labor to be inversely related. The shift in demand occurs along the supply of WiHo. Therefore if, for example, women's demand for men's WiHo occurs where men's supply of WiHo is flat, there will be a large increase in men's WiHo time and a small increase in their reservation wage and labor supply. In contrast, if the shift in demand occurs where men's supply of WiHo is close to vertical, there will be little change in men's WiHo time and a large increase in reservation wage and labor supply. The same holds for changes in men's demand and women's WiHo and labor supply.

Cross-wage elasticities are more complex if there are many types of men and women (see the next chapter).

## Sex Ratio Effects on Labor Supply

Sex ratios are defined as the ratio $N_m/N_f$ (see Henry 1975). Becker (1973) was the first to incorporate this variable in economic analyses of marriage, but his focus was on explaining marriage rates and polygamy. Testable implications regarding sex ratio effects on labor supply were first derived theoretically in Grossbard-Shechtman (1984).[3] Sex ratios and women's labor force participation are connected to the extent that sex ratios influence the equilibrium $y$, the price of WiHo is determined in a WiHo market and influences reservation wage $w^*$. It follows from general equilibrium Eqs. 2.10–2.15 *plus* two labor demand equations (see Chap. 2) that the number of women $N_f$ and the number of men $N_m$ are parameters likely to influence not only equilibrium wages of men and women in labor markets but also equilibrium prices of WiHo.

*Testable Implication TU6: Sex Ratios and Women's Employment: Relative to situations of low sex ratios or balanced marriage markets, high sex ratios are expected to be associated with lower labor supply of women.* We start by assuming an increase in $N_m$, the number of men, for instance due to a wave of all-male immigration, which implies increases in both sex ratio and population size. If population is to remain constant, which is necessary if we want to examine the effect of a pure sex ratio change, the increase in number of men $N_m$ has to be accompanied by a drop in the number of women $N_f$. An increase in $N_m$ and drop in the number of women $N_f$ affect the system of Eqs. 2.13–2.15 as follows: men's aggregate supplies of labor and their demand for a wife's WiHo all shift to the right; women's aggregate supplies of labor and their demand for husband's WiHo shift to the left.[4] These shifts then cause the following initial and secondary effects on wages and WiHo prices, in turn affecting labor supply.

Equation 2.15 implies that an increase in $N_m$ causes an increase in men's aggregate demand for female WiHo, illustrated as a shift to the right from $D$ to $D'$ in panel *a* of Fig. 4.4. In addition, decreases in male equilibrium wages $\overline{w}_m$ and prices for men's WiHo $\overline{y}_m$ originate from increases in supply in panels *b* and *d* (although downward wage rigidity may limit these drops in both the labor market and the market for WiHo). At the same time decreases in the number of women also affect the markets. In the market for women's WiHo (panel a) there will be an increase in the market-established $y$ from $\overline{y}_f$ *to* $\overline{y}_f'$ due to both an increase in men's demand and a decrease in women's supply.

Initial wage effects in turn lead to lower male income: reductions in both equilibrium male wage $\overline{w}_m$ and price of men's WiHo $\overline{y}_m$ tend to push the aggregate demand for female WiHo, $H_f$, back down.[5] Moreover, a lower male wage $w_m$ also tends to lead to a reduction in men's aggregate demand for WiHo $H_f$ due to a substitution effect in home production and consumption (assuming male and female WiHo are substitutes). This factor will be minor if men do not engage much in WiHo, as is the case in many traditional societies. For simplicity such possible secondary effects shifting men's demand for $H_f$ are ignored and it is assumed that the rightward shift from $D$ to $D'$ is final. Due to this increased demand as well as to

[3] Another early study of sex ratios and women's labor supply is South and Trent (1988).

[4] It is assumed that the influx of men does not affect the aggregate demand for total labor and the level of nonwork income $V$.

[5] It is assumed that the goods and services that men produce with the help of women's WiHo have a positive income elasticity.

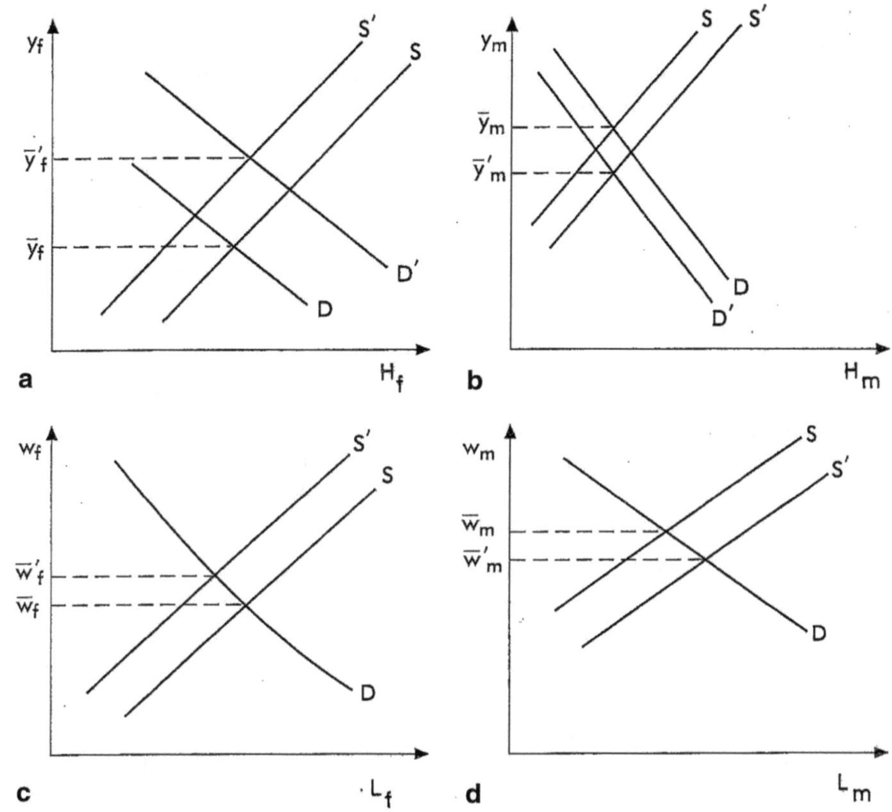


**Fig. 4.4** Markets for **a** women's WiHo, **b** men's WiHo, **c** women's labor, and **d** men's labor

a drop in women's supply the equilibrium $\bar{y}_f$ ends up increasing in comparison to its pre-immigration level, for instance to post-immigration price of women's WiHo $\bar{y}_f'$ in Fig. 4.4 (panel *a*).

This change in WiHo price in turn affect *labor supply.* If women can obtain higher prices for their WiHo their supply of work in the labor force will drop in accordance with Eq. 2.8. This implies that women's supply of labor will shift leftwards to *S'* in panel *c* in Fig. 4.4, in addition to the decrease in supply due to a reduction in the number of women. In addition, lower wages $w_m$ for male workers may induce employers to substitute male workers for female workers, possibly leading to a downward shift in the demand for female workers (not shown). This reduction in supply of women's labor leads to a reduction in total employment of women in the labor force (and if the demand for their labor also drops there will be an even greater reduction in women's employment in the labor force).

Overall an increase in sex ratio is predicted to lead to a larger increase in women's price of WiHo, $y_f$, than in their wage in the labor force $w_f$. Therefore, higher sex ratios are expected to be associated with a decrease in women's employment in the labor force.

The aggregate employment levels in Fig. 4.4 do not determine the division between total number of workers and hours of work per worker. The effect of a high sex ratio is likely to operate in one or both dimensions of labor supply: (1) reduced labor force participation and/or (2) reduced number of hours of work. If not all women participate, a representative woman will be indifferent between being in or out of the labor force.

A prediction similar to TU6 can be found in Guttentag and Secord (1983), who hypothesized independently that women (both married and unmarried) are more likely to work when sex ratios are low. However, Guttentag and Secord never looked separately at sex ratio effects on married women, as I do in Chap. 6. When married and unmarried women are combined, negative associations between sex ratio and women's labor force participation could simply follow from the fact that (a) higher sex ratios imply higher marriage rates for women and (b) married women typically work less than unmarried women, and such negative associations do not necessarily imply that women's price in marriage varies with sex ratio.

*Testable Implication TU7: Sex Ratios and Men's Employment: Relative to situations of low sex ratios or balanced marriage markets, high sex ratios are expected to be associated with more labor supply by men.* Higher sex ratios are also likely to affect men's labor supply. With population constant there will be more men and fewer women. As stated above one of the initial effects of a higher number of men is that men's aggregate demand for women's WiHo increases, which makes women's WiHo more expensive for men and reduces their real income. To the extent that men also supply WiHo they will get a lower price for it. Both income and substitution effects will lead to more labor supply on the part of men. Furthermore, the decrease in number of women associated with higher sex ratios and constant population implies a decrease in aggregate demand for men's WiHo, implying a further decrease *y* (subscript m), the price of men's WiHo, and therefore in men's real income. The only reason why reduced numbers of women could possibly lead to the opposite result is that women's wages will increase if their supply of labor goes down, and with higher incomes their individual demand for men's WiHo will increase. However, to the extent that men's WiHo is limited relative to that of women and that men and women are good substitutes in the labor force this effect is likely to be limited.

Evidence about testable implications TU6 and TU7 is presented in Chap. 6.

In this chapter implications were derived from a macro-level model based on the assumption that there is only one type of woman and one type of man. In the following two chapters new insights on labor supply are derived assuming hedonic models with multiple types of people. Chapter 6 reexamines the testable implications that were derived in this chapter and that deal with income effects, wage effects, and sex ratio effects.

## References


Apps, Patricia, and Ray Rees. 1988. Taxation and the household. *Journal of Public Economics* 35:355–369.

Becker, Gary S. 1973. A theory of marriage: Part I. *Journal of Political Economy* 81:813–846.

Becker, Gary S. 1981. *A treatise on the family*. Cambridge: Harvard University Press.

Becker, Gary S. 2004. Communication by email to Shoshana Grossbard, Oct 12.

Bloemen, Hans, and Elena Stancanelli. 2015. Toyboys or supergirls? An analysis of earnings and employment outcomes of spouses. *Review of Economics of the Household*. http://link.springer.com/article/10.1007/s11150-013-9212-y, forthcoming.

Chiappori, Pierre-Andre 1988. Rational household labor supply. *Econometrica* 56:63–90.

Dessing, Maryke 2002. Labor supply, the family and poverty: The S-shaped labor supply curve. *Journal of Economic Behavior & Organization* 49 (4): 433–458.

Gregg-Lewis, H. 1973. Lectures in labor economics. Classnotes taken by S. A. Grossbard.

Gronau, Reuben. 1977. Leisure, home production, and work—The theory of the allocation of time revisited. *Journal of Political Economy* 85:1099–1124.

Grossbard-Shechtman, Amyra. 1984. A theory of allocation of time in markets for labor and marriage. *Economic Journal* 94:863–882.

Grossbard-Shechtman, Shoshana. 1993. *On the economics of marriage*. Boulder: Westview.

Grossbard-Shechtman, Shoshana. 2003. A consumer theory with competitive markets for work in marriage. *Journal of Socio-Economics* 31 (6): 609–645.

Guttentag, Marcia, and Paul F. Secord. 1983. *Too many women: The sex ratio question*. Beverly Hills: Sage.

Henry, Louis. 1975. Schema d'Evolution des Marriages apres de Grandes Variations des Naissances. *Population* 30:759–779.

Killingsworth, Mark R., and James J. Heckman. 1986. Female labor supply: A survey. In *Handbook of labor economics,* ed. O. Ashenfelter and R. Layard. Amsterdam: North Holland.

Link, C. R., and Russell F. Settle. 1981. Wage incentives and married professional nurses: A case of backward-bending supply. *Economic Inquiry* 19:144–156.

Lundberg, Shelly, and Robert A. Pollak. 1993. Separate sphere bargaining and the marriage market. *Journal of Political Economy* 101:988–1010.

McElroy, Marjorie B. 1990. The empirical content of Nash-Bargained household behavior. *Journal of Human Resources* 25:559–583.

McElroy, Marjorie B., and M. J. Horney. 1981. Nash bargained household decisions: Toward a generalization of the theory of demand. *International Economic Review* 22:333–349.

Robbins, Lionel. 1930. On the elasticity of demand for income in terms of efforts. *Economica* 10:123–129.

Sevilla-Sanz, A., J. I. Gimenez-Nadal, and C. Fernandez. 2010. Gender roles and the division of unpaid work in Spanish households. *Feminist Economics* 16 (4): 137–184

South, Scott J., and Kathrine Trent. 1988. Sex ratios and women's roles: a cross-national analysis. *American Journal of Sociology* 93:1096–1115.

Willis, Robert J. 1974. A new approach to the economic theory of fertility behavior. In *Economics of the family,* ed. T. W. Schultz. Chicago: University of Chicago Press.

# Chapter 5
# Compensating Differentials in Marriage Markets and more New Implications for Labor Supply Based on a Marshallian Marriage Market Analysis

Chapter 4 analyzed labor supply, assuming that there is only one type of man and one type of woman. The analysis here is at the micro level, in line with Chap. 3: it is assumed that there are many types of substitutable individuals participating in multiple markets for work-in-household (WiHo; defined in Chap. 2). A price mechanism based on market values of WiHo facilitates selection of spouses into marriages, assists individual household members in coordinating their time use decisions, and influences distribution of resources within the household. It is shown how individual characteristics such as age, race, and education may be associated with variation in WiHo prices and therefore labor supply. Characteristics of the self and the spouse are examined separately and implications for estimation methods are discussed. The model also calls for examination of the effect of laws and regulations affecting marriage market conditions. In the next chapter it is shown how this hedonic market model offers new insights on income and wage effects on labor supply. The sex ratio effects presented in Chap. 4 are also revisited.

There are more types of couples than types of individuals, given that each individual type can potentially combine with each other type. One way to categorize couples is according to the type of arrangement used to organize household production, including WiHo. Some couples may opt for an egalitarian arrangement, with both members of the couple working outside and supplying WiHo to each other to similar degrees. This implies little need for one spouse to pay for the other's WiHo. In contrast, in cases of specialized division of labor, with one member working more in the labor force and the other working more at WiHo, it is more likely that there will be a transfer of money or goods from the spouse who benefits from the extra WiHo to the spouse who performs it. In the context of a traditional division of labor this entails more WiHo performed by the wife, the husband earning more than the wife, and the husband making some or all of his income available to his wife.



S. Grossbard, *The Marriage Motive: A Price Theory of Marriage*,
DOI 10.1007/978-1-4614-1623-4_5

## Own Productivity in WiHo, Discrimination in WiHo Markets, and Labor Supply

Previous economic analyses of labor supply have looked at how demographic characteristics of *households*, such as number and age of children or number of adults, determine the value of women's time and their labor supply (for instance, Gronau 1973; Heckman 1974). They have also examined effects of *individual* characteristics on such supply, including that of demographic characteristics such as age and race. However, they have typically ignored possible effects of individual demographic traits on labor supply due to effects on WiHo productivity and WiHo price. They have also ignored discrimination in marriage markets.

Labor supply has been analyzed in the previous chapter as a choice between two occupations: work and WiHo. Therefore, the reservation wage depends on the price an individual can get for supplying WiHo. When there are many interrelated hedonic markets for WiHo, an individual *i* has a separate reservation wage $w_{ij}^*$ associated with each potential spouse *j*. Accordingly,

$$w_{ij}^* = y_{ij} + \frac{MU_{hij}}{MU_{xi}} - \frac{MU_{li}}{MU_{xi}}, \tag{5.1}$$

which is adapted from Eq. 2.8 presented in Chap. 2. The higher $y_{ij}^e$, the equilibrium price in a WiHo market for types *i* and *j*, the higher the actual WiHo price $y_{ij}$ and the higher the reservation wage of individual *i* forming a couple with a type *j*. It also follows from Eq. 5.1 that the higher $MU_{hij}$, the marginal utility that *i* derives from performing WiHo work for *j*, the higher the reservation wage.

Furthermore, the labor supply of a spouse not willing to supply WiHo, but willing to pay for it, will also be influenced by how much of their own income goes to the spouse performing most WiHo (the WiHo worker). However, as in Chap. 4 the focus here is on explaining women's labor supply given that women continue to be their households' WiHo workers more often than men (see Chap. 2) and that the variability in women's labor supply considerably exceeds that of men's labor supply.

Any individual or group characteristic $Z_i$ or $Z_j$ that possibly has an impact on WiHo price $y_{ij}$ will affect the reservation wage and therefore labor supply. More specifically, holding other characteristics constant, a factor $Z_i$ that has a positive influence on $y_{ij}$ will lead to a higher reservation wage $w_{ij}*$ and therefore to lower labor supply. Such factors could be associated with higher WiHo productivity and therefore with higher demand for WiHo. In turn, WiHo productivity could be a function of current age, education, place of birth, and birth cohort. Discrimination can also affect value in WiHo markets. When testing the theory it is best to use *Z* factors that are as exogeneous as possible, which gives "age" and "place of birth" an advantage over "education".

**Age** *Testable Implication TU8: Individual suppliers of WiHo who are closer to the age of maximum reproductive capacity are less likely to supply labor in labor markets.* Age affects labor supply not only because of its potential impact on productivity at work, and therefore wage, but also due to its possible effect on productivity in WiHo and therefore value in WiHo markets.[1] Women's WiHo may include willingness to be pregnant with a particular man's child, and both men's and women's WiHo may include willingness to parent a spouse's child. In turn, this kind of WiHo is a function of productivity at reproducing and parenting and how close the person is to the age of optimum parenting capacity. Individuals further from that optimum will be less in demand than those at the optimum, and therefore they will obtain a relatively lower price for their WiHo. Given gender differences in reproductive capacity, the age at which men's demand for women's WiHo peaks is likely to be lower than the age at which women's demand for men's WiHo peaks. WiHo suppliers closer to the optimal age for reproduction and parenting will get higher their WiHo price $y_{ij}$ and therefore will be less likely to supply labor $l_{ij}$. The impact of age may not be linear, especially since it is difficult to separate various effects of age. Effects of reproductive capacity also need to be separated from effects of actual reproduction history. If children are present this is likely to increase the preponderance of traditional gender roles as women are more likely to engage in WiHo and less in labor in the labor force, and men are more likely to work in the labor force.

Suggestive evidence for this implication is that US women are more likely to be in the labor force between ages 40 and 44 (75.8 % in the labor force) than between ages 30 and 34 (73.7 % in the labor force in 2012). This makes sense since in the USA in 2012, the average age at which women gave birth was 28.6 (see Weeks 2011). Labor force participation for women in their early 40s had also been higher than that of women in their early 30s for every single year in the period 2003–2011.

This age differential in women's labor force participation was higher prior to the recession of 2008 than after that recession. Could it be that men had less of a demand for women's reproductive WiHo after the recession than before? In contrast to the age differential for women, in every single year in the period 2003–2012 men had a higher participation rate at ages 30–34 than at ages 40–44. For instance, in 2012 their labor force participation rates at ages 30–34 and 40–44 were respectively 90.7 and 90.1. That small age differential could reflect men's extra labor supply when their wives and partners are having children, or it could indicate higher prices for women's WiHo even if they do not have children but are closer to peak reproductive capacity. I hope that future empirical work will be able to distinguish between these two explanations, possibly by using panel data and focusing on the labor supply of individuals who can be presumed to want to reproduce but have not done so.

**Education** *Testable Implication TU9: To the extent that education is associated with higher WiHo productivity more educated suppliers of WiHo are less likely to supply labor in the labor force.* Years of schooling could affect labor supply

[1] Differences in the age at marriage of men and women are an interesting phenomenon that economists have also tried to explain. For instance, Bergstrom and Bagnoli (1993) and Danziger and Neuman (1999).

**Table 5.1** Percentage of married mothers employed full-time, by race and tier of bachelor's degree. (Source: National Survey of College Graduates 2003 and 2010. Calculations provided by Joni Hersch)

| | All | White | Black |
|---|---|---|---|
| | 1 | 2 | 3 |
| Tier 1 | 43.5 | 40 ($N$=1192) | 90 ($N$=136) |
| Tier 2 | 43.0 | 49 ($N$=1159) | 83 ($N$=68) |
| Tier 3 | 44.6 | 45 ($N$=4335) | 77 ($N$=296) |
| Tier 4 | 55.0 | 54 ($N$=11094) | 75 ($N$=1328) |

by influencing not only labor productivity in labor markets, and therefore wages, but also productivity in WiHo and therefore WiHo price $y$. Education thus has two countervailing effects on labor supply: a positive one via wages and a negative one via reservation wages based on the price of WiHo. The more education raises WiHo productivity relative to its positive effect on labor productivity and wages, the more it is expected to be associated negatively with labor supply. To test this implication it is desirable to select a population with a high willingness to be primary WiHo suppliers in their couple. This is more often the case for women than for men.

*Evidence* Using data from the 2003 National Survey of College Graduates (NSCG) for women aged 23–54, Joni Hersch (2013) found that relative to their counterparts who went to colleges with lower ranking, married mothers with a degree from a top-tier college are more likely to drop out of the labor force when they have children.[2] Her results, based on a pooled data set from the 2003 and 2010 NSCG, show the full-time employment rates reported in column 1 of Table 5.1.

One expects that, relative to a college degree from a lower-tier school, a top-tier college degree will add to productivity at both work and WiHo, and therefore be associated with a higher wage and a higher price of WiHo. If the net effect of that degree is a lower rate of labor force participation, and especially full-time labor force participation, this possibly indicates that a degree from a better-ranked college adds more to price of WiHo than to wage (because it adds more to WiHo productivity than to labor productivity). Hersch's finding was restricted to mothers, which suggests that childrearing is a particularly important component of WiHo and/or that education adds to productivity in WiHo.

**Race and Ethnicity** *Testable Implication TU10: Individuals belonging to groups that are discriminated against in marriage markets will be less in demand in markets for WiHo, the price of their WiHo will be lower and they will be more likely to supply labor in the labor force.* For example, if colorism (see Burke 2008) prevails in marriage markets, and there is a bias against dark skin, prices for the WiHo of

[2] Hersch (2013) defines the four tiers as follows: Tier 1 are highly-selective, private research-intensive universities; Tier 2 are selective private liberal arts colleges; Tier 3 are selective, public research-intensive universities; and Tier 4 are public and private colleges and universities that are not research intensive, grant few or no doctoral degrees, and are not highly selective.

dark-skinned men and women will be lower in equilibrium than that of people with light skin. Historically such discrimination was practiced against blacks in the USA. That anti-miscegenation laws were instituted by whites in many US states reflects marriage market discrimination against blacks (see Fryer 2007). Another example is that in a society discriminating against WiHo suppliers belonging to certain religious groups, one expects that ceteris paribus, women from these religious groups get lower equilibrium $y$ for their WiHo. If the WiHo suppliers are mostly women, and women from lower status groups obtain lower WiHo prices $y$ relative to women from higher status groups, their reservation wage will be lower and they will be more likely to be in the labor force. To the extent that men are WiHo workers this also applies to them.

*Evidence* It is best to examine statistics for married mothers, who are most likely to provide WiHo. Therefore the price of WiHo is most likely to affect them. The same 2003 and 2010 NSCG data mentioned above (columns 2 and 3 in Table 5.1) indicate that black married mothers with a college degree were considerably more likely to work full time than their white counterparts, regardless of whether they obtained their degree in a college belonging to tier 1, 2, 3, or 4. The racial gap is quite large: 40 % (white) versus 90 % (black) working full time for women who went to a tier 1 college and 54 % (white) versus 75 % (black) working full time for women who went to a tier 4 college. In 2012 the racial gap in full-time year-round employment for all women aged 30–49 with a college degree (or more) was 58.9 % for whites versus 68.9 % for blacks. There was practically no gap in full-time year-round employment for women who only went to high school or had the equivalent of a high school education: 44.6 % (whites) versus 45.1 % (blacks).[3] In 2013 racial gaps in labor force participation of women aged 30–49 went in the same direction: 82.4 % (white) versus 87.0 % (black) for those with at least a college degree and 69.6 % (white) versus 72.1 % (black) for those with only high school. Higher rates of labor force participation for black women have also been reported in the past (e.g. in Blau and Ferber 1992; Jacobsen 1994).

This black/white difference is consistent with the existence of discrimination against black women in WiHo markets in the USA, leading to lower WiHo prices and therefore higher likelihood of participation in the labor force and full-time employment. An alternative explanation is that black women like work more than white women. However, this theory does not explain why the racial gap for mothers who went to elite colleges is so much larger than that for women in other categories. My explanation is that women who graduated from these colleges are more valued by marriage markets, and more so in the case of white women. What else explains that black women who graduated from elite colleges were more than twice as likely to work full-time than their white counterparts? It is certainly unlikely that in this group black women earned wages twice as high.

Next, I present testable implications regarding combinations of race (ethnicity) and other variables.[4]

---

[3] These calculations are based on calculations using the Current Population Surveys, US Census, Table Creator, at http://www.census.gov/cps/data/cpstablecreator.html.

[4] This part is adapted from Grossbard-Shechtman (1996).

**Race (ethnicity) and Education** *Testable Implication TU10′: A racial gap in WiHo workers' labor supply is more likely to occur among those with high education than among those with low education. Therefore, it is predicted that education will have a larger positive effect on the labor supply of women belonging to a group suffering from discrimination in marriage markets than on the labor supply of women not suffering from such discrimination.* Education is expected to have a positive effect on both wage and WiHo price. The more it increases wage, the more it will be associated with higher labor force participation. The more it increases WiHo price, the less it will be associated with higher labor force participation. If black women are discriminated against in marriage markets and therefore get lower WiHo prices than white women, and their WiHo price benefits less from education than in the case of white women, but there is no racial gap in the effect of education on wages, it follows that education will have a more positive effect on black women's supply of labor in the labor force. Also, education will have a more positive effect on labor supply for black women than for white women. More generally, viewing both men and women as potential WiHo workers, to the extent that in the US blacks suffer from discrimination in marriage markets (markets for WiHo), it follows that racial gaps in labor supply will be larger among more educated WiHo workers than among WiHo workers with low education.

*Evidence* The black/white contrast apparent from Table 5.1 is most striking for graduates of tier 1 schools, the colleges with the highest ranking. A white woman who graduated from a Tier 1 college has a 40 % likelihood of being employed full time. For her black counterpart that likelihood is more than double and stands at 90 %. It is striking that a white woman with a degree from a tier 1 college is less likely to be working full time in the labor force than her counterpart with a degree from a lower-tier college, whereas the opposite is true for a black woman. A number of earlier studies have documented a larger effect of education for black women than for white women in the USA. (Carliner 1981; Lehrer 1992).

The recent finding by Hersch reported above may indicate that the effect of a degree from a tier 1 school on women's WiHo price is considerably higher for white women than for black women. It is even possible that in contrast to white women, black women with a tier-one degree do not get a higher price for their WiHo than black women who went to a lower-tier college. The marriage market benefit of such elite schooling may be limited to white women. More generally, black women's education may not carry the marriage-related benefits that it carries for white women in the USA. The presumed lower WiHo price for black women could be the result of discrimination. Alternatively, it could be the result of endogamy among both blacks and whites and a lower sex ratio among blacks with the most valuable education than among whites with such education (see Goldman 1977).

**Race (ethnicity) and Divorce Probability** *Testable Implication TU10″: Predicted divorce is expected to have less impact on black women's labor supply than on white women's.* If black women get a lower WiHo price than white women, and a higher WiHo price implies larger transfers of income from husband to wife, it follows that on average a divorce will not involve as much of a loss of transfers from the spouse for black women as it will for white women. Relative to their counterparts who expect their marriage to last, married WiHo workers expecting a divorce are more likely to participate in the labor force and are likely to work more hours because they have to make up for the expected loss in transfers from their spouse. To the extent that married black women anticipate less of a loss in income than their white counterparts, it follows that expected divorce will have less impact on black women's labor supply relative to its impact on white women.

*Evidence* Based on a longitudinal study, Johnson and Skinner (1986) showed that married women anticipating divorce had a higher labor supply than married women who do not anticipate divorce. The higher the likelihood of a future divorce the more women participated in the labor force while married. This was more likely to be the case for white women than for black women, which is consistent with WiHo prices being higher for white women than for black women.

**Weight** *Testable Implication TU11: To the extent that being overweight is associated with lower WiHo productivity, suppliers of WiHo closer to an optimal weight are less likely to supply labor in the labor force than their overweight counterparts.* This effect is expected to operate via markets for WiHo and WiHo price. Women and men who are not overweight are expected to fetch a higher price for their WiHo than those who are overweight, which will raise their reservation wage and discourage their labor supply. Since it is also known that overweight workers earn less in the labor force (especially in the case of women, see Cawley 2004), the effects of weight on productivity in the labor force and at WiHo may cancel each other out. The larger the negative effect of weight on WiHo price relative to its effect on wage, the more being overweight is likely to be associated with higher labor supply. This is especially likely to hold for WiHo workers belonging to groups who typically get paid well for their WiHo, such as women, mothers, whites and those belonging to high-status religious groups.

*Evidence* I have not found direct evidence for this implication, but this analysis could help explain intriguing findings by Lakdawalla and Philipson (2007) regarding weight and occupation: (1) little selection of heavier men into occupations with high strength requirements while women workers who were heavier selected into occupations with more strength requirements; and (2) work in the most fitness-demanding occupations for 18 years leaves men leaner than if they worked in the least-demanding occupations, but this was not found for women. One of the explanations that Lakdawalla and Philipson offer for these gender differences is that "women expect less lifetime labor force attachment and engage in relatively more leisure-time or home production activities that have their own levels of exercise" (p. 109). An alternative explanation in light of a possible link between weight and WiHo prices is that heavier women obtain lower WiHo prices and consequently have lower reservation wages relative to leaner women. This may lead heavier women to be more likely to choose jobs with more strenuous demands, and thereby earn higher wages. These jobs may also be less compatible with simultaneous supply of WiHo and labor in the labor force.

## Compensating Differentials in Marriage and Labor Supply

Any positive characteristic of a (potential) spouse $Z_j$ valued in WiHo markets will be associated with a lower $y_{ij}$ that an individual WiHo worker *i* "charges" for WiHo supplied to spouse *j*, as discussed in Chap. 3: $\frac{\partial y_{ij}^e}{\partial Z_j} < 0$. Individuals with a trait valued in marriage markets thus have to pay less for a spouse's WiHo relative to those without that trait. As first stated in Grossbard-Shechtman (1984) this implies this WiHo worker *i* will have a lower reservation wage $w_{ij}^*$ if married to some of type *j* than if married to someone with a less desirable characteristic (see Eq. 5.1). In turn a lower reservation wage implies a higher labor supply, assuming that other characteristics of both individuals are held constant (including spouse's income) and that spouses do not automatically share a fixed proportion of their income.[5]

**Age-Gap** *Testable Implication TU12: Women who are young relative to their husbands are likely to supply less labor to the labor force.* An individual's age relative to his or her spouse may affect labor supply via its effect on WiHo prices $y_{ij}$ associated with different age gaps between men and women, conditional on one spouse's age. For instance, consider a market for WiHo supplied by women of type *i*. Assume that the women are clearly "young" relative to men of type *j* and that men have a preference for WiHo supplied by younger women. Therefore men's demand for women in this market will be high compared to demand by the same type of men in markets for women closer to their own age. More specifically, consider a market for women's $h_{30,50}$, WiHo supplied by 30 years old women to 50 years old men. Men's preference for young wives implies that relative to the market for $h_{30,30}$, where men as well as women are 30, the demand by 50-year-old men for the WiHo of 30-year-old women is high. Furthermore, the willingness of 30-year-old women to supply WiHo to 50-year-old men is likely to be low relative to their willingness to supply WiHo to 30-year-old men as they are likely to prefer men their own age (e.g., in order to minimize the prospect of early widowhood). With lower supply and higher demand relative to the market for $h_{30,30}$, equilibrium WiHo price $y_{30,50}$ in the $h_{30,50}$ market is likely to be high relative to price $y_{30,30}$ established in the $h_{30,30}$ market. Let us call *age-gap premium* the difference between the WiHo price in a young woman/old man marriage and that paid when two people are close in age, which is in this case, $y_{30,50} - y_{30,30}$. We do not have measures for WiHo prices, but a gap in WiHo price could for example take the form of married women's more luxurious lifestyle if they are married to older men than if they are married to men close to their age. The concept of trophy wife conveys this idea. The connotation is that she is like a trophy that her husband obtained thanks to his money. The American reality TV show *Trophy Wives* typically features wives who are considerably younger than their husbands and who enjoy a standard of living considerably higher than that of the average American.

---

[5] This assumption is also found in Becker's (1973) section on the division of marital output.

Equation 5.1 implies that if $y_{30,50} > y_{30,30}$ then $l_{30,50} < l_{30,30}$; that is, the labor supply of 30-year-old women married to 50-year-old men will be low relative to $l_{30,30}$, the labor supply of 30-year-old women married to men their own age. Again, using the example of the TV series *Trophy Wives*, these women typically do not participate in the labor force.

When testing for age gap effects on labor supply in a rigorous way one needs to control for wife's or husband's age. The relationship between age and age-gap premium could be nonlinear for a number of reasons. Given biological and legal constraints a large age-gap premium is not possible when men are very young. Also, if men are young themselves, they do not derive externalities from their wife's youth and men's willingness to pay a youth premium may be limited. Young men may also be less able to afford a youth premium even if men's income is controlled for. Furthermore, at age 20, with the likelihood of widowhood further into the future, women may be more willing to marry a man who is 10 years older than at age 30. To capture such nonlinearities it may be a good idea for models of women's labor supply to include a square term of age-gap and of the interaction between age and age-gap. Furthermore, when testing the prediction it is important to define 'age-gap' in the appropriate cultural context. In some societies the average age difference between husband and wife is 13 years, whereas in the USA it is currently 1.5 years. The more common and acceptable the age-gap, the less young women are likely to obtain a premium for marrying older men and the less their labor supply is likely to be affected.

*Evidence* Shoshana Neuman and I used a sample of Israeli Jewish women with a high school education or less, as we wanted to focus on women unlikely to go to work because their job is interesting. We found that for each year of husband/wife age difference beyond 3 or 5 years (depending on the cultural norm prevalent for European/American Jews and Asian/African Jews) there was a lower probability that the wife participated in the labor force (Grossbard-Shechtman and Neuman 1988). This is consistent with the existence of an age-gap premium in the price for women's WiHo. Using French data from 1990 to 2002, Bloemen and Stancanelli (2015) found that an age gap of 5 or more years in either direction was associated with lower labor force participation of both partners. The finding of lower labor supply by relatively young wives and husbands is in line with implication TU12. They seemed to find both "trophy wives" and "trophy husbands"! However, the finding of lower labor supply by men and women married to considerably younger spouses does not corroborate TU12: instead I would expect that the spouse of the trophy wife or husband works more in the labor force to pay high transfers for the WiHo they use. It could be that those marrying younger spouses have more personal wealth and that this wealth, not properly measured in the data, is negatively related to observed labor supply.

**Weight of Self and Spouse** *Testable Implication TU13: Men and women who are thin relative to their spouses are likely to supply less labor to the labor force.* To the extent that marriage markets place a penalty on being overweight WiHo workers who are thin relative to their spouse will earn a relatively high WiHo price relative to their counterparts married to equally thin people. This also follows from the same logic of compensating differentials the lead to the previous implications. As for WiHo users who are thin relative to their spouse they will benefit from a compensating differential: he or she will pay less for spouse's WiHo, which implies working fewer hours in the labor force. In traditional marriages, where women are the WiHo workers, it follows that women overweight relative to their husband will get paid less for their WiHo than their counterparts whose weight is similar to that of their husband. This implies more hours of work in the labor force on their part, controlling for spouse's income. In contrast, in nontraditional marriages women who are overweight relative to their husband will work more hours in the labor force to pay compensating differentials to their WiHo-supplying husbands.

**Evidence** Using US panel data Oreffice and Quintana-Domeque (2012) found that husbands who are thinner relative to their wives work fewer hours, while wives who are heavier relative to their husbands work more hours in the labor force. They measure relative thinness in terms of the body mass index (BMI), of one spouse relative to that of the other. Furthermore, they find that wives who are relatively heavier than their husbands are 6 % more likely to work more hours than the average wife, while husbands who are relatively thinner than their wives are 8 % less likely to work more hours than the average husband. These findings are consistent not only with TU12 presented here but also with the collective model (Chiappori 1992), where the relative physical attractiveness of one spouse with respect to the other increases individual bargaining power inside the household. Both my model and that of Chiappori imply that effects of weight will differ depending on whether individuals are coupled/married or not. The reason why marriage matters here in terms of my theory is that the reservation wage of unmarried people is less likely to be tied to WiHo prices, and therefore to the value of thinness in markets for WiHo, than the reservation wage of married people.

Oreffice and Quintana-Domeque (2012) also test for the effects of the relative mean and relative standard deviation of BMI in various marriage markets. Given that such relative mean is available, the following implication can also be tested.

*Testable Implication TU13": The lower the mean BMI for men in a marriage market the larger the effect of husband's relative BMI on wife's and husband's labor supply (in absolute terms).* TU12 stated that if a husband is relatively fat he has to pay for it in terms of working more in the labor market to pay a higher $y$. But if most men are fat in the marriage markets in which they participate, then this particular fat husband does not have to pay his wife as much extra for her WiHo as in the case where other men are thin: the compensating differential will not be as large. Her labor supply will not drop as much and his labor supply will not rise as much. One way to test this is to include an interaction term of "husband's BMI relative to the wife" and "men's BMI in the surrounding marriage market" in the regression models.

Likewise, I expect the effect of husband's relative BMI on wife's and husband's labor supply to be a function of the mean BMI for women in that particular wife's marriage market.

**Race, Ethnicity or Religion of Self and Spouse** Assuming Women Are the WiHo-Workers: *Testable Implication TU14: Assume that one group—let us say blacks or Jews—is discriminated against in markets for WiHo and that discrimination is one-sided or asymmetric. It is predicted that black (Jewish) women married to white (Christian) men will be more likely to supply labor in the labor force than their counterparts married endogamously. Also, white (Christian) women married to black (Jewish) men will be less likely to supply labor in the labor force than their counterparts married endogamously.* These implications can be extended to any two groups, where one discriminates more against the other.

Individuals belonging to groups that are discriminated against in marriage markets will be less in demand in their WiHo markets and the equilibrium price of their WiHo will be lower. Historically such discrimination was practiced against blacks in the USA (its strongest expression taking the form of miscegenation laws, see Fryer 2007). Christians have also often discriminated against Jewish potential marriage partners. Some blacks may also discriminate against whites and some Jews against Christians, but I am assuming asymmetric discrimination. In such circumstances and ceteris paribus, a black woman married to a white man is more likely to participate in the labor force than her counterpart married endogamously; a white woman married to a black husband is less likely to participate in the labor force than her counterpart married endogamously; a Jewish woman married to a Christian husband is more likely to participate in the labor force than her counterpart married endogamously; a Christian woman married to a Jewish husband is less likely to participate in the labor force than her counterpart married endogamously. In Hawaii it appears that Hawaiians are discriminated against in marriage markets; consequently the prediction is that a Hawaiian woman married to a white husband is more likely to participate in the labor force than her counterpart married endogamously, and a white woman married to a Hawaiian husband is less likely to participate in the labor force than her counterpart married endogamously. Among Israeli Jews, those of African or Asian descent were discriminated against in marriage markets in the 1970s. Accordingly the prediction is that an Asian–African woman married to a European husband is more likely to participate in the labor force than her counterpart married endogamously; and a European woman married to an Asian or African husband is less likely to participate in the labor force than her counterpart married endogamously.

*Evidence* The implications for ethnic differences were tested with data from Hawaii and Israel. In Hawaii Xuanning Fu and I found that Caucasian women married to Hawaiian men were less likely to be in the labor force than endogamous Caucasian women and that Hawaiian women married to Caucasian men were more likely to be in the labor force than endogamous Hawaiian women (Grossbard-Shechtman and Fu 2002). Both these findings support implication TU15. We found similar results for Caucasian–Black and Caucasian–Filipino intermarriages, two other groups with status lower than that of Caucasians in Hawaii.

Using a sample of Israeli Jewish couples Shoshana Neuman and I found that women from a higher status ethnicity (European/American) were less likely to be in the labor force if their husband belonged to a lower-status ethnicity ("born in Asia or Africa") than if they were both European/American (Grossbard-Shechtman and Neuman 1988).

Data on labor supply in the USA do not include information on religion, so I could not test this prediction on labor supply using data on religious intermarriage. Compensating differentials in marriage have been documented in the context of religious intermarriage in Grossbard-Shechtman (1983) and Chiswick and Lehrer (1991).

**Education of Self and Spouse** The gap between two spouses' education could also play a role, but due to the multiple possible effects of education on productivity at work, WiHo productivity, and marginal utility of the two types of work, no clear prediction is derived. To distinguish the two productivities one could perhaps rely on whether individuals completed studies more likely to influence productivity in WiHo relative to productivity in the labor market.

## WiHo Price and the Need for Simultaneous Estimations of Couples' Labor Supply

One reason why the error terms in the labor supply equations of the two members of a couple are correlated is that information on the same prices of WiHo is missing in both equations. In the case of a traditional specialized heterosexual couple, the price he is paying for her WiHo appears in both her labor supply (as she is comparing that price to the wage she can get in the labor force) and in his labor supply (as it influences his real income). The same conclusion holds for heterosexual couples where most WiHo is performed by men and for specialized same-sex couples.

In cases where each member of a couple performs WiHo for each other's benefit the price of each person's WiHo influences labor supply for at least these two reasons (choice between two occupations and effect on real income). In all cases it can be expected that estimation of an individual's labor supply will be improved if it is estimated simultaneously with that of a live-in partner or spouse. Joint estimations such as Duguet and Simonnet (2007) and Bloemen and Stancanelli (2015) are therefore of great value. Both of these studies used a French survey that collected extensive information on the time uses of two members of heterosexual couples. Unfortunately, most surveys do not simultaneously interview two members of a couple.

## References

Becker, Gary S. 1973. A theory of marriage: Part I. *Journal of Political Economy* 81:813–846.

Bergstrom, Theodore C., and Mark Bagnoli. 1993. Courtship as a waiting game. *Journal of Political Economy* 101:185–202.

Blau, F. D., and M. Ferber. 1992. *The economics of women, men, and work.* 2nd ed. Englewood Cliffs: Prentice Hall.

Bloemen, Hans, and Elena Stancanelli. 2015. Toyboys or supergirls? An analysis of earnings and employment outcomes of spouses. *Review of Economics of the Household*. http://link.springer.com/article/10.1007/s11150-013-9212-y, forthcoming.

Burke, M. 2008. Colorism. In *International encyclopedia of the social sciences,* ed. W. Darity Jr., 2 vol. Detroit: Thomson Gale.

Carliner, G. 1981. Female labor force participation for nine ethnic groups. *Journal of Human Resources* 16:286–293.

Cawley, J. 2004. The impact of obesity on wages. *Journal of Human Resources* 39 (2): 451–474.

Chiappori, Pierre-Andre. 1992. Collective labor supply and welfare. *Journal of Political Economy* 100:437–467.

Chiswick, Carmel U., and Evelyn L. Lehrer. 1991. Religious intermarriage: An economic perspective. *Contemporary Jewry* 12:21–34.

Danziger, Leif, and Shoshana Neuman. 1999. On the age at marriage: Theory and evidence from Jews and Moslems in Israel. *Journal of Economic Behavior and Organization* 40:179–193.

Duguet, Emmanuel, and Veronique Simonnet. 2007. Labor market participation in France: Couples' decisions. *Review of Economics of the household* 5:159–180.

Fryer, R. G. Jr. 2007. Guess who's coming to dinner? Trends in interracial marriages over the 20th century. *Journal of Economic Perspectives* 21 (1): 71–90.

Goldman, Noreen. 1977. *The marriage market: Supply and demand of potential spouses in the United States*. Cambridge: Harvard University.

Gronau, Reuben. 1973. The intrafamily allocation of time: The value of housewives' time. *American Economic Review* 63:643–651.

Grossbard-Shechtman, Amyra. 1983. A market approach to intermarriage. In *Papers in Jewish demography 1981,* ed. U. O. Schmelz, P. Gerson, and S. DellaPergola. Jerusalem: Hebrew University Institute Contemporary Jewry.

Grossbard-Shechtman, Amyra. 1984. A theory of allocation of time in markets for labor and marriage. *Economic Journal* 94:863–882.

Grossbard-Shechtman, Shoshana. 1996. Marriage markets and black/white differences in labor, marriage, and welfare. Paper Presented at the Annual Meetings of the Population Association of America, May.

Grossbard-Shechtman, S. A., and X. Fu. 2002. Women's labor force participation and status exchange in intermarriage: An empirical study in Hawaii. *Journal of Bioeconomics* 4 (3): 241–268.

Grossbard-Shechtman, A. S., and S. Neuman. 1988. Women's labor supply and marital choice. *Journal of Political Economy* 96:1294–1302.

Heckman, James J. 1974. Shadow prices, market wages, and labor supply. *Econometrica* 42:679–694.

Hersch, Joni. 2013. Opting out among women with elite education. *Review of Economics of the Household* 11:469–506.

Jacobsen, Joyce. 1994. *The economics of gender*. Cambridge: Blackwell.

Johnson, W. R., and J. Skinner. 1986. Labor supply and marital separation. *American Economic Review* 76:455–469.

Lakdawalla, Darius, and Philipson Tomas. 2007. Labor supply and weight. *Journal of Human Resources* 42 (1): 85–116.

Lehrer, E. L. 1992. The impact of children on women's labor supply. Black/white differentials revisited. *Journal of Human Resources* 27:422–444.

Oreffice, S., and C. Quintana-Domeque. 2012. Fat spouses and hours of work: Are body and Pareto weights correlated? *IZA Journal of Labor Economics* 1:6.

Weeks, John. 2011. *Population*. Belmont: Wadsworth.

# Chapter 6
# Revisiting Labor Supply Effects of Sex Ratio, Income, and Wage. Effects of Marriage-Related Laws

In Chap. 4, testable implications TU1, TU2, and TU3 dealing with income effects on labor supply were presented in the context of a macro model with one type of man and one type of woman. I now reexamine these implications in a micro context, assuming that there are many types of substitutable individuals, and derive further testable implications regarding income effects on labor supply. I also revisit TU4 on wage effects, TU5 on cross-wage effects, and implications regarding sex ratio effects analyzed in Chap. 4 using a macro model. This chapter follows the micro model presented in Chap. 3.

## Income Effects

*Revisiting previously stated implications regarding income effects on Time Use (TU).* Implication TU1 carries over to the case of multiple types of men and women: it is always necessary to consider individual rather than household income when studying labor supply and other outcomes.

TU2 stated that if gender roles are traditional and all nonwage incomes change by the same proportion, these changes are likely to have different effects on men and women's labor supply. Generalizing the applicability of TU2 to the case of multiple types of men and women is more complex. Some individuals who were well matched before income changes may no longer be so after income changes, given that they have the option of divorcing and re-matching with spouses who better suit their new circumstances. For example, they may have new levels of WiHo demanded or supplied at new equilibrium WiHo prices. It is still true that employment levels, wages, and the value of WiHo are all determined simultaneously in interrelated markets for labor and WiHo, but now there are multiple WiHo markets.

The availability of multiple types of men and women implies that when incomes change there is not as much need for adjustment to accommodate spouses, as was the case when there was only one type of spouse. To the extent that women are more



S. Grossbard, *The Marriage Motive: A Price Theory of Marriage*,
DOI 10.1007/978-1-4614-1623-4_6

likely to make adjustments than men, this implies fewer gender differences in the effect of income in the micro case than in the macro case.

As for implication TU3 about the effects of household income on value of time, in the macro model (Chap. 4) representative men and women were indifferent between being in or out of the labor force and between being in or out of marriage. Still assuming traditional gender roles, in a micro model the diversity in types of men and women may lead some types of individuals into the labor force while others may opt out; some couples may consist of dual earners, and others not. The proportion of men or women in the labor force in a particular $h_{ij}$ market will depend on demand and supply of WiHo in that market, the ensuing price for WiHo and the reservation wage that is a function of WiHo prices (see Eq. 3.4 defined for type *i* and Eq. 3.6 defined for type *j*).

All income effects will depend on where the supply lies in case of income effects on demand (for a spouse's WiHo) or where the demand lies in case of income effects on own WiHo's supply. The flatter the demand, the less a supply shift affects WiHo price, reservation wage, and labor supply. The flatter the supply, the less a demand shift affects WiHo price, reservation wage, and labor supply. With multiple markets for WiHo it is much more likely to find diversity in the flatness of demands and supplies, corresponding to diversity in elasticity of demand or supply for different WiHo submarkets.

It was shown in Chap. 5 that rigidity in the price of WiHo can prevent prices from moving up or down, affecting income effects on hours spent in WiHo and labor. Such rigidity may not affect all submarkets for WiHo equally. If it does not—for example, because social norms imposing such rigidity vary across social classes—when incomes rise reservation wages may rise more in some markets than in others, and income effects on the value of time and labor supply will vary accordingly.

*New insights about income effects on labor supply.* Adapting Grossbard-Shechtman and Shoshana Neuman (1988) let us consider a married woman who receives a monetary transfer from her husband

$$k(X)\cdot I,$$

where $I$ is a vector of income from sources other than her work that includes spouse's income, and $k$ the proportion of that income to which the individual has access. Transfers from the spouse to the individual may take the form of monetary transfers, access to credit or in-kind transfers with monetary value. Proportion $k$ is a function of factors $X$.

The following equation states that such transfers are compensations for WiHo. Spouses who benefit from WiHo pay for it out of their income, especially if the WiHo worker does not participate in the labor force.

$$y(X)h = k(X)I, \tag{6.1}$$

where $y$ is the price of WiHo and $h$ are hours of WiHo supplied by the WiHo worker in the household (the wife in a traditional household).[1] In the context of a traditional household Eq. 6.1 states that the wife's earnings from supplying WiHo are a proportion $k$ of the household's income, including the husband's earnings in the labor market. The price of WiHo is a function of the factors $X$ that influence the equilibrium price in the market in which this WiHo worker participates. Likewise, the proportion $k$ of $I$ that is transferred to the WiHo worker is a function of these factors $X$.

Factors $X$ include factors that possibly affect demand and supply of WiHo in the market in which this couple participates. To capture the diversity of marriage markets, it is better to add subscripts for a particular type of man $j$ and a particular type of woman $i$, implying

$$y_{ij}(X)h_{ij} = k_{ij}(X_{ij})I_{ij} \tag{6.2}$$

Assuming traditional gender roles and women performing WiHo, the higher price $y$, the higher $k$ and the higher the proportion of a husband's income transferred to the wife. It is assumed that income is also a function of the characteristics of both members of the couple. Furthermore, a spouse's personal earnings may be influenced by the desire for income and productivity, and both may be a function of spouse's characteristics (see Grossbard-Shechtman 1993, Chaps. 12 and 13). More generally, not thinking only in the context of traditional gender roles, it follows that

*Testable Implication TU15* The higher a WiHo worker's price $y$, the higher $k$ and the more household income (other than WiHo worker's own income) affects the labor supply of a WiHo worker. *Any factor associated with higher market value of WiHo workers is expected to also be associated with more sizeable negative household income effects on the WiHo workers' labor supply.*

*Evidence* We do not have data on WiHo prices. However, there are many comparisons we can make across markets for WiHo and indications that individual WiHo workers belonging to some groups get higher WiHo prices than others. If there is discrimination against black women in WiHo markets (see Chap. 5) it is expected that the price of their WiHo will be lower than that of white women who are otherwise similar, and controlling for spouse's characteristics. It follows that we can expect more sizeable income effects on white married women's labor supply than on that of black women. One of the studies that documented that husband's income has a more sizeable effect on white wives' labor supply than on that of black wives is that of Evelyn Lehrer (1992).

Many more predictions regarding differential income effects on WiHo workers' labor supply could possibly be derived. In Grossbard-Shechtman and Keeley (1993) we explored some of the jointness in income effects on labor supply and divorce.

---

[1] I called this function the *MARRIAGE MARKET CONDITIONED HOUSEHOLD INCOME* effect in Grossbard-Shechtman (2005).

Fig. 6.1 Labor supply elasticity for two groups of women

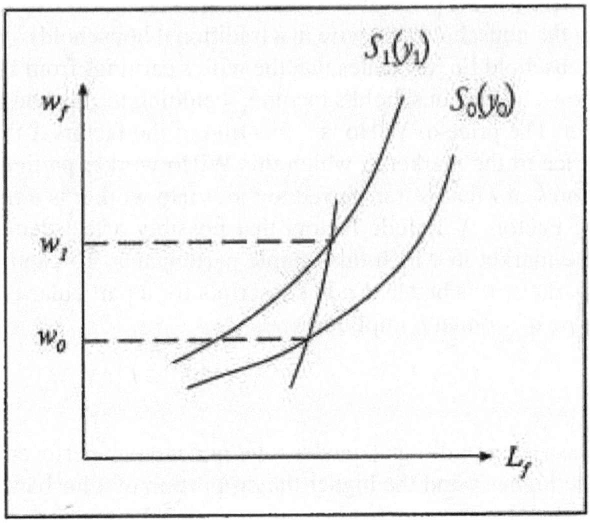


## Wage Effects

### *Wage Elasticity of Labor Supply and WiHo Price*

In addition to the wage effects implications TU4 and TU5 derived in Chap. 5, the following implication can be derived from a microanalysis framework that assumes many types of individuals and continues to assume traditional gender roles.

*Testable Implication TU16 The larger the positive correlation between WiHo price y and wage w in a group of women, the lower the observed elasticity of labor supply.* Factors that influence WiHo prices, such as racial or ethnic origin, will not only cause shifts in the constant term in labor supply regressions, but will also influence the slope of labor supply curves and wage elasticities. The previous literature has explained such racial or ethnic differences in slope in terms of cultural differences or discrimination in labor markets; it did not recognize that conditions in marriage markets can influence the elasticity of labor supply.

Consider the example of two ethnic or racial groups. Figure 6.1 reproduces Fig. 4.1, but now it represents the supply of labor of women from two different groups. Two women, one from each group, initially have identical opportunities in both the labor market ($w_0$) and the (marriage) market for WiHo ($y_0$). They have the same true supply, for constant levels of $y$, denoted by $S$, but all we observe is the labor supply that is based on correlations between $w$ and $y$. We also observe two other women, one from each group, who have a higher wage, $w_1$.

The *observed* elasticity of labor supply, based on a cross-section, depends on the correlation between $w$ and $y$ within each group. If $w$ and $y$ are not correlated the *observed* elasticity is also the *true* elasticity. However, if $w$ and $y$ are positively correlated, for instance due to unmeasured ability leading to higher wages and WiHo prices, an increase in wage from $w_0$ to $w_1$ implies simultaneously a movement along the supply curve (keeping $y$ constant) and a leftward shift of the supply curve (due to the higher $y$ associated with a higher $w$, which leads to a substitution effect and an income effect away from work in light of Eq. 5.1). The observed elasticity—that of the "envelope supply" linking the relevant points on both true supply curves—will then be lower than the true elasticity. If the correlation between $w$ and $y$ is negative, the opposite will be the case: the observed elasticity will be larger than the true elasticity.

*Evidence* Gronau (1981) found that in Israel the labor force participation of Jewish women of Asian–African (AA) origin was more sensitive to changes in wage (actual or potential) than that of European–American (EA) women. He explained AA women's higher observed elasticity of labor supply in terms of this group giving more weight to pecuniary rewards than their EA counterparts. Alternatively, the different elasticities could be interpreted as evidence for implication TU16. There may be less of a positive correlation between $y$ and $w$ for AA women than for EA women due to the lower prevalence of traditional gender roles among the Jews from Europe and America who were more exposed to modern ideas (Stricter adherence to traditional gender roles among AA Jews has been documented, for instance by Yogev and Ayalon (1982)). In contrast, EA women may have more opportunities to balance work in the labor force with family obligations. If relative to similar EA women, talented AA women are more likely to solely work at WiHo and not outside the home, there will be a lower correlation between $w$ and $y$ for AA than for EA Jewish women. That can account for the difference in observed elasticity reported by Gronau. It is possible that a more positive correlation between women's w and y goes together with a lower proportion of all individuals in a particular group being married. AA Jewish men's higher demand for traditional WiHo would entail both more women solely engaging in WiHo and a less positive correlation between $w$ and $y$ than would be found for EA Jews.

Applying the same reasoning to blacks and whites in the USA, this prediction can help us explain a finding reported by Francine Blau and Lawrence Kahn (2007). They estimated labor supply functions for black and white married women in 2000 and found that for black married women own wage elasticities were in the 0.08–0.18 range, in contrast to 0.36–0.41 for white married women. TU16 explains differences in observed wage elasticities of women's labor supply in terms of the correlation between $w$ and $y$ for women who supply WiHo in each group. The larger the demand for WiHo by men in a particular group, the more women's specialization in WiHo is likely to occur and the less w and y are likely to be positively correlated. Marriage and couple formation have been less prevalent among blacks than among whites in the USA. White women have better opportunities for specializing in WiHo and getting a high $y$ for such work than is the case with black women. This implies that relative to talented black women talented white women are more likely to choose between a high $w$ and a high $y$. In contrast, talented black women are more likely to simultaneously obtain both a high $w$ and a high $y$ than talented white women. Therefore one expects more of a positive correlation between $w$ and unobserved $y$ in a cross-section of black women than in one of white women. This could explain why the observed wage elasticity for black married women (including effects of wages via unobserved $y$'s and correlations between these $y$'s and wages) is lower than for white married women (with unobserved $y$'s and correlations between these $y$'s and wages that differ from those of black women).

## *More on Cross-Wage Elasticity*

In Chap. 4 I derived prediction TU5 based on the assumption that there is one representative man and one representative woman. When there are many types of individuals, wages affect the demand for different types of potential spouses differentially.

TU5 predicted a negative cross-wage elasticity of labor supply due to income and substitution effects of wage on the demand for (potential) spouses' WiHo. That effect depends on the elasticity of those spouses' supplies of WiHo. The less elastic, the larger the effect on the reservation wage and the more labor supply is likely to be affected. This implies that we are more likely to observe negative cross-wage effects on the labor supply of individuals when supplies of WiHo are closer to vertical. These are individuals in markets with high reservation wages and low likelihood of participation in the labor force. It is more likely to hold for women's WiHo markets than for men's, given that many more women appear to choose not to participate in the labor force. So I expect that negative cross-wage elasticities are more likely to be observed for women's labor supply than for men's labor supply. If, relative to men, women have higher cross-wage elasticities of labor supply the absolute value of their cross-wage elasticities of WiHo will be smaller than that of men.

*Evidence* Bloemen and Stancanelli (2014) found that men's hours of household production were more sensitive to their wife's wage than women's hours of household production were to their husband's wage, which suggests that men are on a flatter portion of their WiHo supply than women.

## *More on Sex Ratio Effects*

Chapter 4 based on the macro model presented testable implications TU6 and TU7 stating that sex ratios and women's labor supply will be inversely related whereas the opposite is true for men's labor supply. With many types of men and women the analysis of sex ratio effects is more complex. The representative individual in the macro model is indifferent between being married or not. In contrast, when there are many markets for WiHo sex ratios would ideally have to be calculated in each of these markets. The sex ratio in a particular market will affect not only equilibrium price and quantity in that market but also in all the markets for WiHo that are interrelated to that market due to potential substitution between different types of men and women. In this chapter I only discuss sex ratio effects on women's labor supply by marital status and by education.

**Sex Ratio and Marital Status** *Testable Implication TU6'* Within each marital status category sex ratios are expected to matter. In particular: relative to situations of low sex ratios or balanced marriage markets, high sex ratios are expected to be associated with less labor force participation by married women. Given the larger variation in labor force participation among married women relative to that among unmarried women, and given that the theory focuses on the effect of sex ratio on price of WiHo, it is expected that sex ratios will have more impact on married women's labor supply than on that of unmarried women who mostly participate in the labor force and work full time. However, sex ratios may also have an impact on the labor supply of unmarried women, given that they often prepare themselves for supplying WiHo to a spouse or that they may receive some post-marriage income from WiHo after dissolution through divorce or death.

Implication TU6 and TU6' have been tested using variation across geographical regions and across birth cohorts. The disadvantage of cross-sectional studies is that they make it difficult to distinguish between two alternative causalities: did sex ratios respond to differences in employment opportunities via migration, or are sex ratios causing differences in employment? Cities with higher sex ratios may have attracted men due to better jobs for men; cities with lower sex ratios may have better jobs for women. Luckily for researchers, this migration-related reverse causality does not apply to cohort comparisons: people do not choose when to be born; they are stuck in their birth cohorts.

Sex ratios vary across cohorts, as has been pointed out at least since Glick et al. (1963) and Henry (1975), because (1) on average, women marry men who are generally somewhat older and the age difference does not fluctuate much, and (2) the number of births fluctuates from one birth cohort to the next. For example, in the early 1950s there were more marriageable men than women in many Western countries as a result of declining numbers of births during the Depression that occurred in the late 1920s and early 1930s. Conversely, in the mid-1960s, when the first post-World War II baby boomers reached marriageable age, baby boom women in the USA and other countries with similar demographic trends experienced low sex ratios.

*Thirty-five years of testing for sex ratio effects on labor supply.* Around 1979, when the late sociologist David Heer and I both worked at the Population Research Lab at the University of Southern California (USC) it dawned on me that there may be a negative association between sex ratios and women's labor supply. David had shown me some dramatic demographic and economic changes that had occurred between 1960 and 1975 right after I had heard a talk on sex ratio fluctuations by cohort. This led to Heer and Grossbard-Shechtman (1981), includes a market for women's WiHo (which I then called a market for wives and is very similar to the market for wife-services in Grossbard (1976)). We calculated sex ratios by dividing the number of men aged 19.5–26.49 by the number of women aged 17–23.99, that is using a difference in age at marriage of 2.5 years, which was typical for the period we covered, 1955–1975. We compared trends in sex ratio to trends in women's labor force participation and found that in the late 1960s and early 1970s sex ratios for young women had gone down rapidly, as large numbers of women born after the War found relatively few marriageable men a bit older and born during the War. For example, this sex ratio went down from 1.002 in 1956 to 0.885 in 1965. This means that in 1956 the sex ratio was balanced but 9 years later, in 1965, there were 11 missing men for every 100 women aged 17–23.99. We also found that from 1960 to 1975 labor force participation rates of married women aged 20–24 *rose from 31.7 to 57.0%* implying that unprecedented growth in young married women's labor force participation was accompanied by dramatic drops in sex ratio.

In the late 1970s it was not possible to run regression analyses of women's labor force participation by marital status and as a function of sex ratios: detailed data on labor force participation by age and marital status only became available on a yearly basis after the introduction of the Current Population Survey in 1965. I had to wait for more cohorts to be old enough to enter labor and marriage markets in order to seriously test whether fluctuations in sex ratio helped explain further changes in women's economic activity. In the meanwhile I looked at trends beyond the two points in time that Heer and I had examined: 1960 and 1975. In Grossbard-Shechtman (1985) I compared time trends in sex ratio based on Heer and Grossbard-Shechtman with trends in percent of women employed at ages 25–34, as reproduced in Fig. 6.2. It

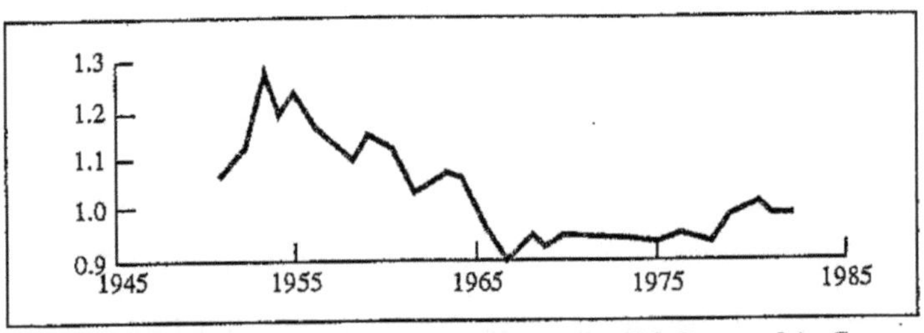


SOURCE: Heer and Grossbard-Shechtman 1981, p. 52; U.S. Bureau of the Census, *Current Population Reports.* Series P-25: Nos. 643, 721, 800, 917, 929, and Series P-20: Nos. 306, 338, 349, 365, 372 and 380.

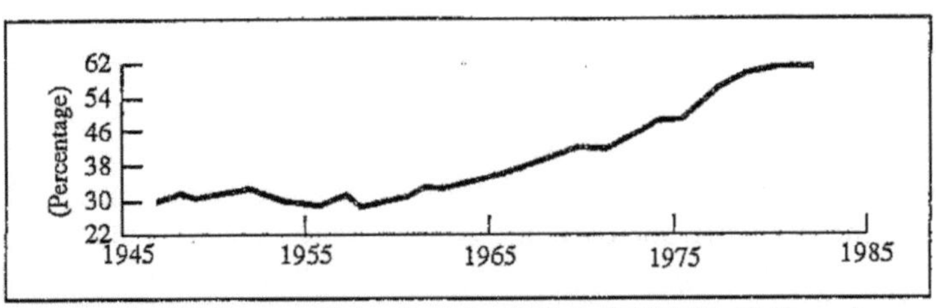


SOURCE: U.S. Bureau of Labor Statistics, Bulletin 2175, Table 15, December 1983.

**Fig. 6.2** Trends in **a** sex ratio and **b** percent of woman employed at ages 25–34

can be seen that the plunge in sex ratio corresponds broadly to the time that young women's employment rose. More precisely the upsurge in employment started in 1963, about the time the sex ratio fell below 1.0. The graphs also show that in the late 1970s and early 1980s the sex ratio started to increase and women's employment surge stopped.

The rapid rise in employment between 1965 and 1975 cannot possibly be explained in terms of higher wages. On the contrary, it occurred "despite a significant slowing of the growth in real wages and dramatic acceleration of the rate of inflation. In fact, between 1973 and 1975, real wages fell in two successive years, yet women's labor force participation continued to grow" (Niemi and Lloyd 1980).

In line with TU6 I had predicted that with rising sex ratios for cohorts born in later baby boom years and during the baby bust there would be a slowdown in the entry of women into the labor force. By the 1990s enough data had accumulated to do a more rigorous study of time series. Clive Granger, who later obtained the 2003 Nobel Prize in Economics for his work on time series, advised me on the econometrics. Based on data for 1965–1990 and controlling for other factors that changed over time Grossbard-Shechtman and Granger (1998) showed that women born in cohorts with lower sex ratios experienced more rapid growth in labor supply. We discovered that women born in the late 1930s (after the New Deal and before feminism became popular) also experienced large increases in participation in the labor force. Sex ratio analysis helps explain that: those born during the New Deal were also a "baby boom" generation, although at a smaller scale than was the case with the post-World War II baby boom.

By the mid-2000s it was possible to analyze employment data for the period 1965–2005, thereby capturing major fluctuations in sex ratio due to the sequence of baby bust, baby boom, baby bust that followed the baby boom, and echo of the post-World War II baby boom. In Grossbard and Amuedo-Dorantes (2007) we calculated sex ratios from Census data for 5-year age groups assuming that the male/female age difference at marriage is, on average, equal to 2 years. This assumption fits the data on age difference at first marriage in the USA well for most of the period we covered (towards the end the difference shrunk to 1.5 years). For each cohort Census data were used to compute sex ratios at the time the women were aged 20–24 or 25–29 and we used the number of men 2 years older.[2] Sex ratios defined for women born between 1926 and 1980 and men born between 1924 and 1978 for the entire country and by US regions are shown in Table 6.1. Each 5-year cohort was given a name related to historical events that occurred around their year of birth.

For the USA as a whole (italic numbers), it can be seen that this sex ratio reached its minimum of 0.87 for the women born at the onset of the baby-boom, in the years 1946–1950 right after World War II, and the men born in 1944–1948, which includes the end of World War II and the beginning of the baby-boom. The maximum

[2] For alternative methods for calculating sex ratios see, for example, Goldman et al. (1984) and Porter (forthcoming).

**Table 6.1** Generations of women, sex ratios, and changes in married women's labor force participation for four regions in the United States

| Year of birth | Generation name | US region | Sex ratio[a] | ΔLFP[b] ages 20–24 | ΔLFP ages 25–29 | ΔLFP ages 30–34 | ΔLFP ages 35–39 | ΔLFP ages 40–44 |
|---|---|---|---|---|---|---|---|---|
| 1926–1930 | Pre-Depression | *USA* | *0.98* | *n.a.* | *n.a.* | *n.a.* | *n.a.* | *4.96* |
| | | NE | 0.95 | n.a. | n.a. | n.a. | n.a. | 2.68 |
| | | Midwest | 1.06 | n.a. | n.a. | n.a. | n.a. | 10.05 |
| | | South | 0.96 | n.a. | n.a. | n.a. | n.a. | 3.07 |
| | | West | 0.99 | n.a. | n.a. | n.a. | n.a. | 3.31 |
| 1931–1935 | Depression | *USA* | *1.00* | *n.a.* | *n.a.* | *n.a.* | *6.69* | *5.65* |
| | | NE | 0.96 | n.a. | n.a. | n.a. | 4.80 | 3.87 |
| | | Midwest | 1.06 | n.a. | n.a. | n.a. | 8.87 | 5.63 |
| | | South | 1.01 | n.a. | n.a. | n.a. | 7.56 | 6.94 |
| | | West | 1.01 | n.a. | n.a. | n.a. | 3.87 | 5.05 |
| 1936–1940 | New deal | *USA* | *0.95* | *n.a.* | *n.a.* | *6.84* | *5.09* | *9.23* |
| | | NE | 0.95 | n.a. | n.a. | 6.02 | 2.18 | 12.61 |
| | | Midwest | 1.02 | n.a. | n.a. | 5.85 | 6.03 | 9.75 |
| | | South | 0.92 | n.a. | n.a. | 8.89 | 3.12 | 6.25 |
| | | West | 0.91 | n.a. | n.a. | 6.22 | 9.75 | 10.35 |
| 1941–1945 | World War II | *USA* | *0.91* | *n.a.* | *5.97* | *5.44* | *10.83* | *4.12* |
| | | NE | 0.90 | n.a. | 7.23 | 5.25 | 12.88 | 1.77 |
| | | Midwest | 0.93 | n.a. | 6.69 | 6.28 | 12.33 | 3.96 |
| | | South | 0.88 | n.a. | 1.74 | 3.34 | 9.34 | 4.52 |
| | | West | 0.92 | n.a. | 9.86 | 7.17 | 9.47 | 5.68 |
| 1946–1950 | Post-World War II | *USA* | *0.87* | *11.28* | *11.84* | *13.51* | *6.61* | *7.05* |
| | | NE | 0.89 | 10.07 | 11.05 | 15.26 | 8.61 | 11.11 |
| | | Midwest | 0.93 | 8.43 | 14.19 | 17.32 | 6.53 | 5.71 |
| | | South | 0.84 | 12.21 | 10.98 | 10.32 | 6.39 | 7.48 |
| | | West | 0.85 | 14.98 | 9.71 | 11.61 | 5.36 | 3.92 |

**Table 6.1** (continued)

| Year of birth | Generation name | US region | Sex ratio[a] | ΔLFP[b] ages 20–24 | ΔLFP ages 25–29 | ΔLFP ages 30–34 | ΔLFP ages 35–39 | ΔLFP ages 40–44 |
|---|---|---|---|---|---|---|---|---|
| 1951–1955 | Korean War | *USA* | *0.95* | *10.47* | *8.25* | *6.06* | *5.28* | *2.85* |
| | | NE | 0.94 | 12.22 | 13.59 | 8.18 | 6.52 | −0.11 |
| | | Midwest | 0.99 | 14.28 | 8.80 | 5.55 | 4.82 | 6.84 |
| | | South | 0.93 | 9.22 | 6.70 | 6.45 | 3.86 | 0.13 |
| | | West | 0.94 | 5.12 | 6.18 | 4.28 | 6.30 | 5.81 |
| 1956–1960 | Sputnik | *USA* | *0.97* | *2.12* | *7.40* | *3.82* | *1.40* | *1.23* |
| | | NE | 0.97 | 2.68 | 5.44 | 2.46 | 0.86 | 2.98 |
| | | Midwest | 1.04 | 2.08 | 6.00 | 4.23 | 2.83 | 0.27 |
| | | South | 0.93 | 1.19 | 7.26 | 5.59 | 2.47 | 3.29 |
| | | West | 0.96 | 5.19 | 9.84 | 2.81 | −0.78 | −2.22 |
| 1961–1965 | Kennedy | *USA* | *1.03* | *4.60* | *3.49* | *3.62* | *−1.84* | *n.a.* |
| | | NE | 1.01 | 6.65 | 2.54 | 4.54 | −0.77 | n.a. |
| | | Midwest | 1.09 | 10.02 | 6.18 | 5.03 | −2.67 | n.a. |
| | | South | 1.01 | 1.79 | 6.90 | 2.98 | −0.58 | n.a. |
| | | West | 1.01 | 1.55 | −2.31 | 2.19 | −2.97 | n.a. |
| 1966–1970 | Moon | *USA* | *1.06* | *−0.23* | *−0.14* | *−2.14* | *n.a.* | *n.a.* |
| | | NE | 1.05 | −3.66 | 2.59 | −0.80 | n.a. | n.a. |
| | | Midwest | 1.16 | −1.66 | 4.28 | −2.00 | n.a. | n.a. |
| | | South | 1.03 | 1.65 | −5.06 | −1.22 | n.a. | n.a. |
| | | West | 1.02 | 1.49 | −0.38 | −4.45 | n.a. | n.a. |
| 1971–1975 | Roe | *USA* | *1.07* | *−0.23* | *0.76* | *n.a.* | *n.a.* | *n.a.* |
| | | NE | 1.05 | −0.06 | 1.62 | n.a. | n.a. | n.a. |
| | | Midwest | 1.11 | 1.43 | −0.11 | n.a. | n.a. | n.a. |
| | | South | 1.06 | 1.63 | 4.06 | n.a. | n.a. | n.a. |
| | | West | 1.06 | −2.27 | −1.24 | n.a. | n.a. | n.a. |

**Table 6.1** (continued)

| Year of birth | Generation name | US region | Sex ratio[a] | ΔLFP[b] ages 20–24 | ΔLFP ages 25–29 | ΔLFP ages 30–34 | ΔLFP ages 35–39 | ΔLFP ages 40–44 |
|---|---|---|---|---|---|---|---|---|
| 1976–1980 | First echo | *USA* | *1.01* | *0.15* | *n.a.* | *n.a.* | *n.a.* | *n.a.* |
| | | NE | 1.01 | −0.61 | n.a. | n.a. | n.a. | n.a. |
| | | Midwest | 1.08 | −1.95 | n.a. | n.a. | n.a. | n.a. |
| | | South | 0.97 | −1.50 | n.a. | n.a. | n.a. | n.a. |
| | | West | 0.98 | −1.47 | n.a. | n.a. | n.a. | n.a. |

This table was first published in Grossbard and Amuedo-Dorantes (2007)

[a] Ratio of men aged 22–26 to women aged 20–24 or men aged 27–31 to women aged 25–29 calculated based on Census data from 1940 to 2000. The age group depends on the Census year. Sex ratios for last two generations were calculated based on the 1990 Census using younger age groups

[b] ΔLFP, changes in labor force participation rate, Calculated from CPS years 1965–2000.

value of the sex ratio, 1.07, corresponds to the women born in 1971–1975 and the men born in 1969–1973. These women were born right around the passage of *Roe v. Wade*, a landmark ruling that led the number of abortions to increase in the USA.[3] The sex ratio for women born between 1966 and 1970 and men born between 1964 and 1968, the Moon generation, was also high at 1.06.

Table 6.1 also reports changes in labor force participation rates for married women belonging to different age groups, these changes being calculated by comparing the labor force participation for year $t$ (the year at which a birth cohort was observed in a certain age group) and year $t-5$. The table indicates a negative correlation between sex ratio and changes in married women's labor force participation. For example, look at the women of the post-World War II baby boom, who have the lowest sex ratio. At almost every age this cohort experienced faster growth in labor force participation than any other 5-year cohort of women. In contrast, married women of the Moon generation, characterized by some of the highest sex ratios, experienced a drop in labor force participation of 2.14 % points when they entered the 30–34 age group (replacing women born in the Kennedy generation).

Catalina Amuedo-Dorantes and I estimated regressions of women's labor force participation for the USA as a whole and separately for four major US regions. We looked at married women and all women in different age groups separately. We found that cohorts of women with lower sex ratios (women born at onset of baby booms) have experienced above-average labor force participation whereas cohorts of women with higher sex ratios (born at the beginning of baby busts) have experienced below-average labor force participation. This held for all women and for married women in particular, and results were robust to a number of specifications. As for why the increase in women's labor force participation in the USA stopped well before that participation reached levels observed in some other Western countries, that can in part be explained by the relatively high sex ratios observed for young women born in the early 1970s, when fertility dropped dramatically as a result of *Roe v. Wade* (Grossbard and Amuedo-Dorantes 2007).

Could there be alternative explanations for these variations in aggregate labor supply over time? Amuedo-Dorantes and I showed that sex ratio effects on women's LFP were robust to the inclusion of women's wages, education, and presence of young children in the regression models, but the inclusion of these endogenous variables weakens the sex ratio effects. Nevertheless, they remain important. For instance, the effect on LFP of an increase in sex ratio of .10 is comparable to that of two more years of education. Some idiosyncratic factors could possibly help explain periodic change. The surge of the feminist movement also helps explain the large increase in labor supply experienced by the first Post WWII baby-boomers, the generation who bought the first issues of *Ms.* magazine and who filled the first women's studies classes. However, why did big increases in women's labor supply last for 15 and not 25 years? Some may say it was a backlash against feminism. But then why did such backlash occur at that particular time? Furthermore, Heer and I

[3] Links between abortion law changes and changes in fertility in the 1970s have been discussed e.g. by John Donohue and Steven Levitt (2001) and Joshua Angrist and William Evans (1999).

argued that the feminist movement was not an exogeneous factor and extremely low sex ratios also help explain the onset of the feminist movement (Heer and Grossbard-Shechtman 1981).

Sex ratio effects have also been tested at the *city level*. Grossbard-Shechtman (1993, Chap. 6) used US cities in 1930; Grossbard-Shechtman and Neideffer (1997) and Chiappori et al. (2002) used US cities in 1990. These studies all found that where sex ratios are higher women are less likely to work in the labor force. Chiappori et al. (2002) also found that where sex ratios are higher men are more likely to work in the labor force, which is possibly evidence for TU7 (see Chap. 4). However, such cross-sectional results could result from reverse causality: women's migration to cities with more job opportunities for women and men's migration to where men have more good jobs could account for the results.

## Sex Ratio and Education

*Sex Ratio and Education* Societies tend to have separate marriage markets for people differing in education level. A priori it is not so clear where sex ratios are expected to have more impact, among the more educated or the less educated.

Implication TU6 is more likely to hold for couples (1) in which one spouse engages in more WiHo than the other; and (2) for which it can be assumed that the other spouse pays for that WiHo. In terms of Eq. 6.2, the $k$ capturing how much the spouse pays for WiHo is likely to be larger when the amount of WiHo, $h$, is larger. It is also expected to be larger if the price of WiHo is higher. Where there are positive intrahousehold transfers compensating for WiHo, sex ratio variations are more likely to influence WiHo price and therefore labor supply than in cases where there is no WiHo or there is little payment for WiHo.

We do not have data on time supplied to WiHo or on whether the spouse transfers income within the household to pay for WiHo. However, hours of WiHo can be approximated with hours devoted to chores: in couples it can be assumed that at least some of these chores benefited the spouse. We can also make assumptions as to who is more likely to get a positive price $y$ for their WiHo depending on individual characteristics of self and spouse (see Chap. 1). Education tends to be negatively correlated with time doing chores (see Chap. 8), so it can be inferred that, compared to women without college education, college-educated women are less likely to work in WiHo for the benefit of their husbands. However, educated women who work in WiHo are likely to get paid a higher $y$ for it if education makes them more productive. So it is not clear in advance whether sex ratios will have more impact on women with or without education.

*Evidence* In Grossbard and Amuedo-Dorantes (2007) we found that in the West and Northeast, the effects of cohort-based sex ratios on the labor supply of married women were more sizeable for women with less education than for college-educated women. This result was obtained by including interactions of sex ratio and years of schooling, but sex ratios were not calculated separately by education category. For the Midwest, however, we got the opposite result: sex ratio effects on labor supply were more sizeable for educated married women than for their less-educated counterparts. Likewise, Emery and Ferrer (2009) found negative sex ratio effects for college-educated women in Canada over the period 1971–1991. This suggests that the premium for educated married women in the Midwest and Canada is higher than in other regions in the USA: in Canada and the American Midwest $yh$ seems to be higher for college-educated women than for women with less education. Therefore low sex ratios can be more damaging to their earnings from WiHo and high sex ratios can be more beneficial than for their less-educated counterparts. This is intriguing and suggests that some underlying factors that are common to the American Midwest and Canada—but not found in the West and the Northeast of the USA—are associated with higher prices for women's WiHo. Could it be that farmers appreciate their wives more than city dwellers, and even more so if they are educated?

While Grossbard and Amuedo-Dorantes used sex ratios for all education groups (assuming that educated and less-educated people are good substitutes and participate in the same WiHo markets) Negrusa and Oreffice (2010) constructed "quality" sex ratios by education groups. They used variation across metropolitan areas and investigated the impact of these sex ratios on the labor supply of married women and men. They found negative sex ratio effects for wives and positive effects for husbands. Effects for more educated individuals were more sizeable; they found insignificant effects for high school graduates. This also suggests that the value of educated women's WiHo, $yh$, is higher than that of the WiHo of less educated women. The finding of Negrusa and Oreffice for men can be explained in terms of this model as well. When sex ratios are higher and women's WiHo is more expensive, men need to work harder in the labor force to afford the higher $yh$ payments. They need a higher income $I$ (see Eq. 6.2). They may also have a higher $k$ in the sense that they transfer a larger portion of their income to their wife.

## *Labor Supply and Laws and Institutions Governing Couple Formation*

The form in which a couple lives together may reveal important information and may be worthy of further investigation when studying labor supply. Are they married or do they live together without marriage? We can infer whether $y$, the price of WiHo, is relatively high or low by using information on choice of type of relationship where such choice is available and the outcome is observed.

Furthermore, laws and regulations that affect couple formation by providing benefits and costs associated with marriage and its alternatives will also influence price of WiHo and therefore reservation wage and labor supply.

*Labor Supply, Marriage, and Cohabitation* Whether a couple cohabits without marriage or is married may indicate variation in price of WiHo. In the case of a couple with a full-time or part-time WiHo worker the fact that the couple is formally married may indicate that the spouse doing most WiHo (the WiHo worker) is being paid a higher WiHo price *y* than their counterpart who cohabits outside marriage. Where women are the WiHo workers they often prefer the commitment involved in marriage and may prefer to have part of their compensation taking this form (see Grossbard-Shechtman 1993 - chap. 4 and 9). Linking observed marital status to WiHo price helps explain DaVanzo's (1972) finding that in Chile women cohabiting without a formal marriage are more likely to participate in the labor force than women married formally. A formal marriage may indicate a higher *y* and therefore less of a need for women in traditional relationships to participate in the labor force. Since DaVanzo analyzed labor supply, marriage type, and wages simultaneously, an alternative explanation—that working women prefer cohabitation—is not so likely.

*Labor Supply and Divorce Laws* To the extent that some divorce laws give less protection to WiHo workers in case of divorce than other divorce this implies that the total package of compensation for WiHo is lower (the price of WiHo may include payments after separation if there is separation or divorce). A lower price of WiHo implies a lower reservation wage and more labor supply. It is therefore expected that labor supply of women will be higher in legal regimes that offer less protection to WiHo workers (assuming traditional gender roles). The replacement of fault- and consent-based divorce laws with no-fault and unilateral divorce can be considered as forms of lowering the effective price for WiHo. These laws, introduced to most of the USA between 1970 and 1980, may have contributed to the rapid growth in women's labor force participation during the years 1970–1985. However, that rapid growth started around 1965, before the divorce laws started changing. Gray (1998) has shown that the effect of unilateral divorce laws interacted with the effect of laws specifying division of property in case of divorce. In states where community property prevails no-fault divorce laws led to higher labor force participation of women and less household production, but in states without community property no-fault divorce was associated with lower labor force participation and more household production. This is consistent with a larger drop in the price of women's WiHo associated with introduction of no-fault divorce in states with community property than in states without community property regulating division of assets in case of divorce.

*Labor Supply and Polygamy* It is also expected that laws allowing polygamy will affect price of WiHo and reservation wage. When men are allowed to marry more than one wife, but women are only allowed to marry one man and assuming traditional gender roles, there will be a large demand for women's WiHo relative to the supply. This implies higher prices for WiHo and higher reservation wages, thus leading to a lower labor supply of women.

*Labor Supply and Common Law Marriage (CLM)* Some states in the USA offer common law marriage and some do not. Common law marriage is a more accessible form of marriage with lower entry costs. The availability of CLM in a state could possibly affect both the demand and the supply of WiHo. The impact CLM on the labor supply of men and women was analyzed in Grossbard and Vernon (see chap. 7). An adaptation of that article is presented in the next chapter. Our interpretation of CLM is that it acts as some form of minimum price of WiHo. We found ample empirical evidence to support our testable implications.

## References


Angrist, Joshua D., and William N. Evans. 1999. Schooling and labor market consequences of the 1970 state abortion reforms. *Research in Labor Economics* 18:75–113.

Blau, Francine D., and Lawrence M. Kahn. 2007. Changes in the labor supply behavior of married women: 1980–2000. *Journal of Labor Economics* 25 (3): 393–438.

Bloemen, H., and E. Stancanelli. 2014. Market hours, household work, child care, and wage rates of partners: An empirical analysis. *Review of the Economics of the Household* 12:51–81.

Chiappori, P. A., B. Fortin, and G. Lacroix. 2002. Marriage market, divorce legislation, and household labor supply. *Journal of Political Economy* 110:37–71.

DaVanzo, Julie. 1972. The determinants of family formation in Chile, 1960. R-830, AID. Santa Monica: Rand (August)

Donohue, John J. III, and Steven D. Levitt. 2001. The impact of legalized abortion on crime. *Quarterly Journal of Economics* 116:379–420.

Emery, J. C., and Ana Ferrer. 2009. Marriage market imbalances and labor force participation of Canadian women. *REHO* 7:43–58.

Glick, Paul C., John C. Beresford, and David M. Heer. 1963. Family formation and family composition: Trends and prospects. In *Sourcebook in marriage and the family,* ed. M. B. Sussman. Boston: Houghton Mifflin.

Goldman, Noreen, Charles Westoff, and C. Hammerslough. 1984. Demography of the marriage market in the United States. *Population Index* 50:5–25.

Gray, J. S. 1998. Divorce law changes, household bargaining, and married women's labor supply. *American Economic Review* 88:628–642.

Gronau, Reuben. 1981. Wives' labor force participation, wage differentials, and family income inequality: The Israeli experience. Working Paper 668. Cambridge: NBER.

Grossbard, Amyra. 1976. An economic analysis of polygamy: The case of Maieri. *Current Anthropology* 17:701–707.

Grossbard, Shoshana Amyra. 2010. How 'Chicagoan' are Gary Becker's economic models of marriage? *Journal of the History of Economic Thought* 32 (3): 377–395.

Grossbard, Shoshana, and Catalina Amuedo-Dorantes. 2007. Marriage markets and women's labor force participation. *Review of Economics of the Household* 5:249–278.

Grossbard-Shechtman, Amyra. 1985. Marriage squeezes and the marriage market. In *Contemporary marriage: Comparative perspectives on a changing institution,* ed. Kingsley. Davis and A. Grossbard-Shechtman. New York: Russell Sage.

Grossbard-Shechtman, Shoshana. 1993. *On the economics of marriage*. Boulder: Westview.

Grossbard-Shechtman, Shoshana. 2005. A model of labour supply, household production, and marriage. In *Advances in household economics, consumer behaviour and economic policy,* ed. Tran. Van Hoa. London: Ashgate.

Grossbard-Shechtman, S. A., and C. W. Granger. 1998. Women's jobs and marriage, baby-boom versus baby-bust. *Population* 53:731–752. (in French: Travail des Femmes et Mariage du baby-boom au baby-bust).

Grossbard-Shechtman, Shoshana A., and Michael C. Keeley. 1993. A theory of divorce and labor supply. In *On the economics of marriage: A theory of marriage, labor, and divorce,* ed. S. Grossbard-Shechtman. Boulder: Westview.

Grossbard-Shechtman, Shoshana, and Matthew Neideffer. 1997. Women's hours of work and marriage market imbalances. In *Economics of the family and family policies,* ed. I. Persson and C. Jonung. London: Routledge.

Grossbard-Shechtman, A. S., and S. Neuman. 1988. Women's labor supply and marital choice. *Journal of Political Economy* 96:1294–1302.

Heer, David M., and Amyra Grossbard-Shechtman. 1981. The impact of the female marriage squeeze and the contraceptive revolution on sex roles and the women's liberation movement in the United States, 1960 to 1975. *Journal of Marriage and the Family* 43:49–65.

Henry, Louis. 1975. Schema d'Evolution des Marriages apres de Grandes Variations des Naissances. *Population* 30:759–779.

Lehrer, E. L. 1992. The impact of children on women's labor supply. Black/white differentials revisited. *Journal of Human Resources* 27:422–444.

Negrusa, Brighita, and Sonia Oreffice. 2010. Quality of available mates, education, and household labor supply. *Economic Inquiry* 48 (3): 558–574.

Niemi, Beth. T., and Lloyd B. Cynthia. 1980. Money illusion or price illusion: The effects of inflation on female labor force participation. Paper Presented at the 89th Brooklyn College Conference on Society in Change.

Porter, M. 2015. How do sex ratios in China influence marriage decisions and intrahousehold resource allocation? *Review of Economics of the Household.* http://link.springer.com/article/10.1007/s11150-014-9262-9, forthcoming.

Yogev, A., and H. Ayalon. 1982. Sex and ethnic variations in educational plans: A cross-cultural perspective. *International Review of Modern Sociology* 12:1–19.

# Chapter 7
# Labor Supply, Household Production, and Common Law Marriage Legislation

*Adapted from Shoshana Grossbard and Victoria Vernon, "Common Law Marriage, labor supply and time use: a partial explanation for gender convergence in labor supply." Forthcoming, Research in Labor Economics, 2015. We thank the editors, two anonymous referees, and participants at an IZA workshop on gender convergence for helpful suggestions.*

## Introduction

This chapter investigates whether availability of Common Law Marriage (CLM henceforth) in the USA helps explain the variation in the labor force participation, hours of work, hours of household production, and leisure time of men and women over time and across states. To the extent that CLM is associated with less labor supply by women or more labor supply by men, the abolition of CLM could help explain some of the gender convergence in labor supply that has been observed in recent decades.

States that recognize CLM offer their heterosexual residents a choice between entering marriage the conventional way and via CLM. With CLM there is no need for a marriage certificate or ceremony: it is established when couples cohabit and hold themselves out as spouses, by calling each other husband and wife in public; using the same last name; filing joint tax returns; or declaring their marriage on applications, leases, birth certificates, and other documents. A short term cohabiting relationship may also be called "marriage" if both spouses agree. A cohabiting couple with a child almost certainly shows enough intent to be married or to be considered "married" in a CLM state.

CLM is like marriage in that it is accepted by all other states and government institutions dealing with tax collection and redistribution of income. In the event of separation, a CLM requires an official divorce. However, property rights are not as clearly defined in the case of a CLM due to a vaguer determination of whether there was a marriage or not, and if so, when it started. CLM can also be claimed unilaterally by one of the partners with property interest *ex-post*.

Most US states used to offer CLM but have abolished it. As of 2014, common-law marriage could still be contracted in 11 states: Alabama, Colorado, Iowa, Kan-



S. Grossbard, *The Marriage Motive: A Price Theory of Marriage*,
DOI 10.1007/978-1-4614-1623-4_7

sas, Montana, New Hampshire (posthumously for purposes of inheritance), Oklahoma, Rhode Island, South Carolina, Texas, and Utah, as well as in the Navajo Nation and in the District of Columbia.

Data availability on CLM is a problem. There is virtually no official data on CLM marriages published by state or local governments, even though some counties encourage residents to register their CLMs. The internet contains a lot of information and legal advice for couples about CLM, so we know it is practiced.[1] Some indication of CLM's prevalence follows from a legal historian's reporting of about 100 legal CLM-related judgments being issued each decade in each state at the federal level (Lind 2008).

We base our empirical study on comparisons between states that do and do not offer CLM and on variation over time in the availability of CLM. Over the period covered by our data, CLM was abolished by Idaho (1996), Georgia (1997), and Pennsylvania (2005), which provides us with a quasi-experiment that we use in our analysis of state-level and individual-level data.

Our empirical analysis assumes that state laws with respect to CLM and changes in those laws are known to state residents, as this knowledge is transmitted in communities. The wealth of information online supports this assumption. We focus on US-born individuals to increase the likelihood that respondents in our sample are familiar with this law based on the experience of older community members: by excluding foreign-born respondents we focus on people who made their marriage decision in the USA. In some of our analyses we relax the assumption of immediate knowledge transmission and exclude 3 years of data after the abolition of CLM by each of the three transition states. We limit our analyses to respondents under age 36, as they are most likely to be entering marriage. We analyze micro data from CPS-iPums for the period 1994–2011 to investigate labor outcomes and from the ATUS for the period 2003–2011 to study effects on household production and leisure.

Previous research has examined the association between labor supply and laws related to marriage and divorce, but it has focused on effects of the replacement of fault- and consent-based divorce laws with no-fault and unilateral divorce (e.g., by Peters 1986; Gray 1998; Stevenson 2007; Genadek et al. 2007). Labor supply effects of laws regarding alimony rights in Canada have also been examined (Chiappori et al. 2011). Our research is innovative, in that we examine labor supply effects of changes in CLM availability. We also contribute to the studies of labor supply comparing married and cohabiting couples (e.g., Stafford et al. 1977; Moreau and El Lagua 2011), and to the household bargaining literature that links variation in legal regimes to time in household production and leisure (Gray 1998).

[1] http://www.co.travis.tx.us/dro/common_law.asp.Popular sites with information on CLM:http://video.about.com/marriage/How-to-Qualify-for-a-Common-Law-Marriage.htm; http://www.answers.com/topic/common-law-marriage; http://www.unmarried.org/common-law-marriage-fact-sheet.html;Common Law Marriage Handbook for government employees who handle claims: http://www.dol.gov/owcp/energy/regs/compliance/PolicyandProcedures/CommonLaw_Marriage.pdf.

Our CPS results indicate significant effects of CLM availability on labor supply of married women. Average weekly hours drop by 1–2 h among married women if CLM is available. A negative effect is found for married women who are White, Hispanic, college-educated, or mothers. These findings are robust to exclusion of 3 years following CLM abolition. When our models allow for adjustment time we also find that married men's labor supply is higher if CLM is available. To the extent that it increased labor supply among married women and decreased labor supply among married men, the abolition of CLM in three states contributed to the convergence in labor supply of men and women. We find no robust significant effects of CLM on household production and leisure time of men and women.

## Why Would CLM Affect Labor Supply?

The conceptual framework is based on the concept of Work-In-Household (WiHo) defined as work in household production benefiting a spouse or partner (see Chap. 2). When we add the assumption of traditional gender roles our model helps explain gender differentials in the effects of CLM on labor supply, why they are negative for married women and positive for married men (when statistically significant), and why these effects are larger for White and college-educated women than for Black women and women without college education.

It follows from Chap. 4 that individual reservation wages are based on value in the marriage markets in which the individuals participate. It is assumed that people either demand or supply *WiHo*, defined as household production work of benefit to a spouse/partner. Therefore, the partner may 'pay' for WiHo in the form of an intra-couple transfer. As in Chap. 5, it is assumed that there are many interrelated WiHo markets defined by personal characteristics of men and women (such as education and age) and that each WiHo market establishes an equilibrium "price". A higher price for WiHo means that the individual WiHo-worker obtains more access to the gains from marriage and has higher bargaining power.

When traditional gender roles prevail, women do more WiHo and earn less in the labor force than men. WiHo markets are then markets for women's WiHo. (A man may also supply WiHo to his wife, especially if he earns less than she does. The following analysis then needs to be adapted). Traditional men could pay for this WiHo with love, but most women also expect a material compensation, a price for the WiHo they supply. Men are thus on the demand side, willing to pay the price of women's WiHo in the form of transfers of some of their higher personal income or of goods consumed by the WiHo-worker. Women's supply of WiHo is upward-sloping: the higher the price paid for WiHo, the more WiHo women are willing to supply. The demand is downward-sloping: the more expensive WiHo, the more men will look for substitute ways of fulfilling their needs for clean clothing, meals, etc.

Men will prefer to pay less for women's WiHo; women will prefer to earn more for that kind of work. These conflicting interests possibly lead to bargaining within heterosexual couples. They also affect prices in markets for WiHo as women com-

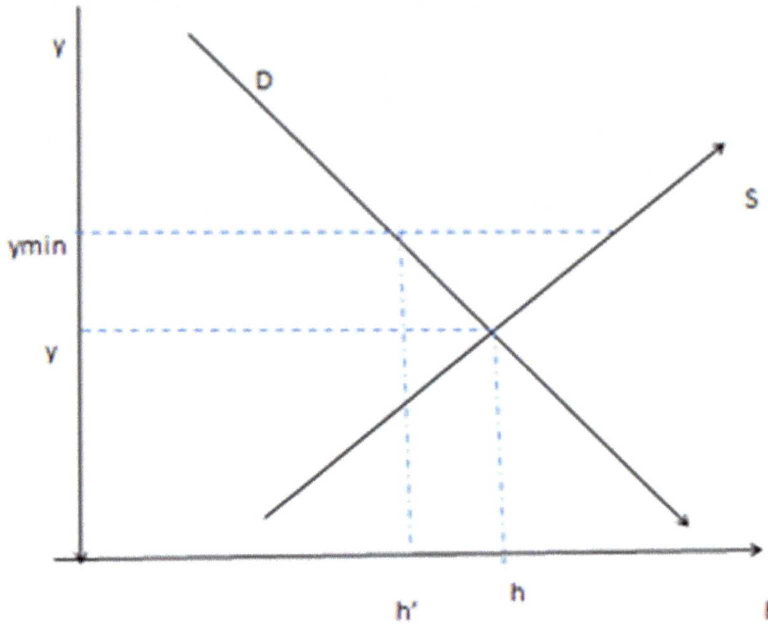


**Fig. 7.1** Market for women's WiHo, comparing CLM states to non-CLM states. *ymin* with *CLM* (Common Law Marriage), h stand for *WiHo* (Work-In-Household)

pete with each other and men compete with each other. Figure 7.1 represents this graphically. It shows a market for WiHo supplied by women; *h* denotes WiHo and *y* denotes its price. Supply *S* is by women working in WiHo and demand *D* is by men willing to pay for this WiHo. It is assumed that many women are sufficiently alike to be substitutable and the same is true for many men.

The higher the price women get for their WiHo, the higher their reservation wage and they are less likely to be in the labor force. As for traditional men who have a demand for women's WiHo, the more they need to pay for WiHo, the more they need to work in the labor force in order to afford that WiHo. Their total expenses on WiHo depend on both the amount they use and the price of WiHo. If at higher WiHo prices women's hours of WiHo decrease, then the total amount men need to earn to pay for a wife's WiHo does not necessarily go up. Therefore, men may not necessarily work more in the labor force if the price of women's WiHo rises.

CLM laws raise expected future compensations to WiHo workers in case of dissolution or death, as some WiHo workers would otherwise be cohabitants and not be eligible for the protection that marriage and divorce laws offer WiHo workers. To the extent that WiHo markets are modeled in a one-period model, it follows that CLM laws offer WiHo workers higher material life-time benefits. CLM laws mean that the option of a cohabitation arrangement implying a low price of WiHo is less available: it is more likely that the WiHo workers will get the benefits of marriage, implying a higher price for WiHo. In that sense CLM legislation acts as the equivalent of minimum wage laws and the effect of CLM on WiHo markets can be analyzed as that of minimum wage laws on labor markets.

This is shown in Fig. 7.1 where the minimum price of WiHo has been set above the market-clearing *y*, at level *ymin*. At this higher *y* women are willing to work more at WiHo in marriage or cohabitation, implying that they would like to move up their supply of WiHo. However, at the higher *ymin* men are less willing to obtain WiHo than they were when the price of WiHo was set at the equilibrium of demand and supply. This is based on both a price effect and an income effect.

At the new equilibrium associated with *ymin* the total amount of WiHo supplied will be the amount demanded and will be smaller than the previous total amount of WiHo supplied, as long as the demand is downward-sloping. The women who do have a 'WiHo job' and are observed as married or cohabiting will get paid more for it, implying a higher reservation wage and lower labor supply. The total number of women employed in WiHo is likely to shrink (see Grossbard and Vernon forthcoming, 2015).

Assuming traditional gender roles we expect that:

*Prediction TU17* When CLM is available women who are in couple are likely to have a lower labor supply than when it is not available. This follows from a higher reservation wage.

*Prediction TU17′ The negative effect of CLM on the labor supply of women who are in couple is likely to be larger (in absolute value) for married women than for cohabiting or single women.* All women could possibly be affected by the state's imposition of *ymin*, even those who are not in couple. However, the positive effect of CLM (*ymin*) on price of WiHo is likely to be most sizeable for women who are in couple: it is for that group that the reservation wage is most likely to increase. When CLM is available women who would otherwise earn a lower price of WiHo and therefore would have a lower reservation wage may not be in couple and be a part of our samples of married and cohabiting women. As a result, CLM effects on women's labor supply are likely to be more sizeable for married women than for women who either cohabit or are single. At the same time we do not rule out effects of CLM on cohabiting and single individuals: they also participate in WiHo markets and may be influenced by the level of opportunities available to them if they form couples. If there are CLM effects on their labor supply they are expected to be negative too.

As for the labor supply of traditional men, CLM implies a higher price for women's WiHo, which leads men to demand a smaller amount of WiHo. The total expenses of married men on WiHo may rise or drop, depending on the elasticity of their demand for women's WiHo. If their total expenses on WiHo rise they will need to work more; if their total expenses on WiHo decrease, they will need to work less. The more elastic that demand, the more possible it is that men's need for income will drop when CLM is available and that they will have a lower supply of labor. The opposite holds if men's demand for women's WiHo is inelastic. This reasoning mostly applies to married men (and CLM is also likely to affect men's willingness to enter marriage or cohabitation). Therefore, if women are the WiHo workers:

*Prediction TU18 The predicted effect of CLM on married men's labor supply is not clear.*

If men are the WiHo workers we predict a negative effect of CLM on married men.

Comparing these predictions implies that, if gender roles are traditional, in absolute terms CLM will have a greater impact on women's labor supply than on men's. An additional reason why one expects more effects of CLM on women's than on men's labor supply is that men tend to be closer to the physical limit to which they can work. There is less room for variation and thus CLM effects on labor supply are also expected to be smaller for men than for women.

This also follows from the analysis presented here:

*Prediction TU19 Parents' labor supply will be more affected by CLM than that of childless respondents.* Parenting is often a form of WiHo, especially if a child is a joint child. If CLM raises the price of parental WiHo, it will be associated with lower labor supply of women. Again, it is not so clear what the effect of CLM will be on fathers.

A minimum $y$ imposed by CLM laws is likely to have more effect on the price of some WiHo workers than on that of others'. WiHo workers whose WiHo is more valuable in the markets in which they participate are more likely to benefit from *ymin* laws such as CLM. This is similar to highly skilled workers benefiting more from minimum wage laws than low-skill workers who are likely to be displaced by capital and more skilled labor when their employers are forced to pay them more. We expect that married educated women are also more likely to benefit from CLM than married women with low education: they are likely to get paid more for their WiHo than if CLM is not available. Higher WiHo price implies higher reservation wage and therefore:

*Prediction TU20 Relative to low-education women, women with a college education are more likely to experience a negative effect of CLM on their labor supply.*

Neumark and Wascher (2011) have shown negative employment effects of minimum wage for Black or Hispanic teens, but not for White teens. This could be due to discrimination in labor markets leading to a larger gap between the minimum wage and the equilibrium wage for Blacks than for Whites (not just teens). Likewise, it is possible that there is discrimination against Blacks in marriage markets, as suggested by Goldsmith et al. (2007). Therefore, Black WiHo workers could suffer larger losses in 'WiHo employment' than White WiHo workers. This holds regardless of who discriminates against Blacks, be it Blacks or Whites. Increased demand for White WiHo workers due to discrimination in favor of Whites implies that relative to Blacks, Whites would experience larger increases in price of WiHo and reservation wage. The following prediction follows:

*Prediction TU21 Relative to Black women, White women are more likely to experience a negative effect of CLM on their labor supply.* This racial gap is likely to be limited to married women.

To the extent that among Blacks it is women who pay men for WiHo (see Cherry 1998), then it is possible that when CLM is available Black women will pay more for men's WiHo. If their demand for men's WiHo is not very elastic they will have higher labor force participation rates under CLM in order to pay more for men's WiHo.

As for predicted effects of CLM on time that men and women spend on leisure, it is predicted that:

*Prediction TU22 Under CLM married women will spend more time in leisure than when CLM is not available.* CLM effects on the leisure of married women will be positive, especially if they are White and educated. This is because at higher price of WiHo their personal disposable income is higher (it includes higher transfers from husbands) and income effects on leisure tend to be positive.

As for CLM's effect on married women's time in household production, it is likely to decrease as husbands' demand for their WiHo time decreases and their personal disposable income, including transfers from husbands, decreases and with higher income they may prefer to perform less work of all kinds, including less WiHo work.

## Data and Sample Means

We use micro data from CPS-iPums 1994–2011 to estimate labor market outcomes and micro data from ATUS 2003–2011 to estimate determinants of household production time and leisure. CLM status is not reported in either of these surveys. It is a legal form of marriage so we assume that most CLM-married individuals refer to themselves as "married" in surveys. However, it is conceivable that some couples who satisfy the requirements of being common-law married report themselves as "cohabiting".

### *CPS-March 1994–2011*[2]

This is a large nationally representative dataset with information on demographic characteristics, labor market status, and identifiable cohabiting relationships. Three states abolished CLM over the time covered by this data: Idaho (1996), Georgia (1997), and Pennsylvania (2005). The main drawback is that not all cohabiting couples can be identified prior to 2007, because only relationships between household heads and their partners were recorded, while other household members are assigned either married or single status. In 1994 data, cohabiting partners cannot be distinguished from roommates. We experiment with dropping that year in our analysis of cohabiting men and women. The fact that our sample underestimates the share of cohabiting couples in the population for 1994–2006 should not be a problem as long as the designation of a household head and the composition of other

[2] https://cps.ipums.org/cps/.

family members do not vary systematically by CLM status, because our variable of interest is not the time trend but the difference between CLM and non-CLM states.

We choose to focus on young individuals aged 18–35. Younger people are more likely to be affected by the change in the marriage law as they are more likely to transition in and out of marriage and cohabitation.

We excluded foreign-born young adults as we want to increase the likelihood that our sample consists of individuals who were likely to respond to a change in CLM legislation in their state of residence. This resulted in a disproportionate loss of married individuals since first generation immigrants are more likely to be married and less likely to cohabit compared to the rest of the US population. This selection affected the Hispanic sample the most: it shrank by more than one-third. We also excluded same-sex cohabiting couples from our sample for in this case it is even harder to determine *a-priori* who is the WiHo-worker.

Our sample includes 339,499 women and 308,513 men, of which 21.7 % live in CLM states. According to Table 7.1 of weighted sample means, CLM states have a slightly higher proportion of married and a lower proportion of cohabiting residents. Respondents from CLM states are on average less educated, more likely to have children, be Hispanic, and work full time in the labor force. CLM states are more likely to offer lower welfare payments, have lower unemployment rates, lower proportion of college-educated adults, lower share of urban population, and lower median household income. All differences by CLM status are statistically significant due to the large sample sizes. CLM is defined as whether the state had the corresponding law in effect at the time of the survey.

We use the following measures of labor supply in our analysis:

1. Employment status last year. We set this variable to equal one if the respondent worked for more than 1 h a week and for more than 2 weeks in the year prior to the survey.
2. Full time employment status last year. It is measured by usual weekly hours of work with 35 hours as a cutoff between full-time and part-time status. Hours of work refer to total hours from all jobs.
3. Average weekly hours of work last year. This is our preferred measure computed as usual hours times the number of weeks worked, divided by 52 weeks, and adjusted for part-time work. A fraction of full-time employees report working part-time for a certain number of weeks. Since we don't know their part-time hours, we adjust average hours by subtracting one-third from their usual weekly hours for the number of weeks reported as part-time work. Similar results are obtained when we subtract one-half of usual hours during part-time weeks.
4. Usual hours of work last year. It is the reported number of usual weekly hours worked at all jobs. It is a popular measure in the labor supply literature, thus it is also reported. However, it is not adjusted for part-time work.

All these measures, collected in March, refer to the previous calendar year. Figure 7.2 illustrates average weekly hours of work among married, cohabiting, and single men and women living in CLM and non-CLM states. Weekly hours range between 21 and 27 h for women, with the longest work week reported by women

**Table 7.1** Sample means. CPS 1995–2011 and ATUS 2003–2011. US born respondents age 18–35

| | Women | | | | Men | | | |
|---|---|---|---|---|---|---|---|---|
| | CPS, CLM 21.6 % | | ATUS, CLM 19.8 % | | CPS, CLM 21.8 % | | ATUS, CLM 20.1 % | |
| | Non-CLM | CLM | Non-CLM | CLM | Non-CLM | CLM | Non-CLM | CLM |
| *Individual characteristics* | | | | | | | | |
| Married | 0.380 | 0.427 | 0.434 | 0.495 | 0.317 | 0.362 | 0.358 | 0.412 |
| Cohabiting | 0.087 | 0.073 | 0.078 | 0.062 | 0.080 | 0.069 | 0.073 | 0.064 |
| Age | 26.4 | 26.5 | 26.9 | 27.2 | 26.4 | 26.5 | 26.6 | 26.6 |
| No high school diploma | 0.115 | 0.128 | 0.080 | 0.086 | 0.138 | 0.151 | 0.099 | 0.122 |
| Some college | 0.366 | 0.358 | 0.362 | 0.355 | 0.329 | 0.326 | 0.358 | 0.322 |
| College degree | 0.183 | 0.175 | 0.238 | 0.253 | 0.158 | 0.151 | 0.206 | 0.194 |
| Graduate degree | 0.052 | 0.041 | 0.087 | 0.062 | 0.040 | 0.038 | 0.058 | 0.058 |
| Black | 0.159 | 0.151 | 0.109 | 0.097 | 0.137 | 0.131 | 0.081 | 0.071 |
| Hispanic | 0.082 | 0.132 | 0.082 | 0.154 | 0.085 | 0.133 | 0.080 | 0.139 |
| Asian | 0.019 | 0.007 | 0.018 | 0.004 | 0.020 | 0.008 | 0.024 | 0.008 |
| Other race | 0.013 | 0.013 | 0.048 | 0.037 | 0.013 | 0.012 | 0.055 | 0.043 |
| Employed last year | 0.774 | 0.780 | 0.733 | 0.732 | 0.851 | 0.871 | 0.817 | 0.846 |
| FT employed last year | 0.533 | 0.548 | 0.503 | 0.512 | 0.703 | 0.730 | 0.675 | 0.709 |
| Average hours of work | 23.3 | 23.6 | | | 30.0 | 31.4 | | |
| Usual hours of work | 27.4 | 27.8 | 26.3 | 26.7 | 34.1 | 35.5 | 34.2 | 36.1 |
| Presence of children <6 | 0.288 | 0.315 | 0.365 | 0.406 | 0.182 | 0.211 | 0.236 | 0.273 |
| Children 6–17 | 0.149 | 0.167 | 0.115 | 0.128 | 0.069 | 0.080 | 0.056 | 0.063 |
| Number of children | 0.833 | 0.935 | 0.843 | 1.010 | 0.464 | 0.556 | 0.492 | 0.584 |
| Student | 0.189 | 0.172 | 0.232 | 0.202 | 0.178 | 0.169 | 0.197 | 0.203 |
| Metropolitan residence | | | 0.833 | 0.798 | | | 0.829 | 0.787 |
| Metro: central city | 0.267 | 0.266 | | | 0.259 | 0.260 | | |
| Metro: outside central | 0.557 | 0.525 | | | 0.565 | 0.525 | | |
| Unearned income | 53,331 | 49,324 | 44,588 | 40,975 | 49,601 | 43,524 | 43,911 | 39,805 |

**Table 7.1** (continued)

| | Women | | | | Men | | | |
|---|---|---|---|---|---|---|---|---|
| | CPS, CLM 21.6 % | | ATUS, CLM 19.8 % | | CPS, CLM 21.8 % | | ATUS, CLM 20.1 % | |
| | Non-CLM | CLM | Non-CLM | CLM | Non-CLM | CLM | Non-CLM | CLM |
| *State characteristics* | | | | | | | | |
| Sex ratio | 0.997 | 0.994 | 0.986 | 0.985 | 0.998 | 0.995 | 0.987 | 0.987 |
| College educated adults | 25.7 | 24.5 | 27.4 | 26.5 | 25.8 | 24.6 | 27.3 | 26.5 |
| Unemployment rate | 5.9 | 5.4 | 6.7 | 6.0 | 6.0 | 5.4 | 6.8 | 6.0 |
| Median household income | 51,957 | 49,083 | 51,911 | 49,492 | 52,046 | 49,216 | 51,849 | 49,665 |
| Welfare | 707 | 611 | 692 | 613 | 710 | 614 | 695 | 618 |
| Urban population share | 79.1 | 75.5 | 79.6 | 76.9 | 79.3 | 75.5 | 79.4 | 76.8 |
| *N* | 256,982 | 82,517 | 11,979 | 3263 | 233,934 | 74,579 | 8511 | 2438 |

Means are weighted using weights provided in the survey

CLM is defined as whether the state had the corresponding law in effect at the time of the survey

Differences among CLM and non-CLM states are not statistically significant at 5 % for pairs of mean values in italics

Shares of college-educated adults are obtained from http://www.census.gov/hhes/socdemo/education/data/census/index.html

Median household income is from Table H-8 at http://www.census.gov/hhes/www/income/data/historical/household/

Shares of urban population are from Iowa Community Indicators program http://www.icip.iastate.edu/tables/population/urban-pct-states

We adjust nominal values to 2010 prices using Consumer Price Index from ftp://ftp.bls.gov/pub/special.requests/cpi/cpiai.txt

Unemployment rates are annual averages by state obtained from BLS (http://www.bls.gov/data/)

Sex ratios, overall and separately by race, are calculated from Census annual state population by age and race data found at https://www.census.gov/popest/data/. We divided the number of men in each 5-year age group by the number of women who are 2 years younger. For example, in order to get a sex ratio for women aged 30–35, we divided the number of men aged 32–37 by the number of women aged 30–35

"Welfare" is the maximum TANF + SNAP benefits for a family of two, in 2010 dollars obtained from the University of Kentucky Center for Poverty Research http://www.ukcpr.org/AvailableData.aspx

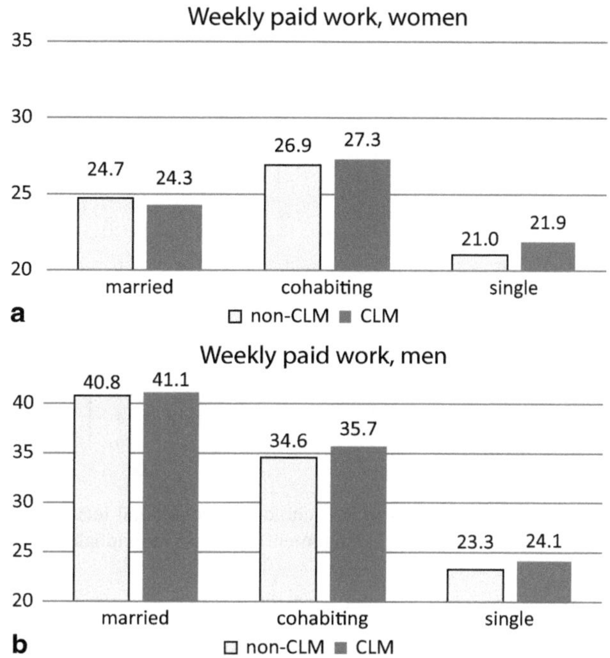


**Fig. 7.2** Average weekly hours of paid work for women and men by presence of CLM and type of living arrangement. US-born individuals ages 18–35, CPS 1995–2011

who cohabit. Men work on average 23–41 h/week, with the longest work hours among married men. Single men and women report the lowest hours of work; this is not surprising since these groups are younger and include more full-time students who are not in the labor force. With the exception of married women, most residents of CLM states report longer workweeks than their counterparts in other states. For example, cohabiting men, single men, and single women in CLM states work about an hour longer per week on average than their counterparts in non-CLM states.

*ATUS 2003–2011*[3] This dataset is a time use supplement to the CPS. The survey is conducted several months after the CPS, and respondents are asked to update the main demographic, labor market, and family status variables. The sample size is much smaller than that of the CPS because only one household member is selected to participate, and the supplement covers a shorter number of years. The shorter time frame makes causal interpretation of our results impossible since only one state changed CLM status during the 8 years of the survey. We therefore examine correlations and interpret our results with caution.

Our sample includes 15,242 women and 10,949 men aged 18–35, 20 % of whom live in CLM states. Survey weights are applied in all estimations to adjust for days of the week. Comparing the ATUS sample means in Table 7.1 to the CPS means in the same table, one notices that ATUS respondents are slightly older, more educated, more likely to be married, and less likely to cohabit. These differences are pos-

[3] http://bls.gov/tus/.

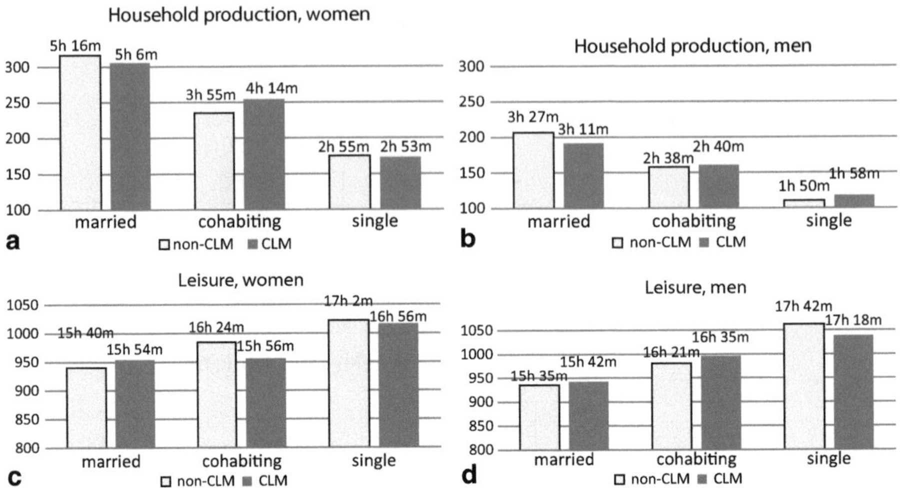


**Fig. 7.3** Daily minutes in household production and leisure for women and men by presence of CLM and type of living arrangement. US-born individuals ages 18–35, ATUS 2003–2011

sibly the result of a higher response rate to the supplement among educated women who are also more likely to be married. The ATUS also contains a lower percent of African-American women and a higher share of students. A somewhat lower proportion of ATUS respondents report being employed and working full-time, but the usual weekly hours of work are about the same across both surveys.

We use two definitions of household production and leisure. In our baseline definitions, household production is broadly defined to include all unpaid work: cooking, cleaning, home repairs and maintenance, food and non-food shopping, paying bills, care of adults, children, and pets, as well as using household and government services. In the same baseline models, leisure includes only active leisure while awake: hobbies, social activities, attending events, taking classes for personal interest, eating out, and all other free time that is not part of household production, education, personal care, or paid work. Both household production and leisure include related travel. We also use alternative definitions of household production and leisure. In this version, household production is more narrowly defined to exclude the following components: all care of pets, half of non-food shopping, half of childcare. Instead these components are added to leisure, along with sleep and personal care to arrive at a broad definition of leisure. Mean values in this section refer to baseline definitions.

Figure 7.3 reports minutes spent in household production and leisure by relationship status (married/cohabiting/single) in CLM and non-CLM states.

Married women in CLM states spend 10 min less in household production and 14 min more in leisure on a typical day compared to married women in non-CLM states. In contrast, cohabiting women in CLM states spend 19 min more in household production and 28 min less in leisure compared to their counterparts in non-CLM states.

Married men from CLM states spend 16 min less in household production and 7 min more in leisure than men in other states. Cohabiting men work about the same time at home and enjoy 14 extra minutes of leisure compared to non-CLM men. Single men from CLM states work 8 min longer around the house and report 25 min less leisure than their counterparts in non-CLM states.

## Empirical Strategy

Our general empirical strategy is to estimate a series of difference-in-difference (DD) models using the CPS data where the outcome of interest *Y* for individual *i* from state *s* in year *t* is a function of CLM and other determinants of a decision:

$$Y_{ist} = \alpha CLM_{st} + \beta X_{ist} + \delta_s + \gamma_t + u_{ist} \tag{7.1}$$

where *Y* is: (1) employment status, (2) full-time employment status, (3) average weekly hours of work, or (4) usual weekly hours worked.

$CLM_{st}$ equals one if state *s* recognized CLM in year *t*. The coefficient of interest is , the estimated impact of living in a CLM state.

The vector of controls *X* consists of:

a. Respondent's demographics. Regressions contain a quadratic function of age, educational level, Black or Hispanic ethnicity, presence of children, presence of preschool age children, and the number of children. We also include into the CPS regressions the log of income of other household members, as well as the log of respondent's own unearned income measured as personal income minus the respondent's labor earnings. Income measures are not included in ATUS models because the corresponding variables have too many missing values. For those under age 25 the CPS asks if they are students and if so full-time or not; we use this information to control for full-time and part-time student status, a variable that greatly affects labor force participation. We also run a set of results where we exclude students. We include two metropolitan residence dummies into the CPS analysis, one for central city and the other for outside central city, with non-identifiable and non-MSA residence being a reference category. In addition, we include an indicator for the presence of a household member in poor health or with a disability limiting work options.
b. State-level time-varying characteristics. This group of variables includes sex-ratio by age and race, which has been shown to affect labor market participation (Grossbard and Amuedo-Dorantes 2007). We included the log of median state household income to account for the aggregate impact of the cost of living. Unemployment rates from last year are included to reflect labor market conditions during past calendar year. Finally, we included the share of college-educated adults age 25 and older, and share of urban population in the state. These variables are likely to affect markets for WiHo and therefore the price of WiHo and value of time.

$\delta_s$ are state-fixed effects. These indicators account for differences in economic, legal, demographic, and cultural environment that are not reflected in state time-varying controls, such as laws regarding child custody, property division and alimony, as well as religiosity of the population, all of which may affect individual choices. When analyzing the ATUS data we also experiment with including three regional dummies (Northeastern, Midwestern, and Western states, Southern being the reference) instead of using state fixed effects.

$\gamma_t$ are time dummies to capture the time trend; and
$u_{ist}$ are i.i.d. error terms.

Standard errors are clustered by state/year to adjust for correlated standard errors that are likely to arise due to common random effects at the state-year level. This is a necessary step because the unit of observation is at the individual-level while the variation is at the state-level.

We estimate the following models using the ATUS for daily minutes spent in household production and leisure:

$$\text{Household Prod}_{ist} = \alpha_1 \text{CLM - P} + \beta X_{ist} + \delta_s + \gamma_t + u_{ist} \tag{7.2}$$

$$\text{Leisure}_{ist} = \alpha_2 \text{CLM - P} + \beta X_{ist} + \delta_s + \gamma_t + u_{ist} \tag{7.3}$$

CLM-P equals one for all respondents in the state of Pennsylvania in years before it abolished CLM. Even though only one state is a treatment state, this approach aims to identify the treatment effect.

We also provide descriptive non-causal evidence on time use differences between CLM and non-CLM states from an alternative version of these regressions where CLM is an identifier of CLM states, with regional dummies but no state-fixed effects. These equations are estimated separately using OLS with clustered errors, with tobit models, as well as with a SUR system of equations.

All Eqs. 7.1-7.3 are estimated separately for married, cohabiting, and single young adults. In accordance with the predictions of Sect. 7.2 we estimate these equations separately by ethnicity (White, Black, and Hispanic), education (college educated or not), and presence of children. All regressions presented in the results section control for the above variables.

Because union formation and dissolution are lengthy processes, it may take time for people to realize that changes in CLM had an impact on their opportunities. Therefore, labor supply changes may not be observed quickly. In an attempt to reduce any possible bias and relax the assumption of quick transmission of knowledge of marriage laws we also estimate regressions on sample from which 3 years of data were removed, starting at each abolition year and immediately after the abolition.

We are also concerned that changes in CLM legislation possibly occurred as a result of previous trends related to changes in labor supply. Also, if trends in labor supply preceded changes in the marriage law, it would be inappropriate to ascribe changes in the labor supply to the abolition of CLM. Figure 7.4 shows average hours of work for married women over time for CLM, non-CLM and the three transition states. Both CLM and non-CLM states are on a similar path that exhibits

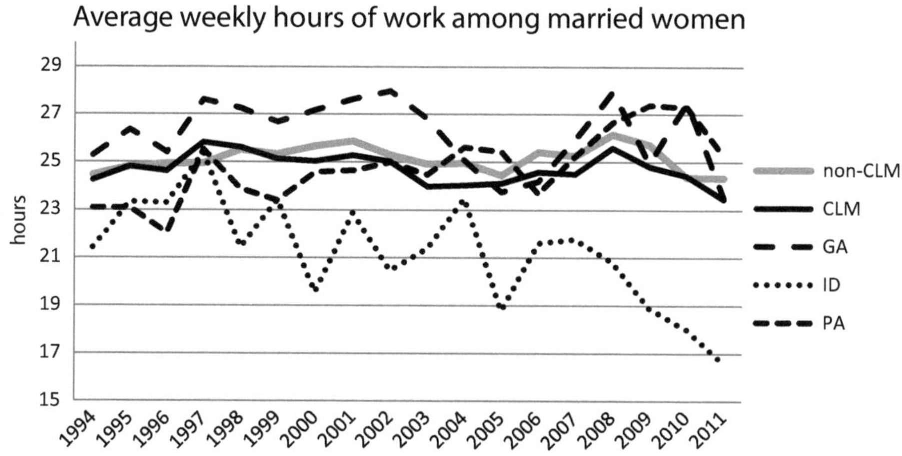


**Fig. 7.4** Married women's average hours of work, CPS 1994–2011

a decline in labor supply during recessionary years. In most years, the line for non-CLM states lies above the line for CLM states. The three transition states differ in their trends. In Idaho hours of work are lower than average and they decline after the abolition of CLM. In Georgia and Pennsylvania, women have higher than average labor supply, and after the abolition of CLM the hours of work increased in the latter, with no clear trend in the former. In an attempt to control for state-specific trends, we produce a set of results that includes state-specific trends as interactions of a trend variable with each state indicator.

## Results

We first present results regarding the effect of CLM on labor supply. Then we present results regarding time in household production and leisure.

### *Labor Supply*

Table 7.2 presents coefficients on CLM in regressions by marital status. Results in Panel A are for the full sample of women and men, Panel B refers to a sample that excludes students, Panel C refers to a sample that excludes 3 years before abolition of CLM (1996–1999 and 2005–2007), and Panel D refers to a sample similar to that of Panel C but it also includes state-specific trends. Table 7.2 only reports CLM coefficients. Full results for regression 1 are found in the Appendix to this chapter.

**Table 7.2** Coefficients on CLM in labor supply regressions, various specifications, CPS 1994–2011

| Women | | | | | Men | | | |
|---|---|---|---|---|---|---|---|---|
| | Probit employed last year | Probit full-time last year | OLS h/week average | OLS h/week usual | Probit employed last year | Probit full-time last year | OLS h/week average | OLS h/week usual |
| | 1 | 2 | 3 | 4 | 1 | 2 | 3 | 4 |
| *A. Full sample* | | | | | | | | |
| Married | −0.031 | −0.045 | −1.181 | −1.533 | −0.005 | 0 | 0.033 | 0.165 |
| | [0.009][a] | [0.017][a] | [0.379][a] | [0.392][a] | [0.006] | [0.008] | [0.383] | [0.370] |
| Cohabiting | 0.022 | 0.02 | 0.914 | 0.969 | −0.01 | −0.021 | −0.011 | 0.5 |
| | [0.023] | [0.029] | [1.111] | [0.950] | [0.016] | [0.024] | [1.011] | [1.146] |
| Single | 0.002 | −0.003 | 0.143 | 0.019 | 0.002 | 0.003 | −0.698 | −0.121 |
| | [0.011] | [0.012] | [0.321] | [0.381] | [0.013] | [0.017] | [0.285][b] | [0.463] |
| *B. Full sample, students excluded* | | | | | | | | |
| Married | −0.032 | −0.044 | −1.158 | −1.542 | −0.006 | 0 | 0.067 | 0.164 |
| | [0.010][a] | [0.016][a] | [0.388][a] | [0.405][a] | [0.005] | [0.007] | [0.383] | [0.362] |
| Cohabiting | 0.015 | 0.026 | 0.913 | 0.995 | −0.011 | −0.025 | −0.016 | 0.394 |
| | [0.025] | [0.032] | [1.259] | [1.102] | [0.017] | [0.024] | [1.080] | [1.185] |
| Single | 0.018 | 0.008 | 0.918 | 0.717 | 0.001 | −0.004 | −0.505 | −0.056 |
| | [0.013] | [0.015] | [0.416][b] | [0.468] | [0.013] | [0.017] | [0.358] | [0.570] |
| *C. Three years after abolition excluded (1996–1999 and 2005–2007)* | | | | | | | | |
| Married | −0.030 | −0.051 | −1.493 | −1.813 | 0.008 | 0.015 | 1.101 | 1.228 |
| | [0.013][b] | [0.020][b] | [0.398][a] | [0.432][a] | [0.004][c] | [0.007][b] | [0.383][a] | [0.344][a] |
| Cohabiting | 0.008 | 0.001 | 0.685 | 0.013 | −0.025 | −0.05 | −0.433 | −0.272 |
| | [0.028] | [0.038] | [1.410] | [1.160] | [0.020] | [0.031] | [1.463] | [1.541] |
| Single | 0.004 | −0.001 | −0.244 | 0.103 | 0.003 | −0.01 | −0.689 | −0.153 |
| | [0.013] | [0.017] | [0.435] | [0.488] | [0.018] | [0.023] | [0.417][c] | [0.713] |

**Table 7.2** (continued)

| Women | | | | | Men | | | |
|---|---|---|---|---|---|---|---|---|
| | Probit employed last year | Probit full-time last year | OLS h/week average | OLS h/week usual | Probit employed last year | Probit full-time last year | OLS h/week average | OLS h/week usual |
| | 1 | 2 | 3 | 4 | 1 | 2 | 3 | 4 |
| *D. Three years after abolition excluded, state-specific trends included* | | | | | | | | |
| Married | −0.009 | −0.045 | −1.417 | −1.690 | 0 | −0.006 | 0.050 | 0.235 |
| | [0.016] | [0.022][b] | [0.441][a] | [0.603][a] | [0.008] | [0.013] | [0.545] | [0.617] |
| Cohabiting | 0.009 | −0.015 | 0.495 | 0.219 | −0.036 | −0.042 | 0.617 | 0.174 |
| | [0.059] | [0.073] | [2.256] | [2.384] | [0.035] | [0.043] | [2.813] | [2.691] |
| Single | 0.007 | 0.006 | −0.214 | 0.005 | −0.018 | −0.02 | −1.062 | −0.654 |
| | [0.018] | [0.028] | [0.760] | [0.814] | [0.031] | [0.028] | [0.646] | [0.872] |

The table shows CLM estimates from Eq. 7.1. Columns (1) and (2) are marginal effects from probit regressions estimated at the mean. Columns (3) and (4) are OLS coefficients from the hours of work regressions. Each coefficient comes from a separate regression. R-sq are between 0.08 and 0.19 in OLS regressions. Standard errors are in brackets

[a] Significant at 1 %. Sample sizes in Panel A are 139,608, 28,660, 171,126 for women and 113,229, 25,740, 169,436 for men among married, cohabiting and single respondents, correspondingly. Panel D has the smallest samples, 90,860, 18,862, 111,169 for women and 73,776, 16,902, 109,667 for men, correspondingly

[b] Significant at 5 %

[c] Significant at 10 %

CLM coefficients in regressions for married women are highly significant for most labor supply outcomes and in all four panels: if CLM is available married women are less likely to be employed, less likely to work in full-time jobs, and they work less in the labor force per week than when CLM is not available. Their average weekly hours of work decrease by 1 in the case of the full sample and by 1.5 when 3 years after abolition are excluded. Results don't change much when we include interactions of a trend variable with each state variable.

Cohabiting and single women's labor supply in CLM states does not differ significantly from that in other states, with the exception of the positive coefficient on the average hours of work among single women in the subsample that excludes students.

Men's labor supply is generally unaffected by CLM. The coefficients in regressions for men are not significant in most regressions, with the exception of positive CLM effects on the labor supply of married men when 3 years after abolition are excluded and negative effects for single men's average hours of work in two of the samples.

The data thus provides robust evidence that the abolition of CLM raised married women's labor supply. The abolition of CLM may have led to a drop in married men's labor supply if we base ourselves on Panel C. This is consistent with predictions TU17 and TU18. We also see primarily effects for married respondents, in accordance with Prediction TU17'.

In Table 7.3 we estimate labor supply regressions for subsamples of married individuals by race, presence of children, and college education. Two sets of results are presented, those using the full sample of married adults (Panel A), and the other where we exclude 3 years after each state's abolition of CLM, but include state-specific time trends (Panel B). It can be seen from both panels that effects of CLM for married women who have at least one child are large compared to those for all married women. Separate regressions, not presented here, indicate that CLM does not have significant effects on the labor supply of childless women. This corroborates Prediction TU19: WiHo markets matter more in the case of parents than in the case of the childless. For married men it does not matter whether they are parents or not: in any event CLM does not have an effect.

Regressions for respondents with a college degree in Panel A show a negative labor supply impact of CLM for married women, a result that is consistent with Prediction TU20 but is not robust to the exclusion of 3 years after abolition and inclusion of state-specific trends (Panel B). However, in Panel B CLM coefficients for married men are positive and significant. In either event, whether we use Panel A or Panel B results, the abolition of CLM seems to have led to a convergence in the labor supply of the college-educated, as well as the whole sample not stratified by education.

Results in both panels suggest that White and Hispanic married women are the groups for which CLM is negatively associated with labor supply. The same is not true for Black women, which is consistent with Prediction TU21. For Hispanic married women CLM coefficients on hours worked are negative and considerably larger in absolute terms than for White women. CLM is associated with less labor

**Table 7.3** Estimates of CLM effect in regressions for married women and men age 18–35, CPS 1994–2011

| | Women | | | | Men | | | |
|---|---|---|---|---|---|---|---|---|
| | Probit employed last year | Probit full-time last year | OLS h/week average | OLS h/week usual | Probit employed last year | Probit full-time last year | OLS h/week average | OLS h/week usual |
| | 1 | 2 | 3 | 4 | 1 | 2 | 3 | 4 |
| *A. Married, full sample* | | | | | | | | |
| White | −0.029 | −0.041 | −0.961 | −1.266 | −0.003 | 0.006 | 0.36 | 0.397 |
| | [0.011]*** | [0.016]*** | [0.403]** | [0.406]*** | [0.006] | [0.008] | [0.436] | [0.403] |
| Black | −0.006 | 0.02 | 0.326 | −0.124 | −0.021 | −0.055 | −0.994 | −0.159 |
| | [0.024] | [0.043] | [1.277] | [1.191] | [0.026] | [0.037] | [1.437] | [1.500] |
| Hispanic | −0.012 | −0.18 | −3.01 | −4.444 | −0.035 | −0.083 | −4.078 | −4.212 |
| | [0.062] | [0.059]*** | [1.717]* | [2.586]* | [0.033] | [0.038]** | [1.933]** | [1.839]** |
| Children | −0.050 | −0.049 | −1.600 | −2.084 | −0.006 | −0.002 | −0.065 | 0.09 |
| | [0.011]*** | [0.016]*** | [0.497]*** | [0.455]*** | [0.006] | [0.009] | [0.433] | [0.416] |
| College | −0.055 | −0.075 | −2.759 | −2.700 | 0.002 | −0.003 | 0.754 | 1.035 |
| | [0.015]*** | [0.027]*** | [0.705]*** | [0.666]*** | [0.007] | [0.015] | [0.562] | [0.600]* |
| *B. Married, 3 years after abolition removed, state specific trends included* | | | | | | | | |
| White | 0.005 | −0.044 | −1.196 | −1.263 | 0.005 | 0.01 | 0.323 | 0.318 |
| | [0.022] | [0.022]** | [0.568]** | [0.743]* | [0.008] | [0.013] | [0.566] | [0.633] |
| Black | 0.041 | 0.079 | 3.636 | 3.067 | −0.024 | −0.119 | 0.018 | 1.411 |
| | [0.033] | [0.063] | [2.156]* | [1.894] | [0.039] | [0.089] | [1.758] | [2.166] |
| Hispanic | −0.214 | −0.270 | −4.976 | −12.165 | −0.139 | −0.073 | −7.535 | −9.187 |
| | [0.097]** | [0.098]*** | [2.555]* | [3.305]*** | [0.124] | [0.073] | [3.586]** | [3.398]*** |
| Children | −0.028 | −0.049 | −1.686 | −2.105 | 0.005 | 0.002 | −0.44 | 0.059 |
| | [0.019] | [0.025]** | [0.718]** | [0.761]*** | [0.009] | [0.015] | [0.555] | [0.527] |
| College | −0.003 | −0.05 | −1.879 | −1.435 | 0.009 | 0.032 | 2.269 | 2.344 |
| | [0.030] | [0.051] | [1.647] | [1.533] | [0.007] | [0.012]*** | [0.894]** | [0.844]*** |

The smallest samples are for married Black women and men, correspondingly 8606 and 7562 in Panel A, and 5624 and 4969 in Panel B. The samples of Hispanics are also relatively small, 8734 and 6729 for women and men in Panel B

* significant at 10%; ** significant at 5%; *** significant at 1%

supply on the part of Hispanic men. From Panel B it appears that Black married women work more hours when CLM is available, which is consistent with Cherry's (1998) theory that Black women pay in order to marry (corresponding to a price for WiHo paid by women to men in terms of our conceptual framework).

Overall, we thus find evidence that is consistent with our analysis of CLM as a law setting a minimum price for women's WiHo. It is necessary to keep in mind, however, that legislation is not random. Why are states moving away from a common law definition of marriage? This is an important question that we are not able to address. If legislation is endogenous with labor supply (the same factors could account for increases in married women's labor supply over time and for the abolition of CLM in a state) our interpretations are less applicable. Changing social norms can be one explanation for how the abolition of the old-fashioned law and an increase in women's labor supply can take place at the same time. As cohabitation becomes more acceptable, states with more tolerance toward cohabitation may be the ones abolishing CLM in favor of its modern equivalent, the cohabiting union. Meanwhile social norms also shift toward more equal division of labor within a household, and educational attainment of women is rising relative to men. Hence, we observe higher labor force participation of women. However, it is possible that CLM is being abolished for reasons unrelated to the labor market. For example, states may have simply found it too expensive to keep CLM on the books as government agencies and private companies have to incur extra costs when verifying marriage-based claims and state courts have to deal with the legal burden imposed by CLM in contested cases where existence of a marriage has to be proven.

## Robustness Checks

Our results are robust to various changes in specification. We introduced several modifications to the main model: we omitted state characteristics and included respondent and spouse's estimated wage. Wages were estimated using Heckman corrected method over all CPS respondents age 18–55, separately for men and women. We also experimented with including partner's age and education in regressions for couples. These changes only had a minor impact on the coefficients of interest. We also tried to exclude New Hampshire from the CLM states, given that it offers CLM only posthumously, and obtained similar results. We also experimented with a specification where we use only demographic controls and state/year fixed effects, omitting state-level time-varying variables; the results are very similar. We also tried a specification sample that includes three transition states, three CLM states and three non-CLM states of comparable size and location to those of the transition states; the results are similar (available upon request).

The difference-in-difference (DD) approach that we used for identification often suffers from a serial correlation problem. Bertrand et al. (2004) have shown that standard errors of DD estimators are often underestimated and thus the statistical significance of the coefficients is overestimated. We repeat their experiment with 'placebo laws' in order to assess whether our results are reliable or could be due to random coincidence. We generate random laws that affect some states and not others, and estimate their effect. In each round of simulations, we first draw 3 years at random from a uniform distribution between 1996 and 2006. Second, we exclude the three transition states from our sample and select three other states at random and designate them as CLM states before the chosen years, and as non-CLM states after; these are designated to be transition states. We leave the remaining states as they are, either CLM or non-CLM. We then estimate Eq. 7.1 on these placebo laws, and repeat this procedure 100 times. This approach simulates results of 100 independent researchers who are studying the same problem and estimating models similar to the one for married women and men in Panel A of Table 7.2. The standard errors lead us to reject the null hypothesis of no effect at the 5 % significance level in 15 % of the cases for average hours of work for women, including seven cases with significantly negative placebo law effects and eight cases of significantly positive effects. This implies that 7 % of researchers would find a significant and negative effect of CLM on married women's labor supply. This is higher than 5 % which we expect might occur randomly in case of consistent standard errors. The power of our results is not ideal, yet this over-rejection rate is relatively low. In regressions for men, over-rejection rate is below 5 % random laws produced significant coefficients on CLM in only 4 cases out of 100.

## *Household Production and Hours of Leisure*

We predicted that under CLM women will spend more time in leisure than when CLM is not available (Prediction TU22). Table 7.4 Panel A provides coefficients on CLM-P from Eqs. 7.2 to 7.3 where CLM-P equals one for respondents from Pennsylvania before the abolition of CLM. None of these coefficients are statistically significant, but the signs of the CLM-P coefficients for women are positive, suggesting that married and cohabiting women spent more time in household production before the abolition of the law. In contrast, negative signs for men suggest that cohabiting and single men spent less time in household production tasks before the abolition of the law. The table shows that cohabiting women enjoyed less leisure under CLM but this result should be interpreted with caution because the survey contains only 47 cohabiting women. We checked robustness of our results in Panel B where alternative definitions of household production and leisure are used. The results are similar. We conclude that there is little evidence of an effect of CLM on couples' non-market time use. We can neither accept nor reject Prediction TU22.

In Panels C to D we present coefficients on CLM in regressions without state-fixed effects. Here coefficients have no causal interpretation: they show average differences between CLM and non-CLM states that could be due to cultural, demographic, political, or religious differences across states. None of the coefficients are statistically significant at 5 % level.

**Table 7.4** Coefficients on CLM in household production and leisure regressions, ATUS 2003–2011

| | Women | | Men | | Sample size | |
|---|---|---|---|---|---|---|
| | h.prod. | Leisure | h.prod. | Leisure | Women | Men |
| | 1 | 2 | 4 | 5 | | |
| *A. CLM-P, baseline definitions of dependent variables* | | | | | | |
| Married | 10.78 | −3.58 | −3.32 | −19.9 | 7121 | 4896 |
| | [31.56] | [37.68] | [14.66] | [17.00] | | |
| Cohabiting | 58.58 | −183.59 | −64.82 | −69.52 | 981 | 738 |
| | [62.69] | [49.52]*** | [46.57] | [63.56] | | |
| Single | −0.76 | 19.47 | −32.12 | −5.35 | 7140 | 5315 |
| | [19.74] | [30.70] | [10.88]*** | [17.71] | | |
| *B. CLM-P, alternative definitions of dependent variables* | | | | | | |
| Married | 17.83 | −6.99 | −0.4 | 26.88 | 7121 | 4896 |
| | [23.26] | [19.17] | [13.26] | [20.29] | | |
| Cohabiting | 39.36 | −120.23 | −43.28 | −82.67 | 981 | 738 |
| | [59.20] | [73.66] | [34.89] | [67.88] | | |
| Single | −4.59 | 40.2 | −24.69 | −53.21 | 7140 | 5315 |
| | [15.92] | [18.90]** | [9.10]*** | [25.71]** | | |
| *C. CLM, baseline definitions of dependent variables* | | | | | | |
| Married | −12.07 | 4.82 | −6.84 | −2.26 | 7121 | 4896 |
| | [6.53]* | [5.96] | [6.59] | [7.84] | | |
| Cohabiting | −3.56 | −23.86 | 13.11 | 19.59 | 981 | 738 |
| | [20.53] | [16.25] | [19.25] | [27.86] | | |
| Single | −9.67 | −10.22 | 7.36 | −4.07 | 7140 | 5315 |
| | [5.81]* | [8.97] | [7.02] | [10.33] | | |
| *D. CLM, alternative definitions of dependent variables* | | | | | | |
| Married | −7.18 | 5.16 | −4.63 | 9.3 | 7121 | 4896 |
| | [5.30] | [5.86] | [5.47] | [8.28] | | |
| Cohabiting | −10.48 | −15.83 | 5.2 | 5.8 | 981 | 738 |
| | [15.99] | [21.11] | [15.14] | [30.55] | | |
| Single | −6.01 | 1.09 | 7.27 | −12.82 | 7140 | 5315 |
| | [5.11] | [9.40] | [6.28] | [10.27] | | |

These are estimates of Eqs. 7.2 and 7.3. The sample includes US born women and men age 18–35. Dependent variables are daily minutes spent in household production and leisure. Household production, leisure, plus the excluded categories of paid work, sleep, personal care, and education add up to 1440 min. Survey weights are applied to account evenly for all days of the week. Household production and leisure regressions are estimated using OLS with clustered errors. Variable CLM-P in Panels A and B is an indicator for years before Pennsylvania abolished CLM. Variable CLM in Panels C and D is an indicator for CLM states in regressions with regional dummies instead of state-fixed effects. R-sq is between 0.09 and 0.29. Baseline definitions are active leisure and broad household production. Alternative definitions are broad leisure and narrow household production

## Robustness Check

We estimate both tobit marginal effects and SUR regressions as alternative specifications to OLS. We find that estimates of the coefficients on CLM are very similar, which is consistent with Stewart (2013). Inclusion of respondent's and spouse's estimated wages, and exclusion of New Hampshire, do not modify the magnitude and significance of the coefficients substantially.

## Conclusions

This paper examined whether the availability of Common-Law Marriage (CLM) helps explain variation in the time use—labor supply, time in home production, and leisure—of young men and women in the USA. An analysis of the CPS for respondents under age 36 revealed that for married women labor supply effects of CLM availability are negative. These results mostly apply to White and college-educated married women and to married women with children. Very few CLM effects on men's labor supply are statistically significant, except in one of our models where we find positive effects of CLM on the labor supply of married men. No effects were found for single and cohabiting respondents.

These results are consistent with a conceptual framework based on the concept of Work-In-Marriage (WiHo), marriage market analysis, and the assumption of traditional gender roles. We argue that CLM raises the price of the WiHo of married women who get paid for their WiHo, and therefore their reservation wage, leading to lower labor supply. Our analysis also explains why CLM's effects on married men's labor supply are not as consistent as the effects we found for women and why CLM effects on labor supply are larger for white and college-educated married women than for their counterparts who are black or without college education. Biological factors such as presence of children also help explain our results.

CLM has strong negative effects on the labor supply of married women and in one of our models for educated married men it is associated with more labor supply. Consequently, it follows that the abolition of CLM in three states may have contributed to the convergence in labor supply of men and women.

Our ATUS results indicate small and generally insignificant effects of ATUS on the non-market time use of men and women, suggesting that many married and cohabiting women did spend more time in household production and leisure before the abolition of CLM.

So far social scientists have paid limited attention to CLM. It may be time to integrate these old-fashioned laws in scientific analyses, not only to shed further light on how they affect time use but also in terms of their effects on other outcomes. It would be particularly interesting to see more state- and individual-level data collected on the type of marriage people enter into in CLM states. Comparisons with the effects of similar legal changes in other countries could also be valuable.

# Appendix

## Full Results for Eq. 7.1. Married Women and Men, CPS 1994–2011

| | Women, $N=139{,}608$ | | | | Men, $N=113{,}229$ | | | |
|---|---|---|---|---|---|---|---|---|
| | Probit employed last year | Probit full-time last year | OLS h/week average | OLS h/week usual | Probit employed last year | Probit full-time last year | OLS h/week average | OLS h/week usual |
| | 1 | 2 | 3 | 4 | 1 | 2 | 3 | 4 |
| **CLM** | −0.03*** | −0.04*** | −1.18*** | −1.53*** | −0.01 | 0 | 0.03 | 0.16 |
| Age | 0.04*** | 0.10*** | 3.75*** | 2.64*** | 0.01*** | 0.02*** | 1.34*** | 0.72*** |
| Age-squared | −0.07*** | −0.17*** | −6.00*** | −4.45*** | −0.01*** | −0.02*** | −1.79*** | −0.95*** |
| No high school | −0.12*** | −0.12*** | −5.51*** | −4.69*** | −0.03*** | −0.07*** | −5.03*** | −3.30*** |
| Some college | 0.05*** | 0.03*** | 1.89*** | 1.73*** | 0.01*** | 0 | 1.38*** | 0.73*** |
| College degree | 0.08*** | 0.08*** | 3.59*** | 3.30*** | 0.02*** | 0.02*** | 2.94*** | 1.71*** |
| Graduate degree | 0.12*** | 0.16*** | 6.78*** | 6.93*** | 0.01*** | 0.01*** | 4.67*** | 3.69*** |
| Black | 0.06*** | 0.15*** | 3.80*** | 4.13*** | −0.03*** | −0.04*** | −3.60*** | −3.01*** |
| Hispanic | 0.02*** | 0.07*** | 1.70*** | 1.56*** | 0 | −0.01 | −1.63*** | −1.56*** |
| Metro: central city | −0.03*** | −0.02*** | −0.79*** | −0.91*** | −0.01*** | −0.02*** | −1.13*** | −1.19*** |
| Metro: outside central | −0.01*** | −0.02*** | −0.48*** | −0.67*** | 0 | 0 | 0.25* | −0.13 |
| Student PT | 0.03* | −0.05** | −0.64 | −0.89 | 0 | −0.03*** | −2.46*** | −2.81*** |
| Student FT | −0.14*** | −0.34*** | −9.49*** | −9.69*** | −0.08*** | −0.30*** | −13.69*** | −12.51*** |
| Log unearned income | 0.00*** | 0 | −0.07*** | 0.11*** | −0.00*** | −0.01*** | −0.47*** | −0.18*** |
| Log income of others in hh | −0.01*** | −0.01*** | −0.47*** | −0.46*** | 0 | −0.00** | −0.14*** | −0.11*** |
| Presence of kids <6 | −0.10*** | −0.15*** | −5.86*** | −4.42*** | 0.02*** | 0.03*** | 1.84*** | 1.47*** |

| | Women, $N=139{,}608$ | | | | Men, $N=113{,}229$ | | | |
|---|---|---|---|---|---|---|---|---|
| | Probit employed last year | Probit full-time last year | OLS h/week average | OLS h/week usual | Probit employed last year | Probit full-time last year | OLS h/week average | OLS h/week usual |
| | 1 | 2 | 3 | 4 | 1 | 2 | 3 | 4 |
| Presence of kids <18 | 0 | −0.03*** | −0.69*** | 0.39* | 0.01*** | 0.02*** | 1.21*** | 1.00*** |
| Number of children | −0.06*** | −0.09*** | −3.24*** | −3.24*** | −0.00*** | −0.01*** | −0.38*** | −0.20*** |
| Disabled present | −0.16*** | −0.14*** | −6.75*** | −5.49*** | −0.13*** | −0.18*** | −10.27*** | −8.41*** |
| Sex ratio | −0.08*** | −0.13*** | −4.98*** | −3.57*** | −0.01 | −0.01 | 1 | 0.75 |
| Unemployment rate | −0.00** | −0.01*** | −0.28*** | −0.23*** | −0.00** | −0.00*** | −0.39*** | −0.25*** |
| Welfare | −0.02 | −0.06*** | −0.75 | −1.32* | −0.01* | −0.01 | −0.07 | 0.12 |
| College educated adults | 0.01*** | 0.01*** | 0.23** | 0.42*** | −0.00** | 0 | −0.28*** | −0.23** |
| Urban population share | −0.00*** | −0.01*** | −0.15*** | −0.20*** | 0 | 0 | 0.13** | 0.12** |
| Log median state income | 0.01 | 0.04 | −0.92 | 0.15 | 0.01 | 0.04* | 1.98* | 1.1 |
| *State dummies* | | | yes | | | | yes | |
| *Time dummies* | | | yes | | | | yes | |
| R-squared | | | 0.17 | 0.14 | | | 0.12 | 0.08 |

* significant at 10%; ** significant at 5%; *** significant at 1%

## References

Bertrand, Marianne, Esther Duflo, and Sendhil Mullainathan. 2004. How much should we trust difference-in-difference estimates. *The Quarterly Journal of Economics* 119:249–275

Cherry, Robert. 1998. Rational choice and the price of marriage. *Feminist Economics* 4:27–49.

Chiappori, Pierre-André, Iyigun Murat, Jeanne Lafortune, and Yoram Weiss. 2011. Are intra-household allocations policy neutral? Theory and empirical evidence. IZA DP No. 5594, March.

Genadek, Katie R., Wendy A. Stock, and Christiana Stoddard. 2007. No-fault divorce laws and the labor supply of women with and without children. *Journal of Human Resources* 42 (1): 247–274.

Goldsmith, A., D. Hamilton, and W. Darity Jr. 2007. From dark to light: Skin color and wages among African Americans. *Journal of Human Resources* 42:701–738.

Gray, J. S. 1998. Divorce law changes, household bargaining, and married women's labor supply. *American Economic Review* 88:628–642.

Grossbard, Shoshana, and Catalina Amuedo-Dorantes. 2007. Marriage markets and women's labor force participation. *Review of Economics of the Household* 5:249–278.

Grossbard, S. and Vernon, V. 2015. Common law marriage and couple formation. *IZAJole* Special issue in honor of Gary Becker. (Forthcoming)

Lind, Goran. 2008. *Common Law Marriage: A legal institution for cohabitation.* New York: Oxford University Press.

Moreau, Nicolas, and Abdel R. El Lagua. 2011. The effects of marriage on couples' allocation of time between market and nonmarket hours. In *Household Economic Behaviors,* ed. J. A. Molina. New York: Springer.

Neumark, David, and William Wascher. 2011. Does a higher minimum wage enhance the effectiveness of the earned income tax credit? *Industrial and Labor Relations Review* 64 (4): 712–746.

Peters, Elizabeth H. 1986. Marriage and divorce: Informational constraints and private contracting. *American Economic Review* 76:437–454.

Stafford, Rebecca, Elaine Backman, and Pamela Dibona. 1977. The division of labor among cohabiting and married couples. *Journal of Marriage and the Family* 39 (1): 43–55.

Stevenson, Betsey. 2007. The impact of divorce laws on marriage-specific capital. *Journal of Labor Economics* 25:75–94.

Stewart, Jay. 2013. Tobit or not tobit? *Journal of Economic and Social Measurement* 38 (3): 263–290.

# Chapter 8
# Labor Supply and Marriage Markets: A Simple Graphic Analysis with Household Public Goods

*This chapter is adapted from Grossbard-Shechtman (2005).*

When modeling labor supply economists tend to be committed to the leisure/goods trade-off model based on Robbins (1930). The model that has been learned and taught by many generations of economists is hard to beat: it has elegant calculus, a simple two-dimensional graph, and it takes into consideration the factors influencing labor supply of most interest to labor economists, such as wage, income, and government transfers. However, the leisure/goods trade-off model does not make room for effects of marriage market conditions. The following model is also simple and is associated with a relatively easy graph that shares many common features with the Robbins model. Its main advantage is that it can handle effects of marriage market conditions on time allocation, including labor supply.

The inability of the Robbins model to incorporate marriage market effects is related to its unitary assumptions: it analyzes the labor supply of individuals in couple as if the couple is one unit. It assumes implicitly that all incomes are pooled and explicitly considers the "household" as the decision-maker. The following model is not unitary. Instead it involves time use decisions by an individual who is influenced by marriage market conditions. It builds on Gronau's (1977) model of allocation of time, even though that model is unitary and makes no room for marriage market effects and does not take account of intra-household income distribution. It also builds on Robert Cherry's marriage model (1998), the first to adapt Gronau's (1977) model to integrate intra-marriage transfers.

The macro and micro models presented in Chaps. 2 and 3 involved many individual participants and diverged in many ways from unitary household decision-making models. But precisely given this individualistic nature they need to be complemented with marriage market analysis, which adds to complexity. The marriage market models presented in the previous chapters do not lead to simple graphs capturing individual labor supply decisions and compatible with familiar leisure/goods models. The following models also have an individual, and not a household, deciding on own labor supply. However, a major individualistic assumption found in the previous chapters was removed in a quest for graphic simplicity. Instead of assuming that all consumption is private, as was the case in the models of Chaps. 2



S. Grossbard, *The Marriage Motive: A Price Theory of Marriage*,
DOI 10.1007/978-1-4614-1623-4_8

and 3, the following models assume a couple's joint consumption of goods produced at home. It is also assumed that all work-in-household (WiHo) goes toward the home production of household-public goods and that only one household member is active in household production. The model applies to the individual supplying WiHo.

I first discuss a simple case in which women do not have the option of participating in the labor force. A traditional division of labor is assumed: the only spouse/producer is the wife and the husband and wife consume the goods she produces. This case is particularly applicable to women in the third world. I then discuss a case where the WiHo worker is also employed in the labor force.

The individual's utility function is simple:

$$U(x,\ s), \tag{8.1}$$

where $x$ stands for goods and $s$ for leisure.[1]

The total amount of goods that the individual consumes includes goods that she produces $x_h$ plus commercial goods $x_c$ that she has access to, i.e., $x = x_c + x_h$.[2] Commercial goods are privately consumed by the individual. Home-produced goods $x_h$ are also consumed by the spouse, i.e., they are household public goods.[3] Therefore, any time $h$ that she devotes to household production is of benefit to the spouse. Applying the definition of WiHo (see Chap. 2) all her household production time is WiHo.

The individual's production function is:

$$x_h = f\ (h),\ with\ f' > 0 \text{ and } f'' < 0 \tag{8.2}$$

It is assumed the spouse does not produce at home.

The individual can also participate in commercial labor markets and supply $l$ hours of labor. The time constraint is

$$T = l + s + h, \tag{8.3}$$

where $l$ is labor in the labor force, but $l$ can be equal to zero. The budget constraint is

$$x_c = yh + wl + Y + I, \tag{8.4}$$

where $w$ is wage, $y$ is hourly compensation for WiHo, $Y$ is an income transfer from the spouse that is not tied to household production work, and $I$ is any other form

---

[1] In contrast with the utility function in Chaps. 2 and 3 that also contained two other own uses of time and WiHo time supplied by the spouse.

[2] For simplicity of exposition the individual is a 'she'. The model is also applicable to men.

[3] However, the individual only derives utility from her consuming the goods, so spouse's consumption does not enter her utility function.

of non-work income. It is assumed that the price of all goods is 1, regardless of whether goods are produced at home or bought.

Maximization of utility subject to the constraints leads to first order conditions and to:

$$w = MUs/MUx = y + f' \tag{8.5}$$

The equality on the left is the first order condition in Robbins' (1930) leisure/goods tradeoff model and corresponds to the point where the budget constraint with slope $w$ is tangent to the indifference curve. The equality on the right in 7.5 states that the marginal rate of substitution between leisure and goods (the slope of the indifference curve) equals the sum of $y$, the compensation for WiHo, and the marginal productivity of WiHo ($h$). That sum is the total personal benefit that the individual derives from engaging in an hour of household production: direct benefits $f'$ in terms of the goods that she produces and also consumes and indirect benefits (she can purchase commercial goods with her WiHo wage $y$).[4]

## Graphic Representation

### *Simple Case: Leisure and WiHo. No Labor Force Participation*

It is assumed that the WiHo worker (let us say the wife) solely chooses between leisure and WiHo ($l$=0). The only form of income available to women is the share of their income that husbands potentially agree to share with them. In turn, this share is a function of the price of WiHo, $y$, which is assumed to be given. It is assumed that the husband enjoys the same goods that the wife produces (i.e., there is joint consumption and the goods that she produces are household public goods) and therefore he is willing to pay her to produce these goods. Husbands can also transfer income to their wife irrespectively of hours of household production work. From the woman's point of view this is a form of non-work income and will be called $Y$.

The budget constraint collapses to $x_c = yh + Y$, where $y$ is the price of WiHo and $Y$ is an income transfer from the husband that is not tied to household production work WiHo. It is assumed that the price of goods is 1 and that other transfers $I$=0.

[4] The equality on the right is similar to the second equality found in Gronau (1977) except that in Gronau's model a married woman does not get paid by her spouse for what she produces in the household. Figure 8.1 looks similar to the leisure/goods trade-off graph in Gronau (1977), except that in Gronau the transformation curve has slope $f'$, and here it has slope $y/p+f'$ (if $p$ differs from 1).

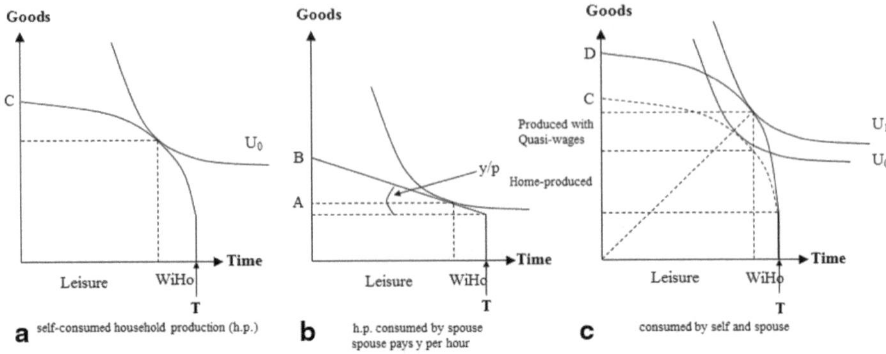


**Fig. 8.1** Allocation of time to leisure and Work-In-Household (WiHo), **a** self-consumed household production (h.p.), **b** h.p. consumed by spouse pays y per hour, **c** consumed by self and spouse

Figure 8.1 represents the leisure/goods trade-off of this woman. There are three panels in Fig. 8.1: (a) own consumption of household-produced goods, the equivalent of a corner solution in Gronau (1977); (b) consumption of commercial goods as a result of spouse's consumption of the same household-produced goods and a consequent payment by the spouse; and (c) combined consumption of household-produced goods and commercial goods resulting from a given amount of hours of household production. This combination is obtained by vertical addition of the budget and transformation lines of Panels A and B.

A household producer is clearly better off when her household production is also appreciated by her spouse, which implies that there is WiHo. Whether more appreciation takes the form of a higher *y*, the compensation for WiHo, or a higher income transfer *Y*, it will increase individual opportunities for consuming goods and leisure. In both cases, there will be an income effect. However, in case the appreciation takes the form of a compensation for time in household production, there will also be a substitution effect between the two kinds of goods. The difference between the effect of a non-work-related transfer *Y* and that of a household production work-related transfer *yh* is similar to the difference between a pure income effect and a wage effect in standard labor supply analysis. It is expected that if appreciation is conditional on household production work performance, people will have more incentives to engage in in-marriage household production (see Grossbard-Shechtman and Lemennicier 1999) than if appreciation takes the form of an income transfer not conditional on work effort.

The analysis implies that allocation of time to household production (WiHo) and leisure is a function of marriage market conditions. Both a non-work-related transfer *Y* and a household production work-related transfer *yh* will affect allocation of time. Next, the model is expanded to include labor supply.

## *Choice Between Leisure, WiHo, and Labor Supply*

In this model, an actual or potential household production worker, let us say a woman, is still maximizing a utility function $U(x)$, where $x$ is defined as above, and she has the same production function for $x_h$, but now she maximizes her utility subject to time constraint $T=l+s+h$, where $l$ is labor and $h$ is WiHo, and budget constraint, $x_c=yh+wl+Y$, where $w$ is wage and $y$ is the price of WiHo. It is assumed that the price of commercial goods is 1 ($p=1$).

Now both sides of Eq. 8.5 are relevant. The equality on the left is the first order condition in Robbins' leisure/goods tradeoff and corresponds to the point where the budget constraint with slope $w$ is tangent to the indifference curve. This is a well-known result obtained by Robbins (1930) and integrated by Gronau (1977). In addition, the equality on the right of this first order condition states that the marginal rate of substitution between leisure and goods also has to equal the sum of $y$, the hourly compensation for WiHo, and the marginal productivity of WiHo ($h$) from the perspective of the household production worker. That sum is the total personal benefit that the WiHo worker derives from engaging in an hour of WiHo: she enjoys that hour of household production *directly* at a level $f'$ in terms of the home-produced goods that she produces and consumes, and *indirectly* in the form of the commercial goods that she enjoys and buys with her earnings from WiHo, at an hourly rate $y$. The person will work in household production if $y+f'>w$. The person will work in the labor force if $y+f'<w$.

This is similar to what Gronau (1977) obtains, except that in Gronau and most other models of household allocation of time (such as the Gregg-Lewis model discussed in Chap. 4) a married woman does not get paid by her spouse according to what she produces in the household.[5] Accordingly, in Gronau (1977) the transformation curve has a slope $f'$, whereas here it has slope $y+f'$ (assuming $p$ is 1).

Figure 8.2 presents this graphically. It shows an expanded opportunity set that includes the set available to individuals in traditional analyses of the leisure/goods tradeoff. In addition, it includes opportunities derived when producing jointly-consumed goods at home. Three components of the possibility curve have been stacked up vertically: the bottom component is a rectangle showing the goods the individual can purchase with non-work income $Y+I$. If this were to be the only consumption, all time would be devoted to leisure $s$. The second component shows how many goods the individual can consume as a result of producing at home. On the vertical axis, after all non-work income has been spent; we first see the private commercial goods bought with the individual's earnings $yh$ from supplying WiHo to the spouse. In addition, working in WiHo leads to home-produced goods $x_h$ also consumed by the individual. The third component, at the top, shows how many commercial goods can be purchased with wages earned in the labor force and is identical to the familiar leisure/goods analysis. Equilibrium is obtained where the indifference curve is tangent to a segment of the opportunity set and can include corner solutions either at

[5] Likewise, Cherry (1998) does not consider the possibility that intra-marriage transfers are a function of the hours that a spouse spends in household production.

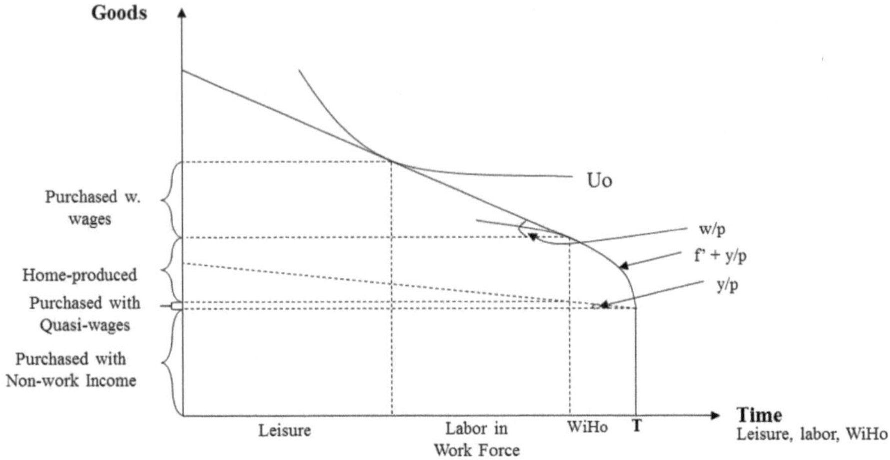


**Fig. 8.2** Allocation of time by spouse/producer when y/p, the price of WiHo is given

the transition between no work and some home production (WiHo) or the transition between home production (WiHo) and work in the labor force.

Figure 8.2 presents a situation where $w>y+f'$ and the individual works in the labor force, as well as in WiHo. If, instead, an indifference curve were tangent to the $y+f'$ segment in the opportunity set the individual would not work in the labor force.

## *Marriage Market Effects*

A household producer (called here a WiHo worker) is better off, when the more his household production $x_h$ is appreciated by the spouse. Whether higher appreciation takes the form of a higher $y$, the hourly compensation for WiHo, or of a higher income transfer $Y$, it will increase individual opportunities for personal consumption of goods and leisure. In the case of income transfers $Y$ higher payments by the spouse only entail an income effect. It is what we call a pure income effect in labor supply analysis. In contrast, a higher price for WiHo ($y$) entails both an income effect and a substitution effect between the two kinds of goods that the individual consumes.

An increase in the WiHo worker's value in marriage markets taking the form of a higher compensation $y$ per hour of WiHo will cause an outward shift in the transformation curve $f'+y/p$ in Figs. 8.1 or 8.2. As a result, the point at which the wage line $w/p$ is tangent to the transformation curve will correspond to a higher amount of hours in home production (h.p). Therefore, *ceteris paribus*, the higher the price of WiHo $y$, the more the individual will spend time in WiHo. A higher price for WiHo thus gives people an incentive to engage in more WiHo and less work in the labor force. Along the same logic, a switch from intra-household transfers unrelated to

WiHo to a system of compensation rewarding time spent on WiHo via higher price of WiHo $y$ will encourage WiHo and household production.

Any factor $X$ that is expected to be associated with a higher price $y$ is expected to lead to more home production WiHo as long as the income effect is smaller than the substitution effect. A factor that is associated with a higher transfer $Y$ is not as likely to lead to more WiHo, due an expected income effect in the direction of more leisure and less work of any kind.

Chapters 3 and 5 mentioned some individual characteristics that may be associated with a higher price of WiHo, including age, education, and ethnicity. Characteristics of partners may also affect the price of WiHo that is used in an exchange of time for money in a particular couple, as discussed in the section on compensating differentials in Chap. 5. As discussed in Chaps. 4 and 6, an important factor that can influence the price of WiHo is the sex ratio in a heterosexual marriage market.

## References

Cherry, Robert. 1998. Rational choice and the price of marriage. *Feminist Economics* 4:27–49.

Gronau, Reuben. 1977. Leisure, home production, and work—The theory of the allocation of time revisited. *Journal of Political Economy* 85:1099–1124.

Grossbard-Shechtman, Shoshana. 2005. A model of labour supply, household production, and marriage. In *Advances in household economics, consumer behaviour and economic policy,* ed. T. Van Hoa. London: Ashgate.

Grossbard-Shechtman, S. A., and B. Lemennicier. 1999. Marriage contracts and the law-and-economics of marriage: An Austrian perspective. *Journal of Socio-Economics* 28:665–690.

Robbins, Lionel. 1930. On the elasticity of demand for income in terms of efforts. *Economica* 10:123–129

# Chapter 9
# Household Production and Racial Intermarriage

*This chapter is adapted from "Racial Intermarriage and Household Production," forthcoming, Review of Behavioral Economics.*

## Introduction

Racial issues have been a prominent topic of research in economics (e.g., Becker 1957; Arrow 1998) and demography (e.g., Semyonov et al. 1984; Wright et al. 2013). In the USA, being black has been associated with a wide range of disadvantages (Burke 2008): Blacks earn less than whites (Bergmann 1971; Smith and Welch 1989; Altonji and Blank 1999; Darity et al. 2001; Goldsmith et al. 2007; Charles and Guryan 2008), and have relatively lower marriage and couple formation rates (Spanier and Glick 1980; Hamilton et al. 2009). According to a recent analysis of Internet dating in the USA, relative to white men, African American men received only about half as many first-contact e-mails from white women (Hitsch et al. 2010).

Many states in the USA openly discriminated against blacks in marriage markets by instituting antimiscegenation laws that led to historically low racial intermarriage rates (Fryer 2007; Chiswick and Houseworth 2011). Increases in black/white intermarriage rates since the 1960s may have resulted from a reduction in such discrimination and the Supreme Court's 1967 decision ruling against antimiscegenation laws.

Furthermore, Spanier and Glick (1980) and Hamilton et al. (2009) have documented that in the USA, black men who marry white women have higher education, income, and occupational status than *endogamous* (marrying within their own group) black men, possibly indicating that black men have to "pay" their way into marriage with white women. Similar differentials were found for immigrants marrying natives in Australia (Meng and Gregory 2005), France (Meng and Meurs 2009), and Germany (Nottmeyer 2011). In all these cases, women seem to prefer men from their own group and expect some "compensation" when marrying minority men.

In this chapter, we test whether in US marriage markets blacks are also disadvantaged in terms of obtaining less chore time from their spouses or spending more



S. Grossbard, *The Marriage Motive: A Price Theory of Marriage*,
DOI 10.1007/978-1-4614-1623-4_9

time on chores when in couple with whites than when endogamous. The conceptual framework is based on the microversion of the market for WiHo model presented in Chap. 3.

The same conceptual framework also leads to the prediction that ethnic intermarriage is linked to participation in the labor force, which was tested in Grossbard-Shechtman and Neuman (1988) and Grossbard-Shechtman and Fu (2002). An advantage of turning to chores as a testing ground for theories linking marriage market analysis with allocation of time is that by definition chores are less desirable than leisure. It is possible that low WiHo price will lead WiHo workers to higher involvement in chore work within the household than to higher labor force participation. In this chapter, we examine whether US whites spend less time on chores when in couple with blacks than when endogamous, and whether blacks spend more time on chores when in couple with whites than when endogamous.

Our empirical analysis builds on a growing literature on allocation of time that includes Gershuny and Robinson (1988), John and Shelton (1997), Bianchi (2000), Sandberg and Hofferth (2001), Hamermesh (2002), Bittman et al. (2003), Kalenkoski et al. (2005, 2007), Aguiar and Hurst (2007), Connelly and Kimmel (2007, 2009), Burda et al. (2008), Sayer and Fine (2011), Sevilla-Sanz et al. (2012), and Bloemen and Stancanelli (2014). While previous US time-use studies have controlled for race or investigated racial differences, our study is the first to focus on how individual allocation of time to household production varies with racial intermarriage. To the best of our knowledge, the link between home production time and intermarriage has not been analyzed in other countries either.

Using the American Time Use Survey (ATUS) 2003–2009, we focus on the association between a spouse's race and the time that respondents allocate to chores. Some of our models take account of selection into intermarriage to address the possible endogeneity of the decision to perform chores and the choice of a spouse of a different race. According to our preferred model, relative to their endogamous counterparts white women in couple with black partners devote 0.38 fewer h/day to chores and 0.64 fewer h/day to housework (chores + basic childcare). The absolute size of these coefficients is similar to the effect of a young child on married women's time devoted to chores. Racial intermarriage differentials in white women's hours of household work are robust to various definitions of black and seem to be more prevalent among the US born than the foreign born. White men also spend less time in housework if intermarried with black women than if endogamous, but estimated effects are smaller than for women and often insignificant statistically. These differentials are viewed as compensating differentials in marriage in the following sense: To agree to marry a black man, a white woman needs to receive more of a compensation than she would get from a white man. The compensating differential in marriage takes the form of extra hours of leisure available to the intermarried white woman.

Even though results for blacks are less robust than for whites due to smaller sample size, they are also consistent with whites' preferred group status in marriage markets: When in couple with whites black women seem to devote more time to chores and housework than when endogamous. Results for black men seem to go in the same direction, but are less conclusive than those for black women.

Taken together, our findings suggest that blacks pay a price for being in couple with whites rather than being endogamous: They are likely to obtain fewer minutes of chores from their white partners and perform more minutes of work themselves. Conversely, relative to their endogamous counterparts, whites in couple with blacks benefit in the form of less own work in chores. They may also obtain more chore work from their black partners.

## Conceptual Framework

Consider a market for WiHo with a particular type of man $M_i$ and a particular type of woman $F_j$ when there are many types of mates available in other markets (see Chap. 3). Assuming supply of traditional gender roles is by women and demand by men, consider a vector of male characteristics $X_i$ that can possibly shift the demand by men $M_i$ and a vector of female characteristics $Z_j$ that can possibly shift the supply by women of type $F_j$ in a particular $F_jM_i$ market. These characteristics will affect the equilibrium prices for women's WiHo:

$$y_{ij}^{0} = f(X_i, Z_j), \tag{9.1}$$

where $y_{ij}^{0}$ is the price that traditional women $F_j$ of type *j* may receive for their WiHo when married to men $M_i$ of type *i* if equilibrium has been established in an $F_jM_i$ market. Applying this framework to markets for WiHo stratified by race, we focus on four markets: Endogamous markets for whites, endogamous markets for blacks, markets for marriages between black men and white women, and markets for marriages between white men and black women. We assume that both blacks and whites prefer endogamy and that preferences for endogamy are stronger among whites than among blacks (possibly due to whites' discrimination against blacks that is not or partially reciprocated by blacks' discrimination against whites).

For example, consider marriage markets in which white women $F_W$ are the WiHo suppliers, and where both *X* and *Z* are dummies for "white." Women $F_W$ are choosing between marrying black men $M_B$ and white men $M_W$. To the extent that some white women prefer to marry white (rather than black) men it follows that white women's market supply to black men in this interracial marriage market will be smaller than their aggregate supply to white men in the market for endogamous marriages.

If all other factors are controlled for and the demand in both markets is the same, comparative static analysis leads to $y_{BW} > y_{WW}$ in equilibrium, implying that white women will obtain a higher price for their WiHo if they are in couple with black men than if they are endogamous. That the demand is the same implies that white men and black men have the same willingness to marry white women. This assumption can be relaxed. $y_{BW} > y_{WW}$ is expected to hold as long as black men's demand for marriage to white women's WiHo does not lie below white men's demand for marriage to white women by an amount equal or higher than the difference between white women's supply to black men and their supply to white men.

To the extent that all participants in a market are influenced by market equilibrium conditions, this inequality holds even for individual women who do not discriminate and do not intend to divorce and threaten their husbands with their relatively high marriage market power.

We cannot measure WiHo prices $y_{ij}$ but we know that most individuals prefer leisure (e.g., relaxing, socializing after work, doing exercise, out-of-home leisure, listening to music) to work, where work includes much home production. Therefore, WiHo workers are likely to translate a higher price for their WiHo into a lighter workload in home production and more leisure(see Grossbard-Shechtman 1984; Lafortune et al. 2012).[1] It is assumed that there are no racial differences in how WiHo price translates into hours of chores: A given differential in WiHo price $y_{BW} - y_{WW}$ translates into a corresponding intermarriage differential in amount of time spent on chores.[2] We therefore expect white women in interracial marriages to perform fewer chores compared to their counterparts in endogamous marriages.

Unobserved intrahousehold payments for WiHo are also a function of income, number of children, and other relevant variables. The better we control for these variables, the more we are likely to find that

*Prediction TU23 White women married to black men will supply fewer hours of chores than endogamous white women.*

Furthermore, if white men prefer to marry white women (and such preference for endogamy is incompletely reciprocated by black women), this amounts to a relatively small demand for black women in interracial marriages relative to the demand for black women by black men. A comparison of markets for endogamous black women and black women married to white men thus implies $y_{BB} > y_{WB}$ and that

*Prediction TU24 Black women in couple with white men will spend more time on chores than comparable endogamous black women.*

Men may also obtain intrahousehold transfers that depend on their intermarriage status. Men's surplus from marriage is inversely related to the $y_{ij}$ they have to pay for their wife's WiHo. The same asymmetric preferences for interracial marriage

[1] Leisure may be more enjoyable than home production to the extent that the former activities provide a higher "experienced utility" to the individuals (Kahneman et al. 2004; Kahneman and Krueger 2006).

[2] This assumption could be relaxed. Our predictions are reinforced to the extent that white women married to black men also have higher ability to translate a given share of gain from marriage into less time in chores. The intermarriage differential in time spent on chores will then be larger than the differential $y_{BW} - y_{WW}$. If the opposite is the case and white women married to black men are less able to translate a given price of WiHo into less time in chores this will weaken the prediction. It will only invalidate the prediction if white women are considerably less able to bargain about chores if married to blacks than if married to whites and the racial intermarriage differential in ability to translate an intermarriage differential in share from gain in marriage into less time in chores is large relative to $y_{BW} - y_{WW}$.

discussed above imply that white men in couple with black women will receive a higher surplus from marriage than their endogamous counterparts, i.e., $y'_{WW} < y'_{WB}$. This implies that

*Prediction TU25 White men intermarried with black women will work less at chores than endogamous white men.*

As for black men, the existence of white own-kind preferences exceeding those of blacks leads us to predict $y'_{BB} > y'_{BW}$ and that

*Prediction TU26 Black men married to white women will work more at chores than endogamous black men.*

All four predictions are more likely to be supported by empirical evidence when household production activities are more likely to be considered as chores. This is more likely:

a. On weekdays than on weekends. On weekends, when both members of a couple are more likely to synchronize household production, performing the same household production activity may be more enjoyable than it is during the week. Also, the type of activities left for the weekend may be more enjoyable than the activities performed on weekdays (Hamermesh 2002; Jenkins and Osberg 2005; Connelly and Kimmel 2009).
b. For married than unwed. Relative to unwed couples, married couples are more likely to establish implicit contracts involving the exchange of WiHo for a payment based on the price of WiHo. Therefore, factors associated with value of WiHo, such as interracial marriage, are more likely to be associated with time spent on chores for married than for unwed couples.
c. When respondents are not employed in the labor force or they have limited working hours. More chore-type activities are likely to be reported by respondents who are not employed or work few hours in the labor force than by fully employed men and women. The more respondents engage in chores or housework, the more we are likely to observe an effect of intermarriage on household production time.
d. When spouses are fully employed than when spouses are not fully employed. Respondents with fully employed spouses are more likely to engage in household production: It is more likely that they have implicit contracts (possibly related to marriage contracts) regarding division of labor, with respondents doing more chores and spouses bringing in more earned income.

The degree to which we expect to observe interracial marriage differentials will vary with skin color, given that Hamilton et al. (2009) found evidence that black women with lighter skin tone who marry have spouses with more desirable characteristics. We do not have information on skin tone, but we know whether respondents defined themselves or their spouses as black only or as one of the following categories found in the Census: "white–black," "white–black–American Indian," "white–black–Asian," and "white–black–American Indian–Asian." We call these various combinations "mixedblack." To the extent that discrimination levels are a function of skin color and if mixedblacks have a lighter skin shade than blacks we predict that the negative coefficient for white wives will be larger if the husband is "black" than if he is "mixedblack."

Furthermore, interracial marriage differentials may also depend on the intensity of racial discrimination in the state of residence. The more racist the white majority in the state the larger the expected compensating differential obtained by a white woman in couple with a black man and the more likely it is that white women in couple with black men work less in chores than endogamous white women. Inspired by Fryer (2007), we use the following dummy to capture the prevalence of white discrimination against blacks in state marriage markets: Is this a state where anti-miscegenation laws were abolished by the 1967 US Supreme Court decision "Loving v. Virginia" (388 US 1)? In a state that never had such law, or abolished it in a state-level political process, racism is presumably less prevalent than where a state waited for the federal-level Supreme Court to overturn its antimiscegenation laws. The prediction is that the negative effect of black husband on hours a white woman spends on chores will be larger (in absolute terms) if she resides in a state that was forced to abolish antimiscegenation laws.

We also investigate whether interracial marriage differentials in time use vary with where respondents and their spouses were born. If there is more black/white racism in the USA than in most countries from which immigrants have arrived the decrease in wife's hours of chores work will be larger if husband is black and she is born in the USA than if husband is black and she is born elsewhere. Alternatively, we examine whether interracial marriage differentials in home production time vary with whether blacks are born in Africa or elsewhere. African blacks may have a different culture or may be treated differently in US marriage markets.

## Data and Methods

*Data and Definitions* We use the ATUS, the first federally administered, continuous survey on time use in the USA for the years 2003–2009 (see Hamermesh et al. 2005). Respondents are randomly selected from a subset of households that have completed their eighth and final month of interviews for the Current Population Survey (CPS). They are interviewed (only once) about how they spent their time on the previous day. We restrict our analyses to non-retired/non-student married or cohabiting respondents between the ages of 21 and 65, who have time diaries that add up to a complete day (1440 min).

We define *chores* in two ways. Following Burda et al. (2008), we define chores as activities that satisfy Margaret Reid's (1934) third-party rule: They can possibly be substituted for market goods and services. In addition, we use a more restrictive definition that only includes activities for which women have negative income elasticities. These are activities that women would rather avoid doing if they can afford to. More precisely, for this more restricted definition we require that elasticities with respect to own years of schooling (a proxy for permanent income) and own actual earnings be below $-0.01$.[3] The following activities fit this more restricted criterion and are called "chores": Interior cleaning, laundry, grocery shopping, kitchen and food clean-up, travel related to housework, travel to/from the grocery store, and food and drink preparation (see Table 9.9 in Appendix for a description of the categories). They correspond to what has been referred to as "female tasks," e.g., by Cohen (1998), Hersch and Stratton (2002), and Sevilla-Sanz et al. (2010).[4] We also perform robustness of our "chores" regressions, including basic childcare in addition to chores.

Given that the time devoted to household production by men in the USA has been shown to be limited relative to that of women (Aguiar and Hurst 2007; Hersch 2009), we use a broader and widely used definition of chores for men: Total time devoted to household production activities excluding childcare. We exclude childcare as a number of studies have found that parents report spending time with their children as being among their more enjoyable activities (Juster and Stafford 1985; Robinson and Godbey 1997; Kahneman et al. 2004; Kahneman and Krueger 2006). We include the following activities in our definition of *total housework:* Meal preparation and cleanup, laundry, ironing, dusting, vacuuming, indoor household cleaning, indoor design and maintenance (including painting and decorating), time spent obtaining goods and services (i.e., grocery shopping, shopping for other household items, comparison shopping), and time spent on other home productions such as home maintenance, outdoor cleaning, and vehicle repair. We also use *Total Housework* in robustness checks for our estimations for women.

We estimated models with alternative specifications of black: (1) "black" including the Census categories "black" and "white–black"; (2) both "black only" and "mixedblack", where mixedblack includes the Census categories "white–black," "white–black–American Indian," "white–black–Asian," and "white–black–American Indian–Asian"; (3) "allblack" defined as "black only" + "mixedblack." White is always defined as "white only."

Table 9.1 shows means and standard deviations for some of the variables used in the analysis for both men and women. It can be seen from columns 1 and 4 that men devote much less time than women to both *chores* and *total housework*: 2.1 and 3.4 daily hours to *Chores* and *Total Housework* in the case of women, versus 0.6 and 1.8 h in the case of men. Black here is defined as "black only" and "white–black." Given that our data includes a much larger number of white respondents than black respondents (17,531 white women and 15,627 white men versus 1305 black women and 1270 black men) we first analyze whites.

Columns 2 and 3 describe the data for white and black women, column 5 for white men, and column 6 for black men. It can be seen that on average white women spend slightly more time on chores than black women (2.1 versus 1.9 h/day). Slightly less

[3] Hamermesh (2007) finds a negative relationship between income and time allocated to household production.

[4] Hersch and Stratton (2002) and Sevilla-Sanz et al. (2010) show that women concentrate on routine and more time-intensive housework, such as cooking and cleaning, whereas men are more active in sporadic, less time-intensive tasks, such as gardening and repairs.

**Table 9.1** Summary statistics. (Source: ATUS 2003–2009)

| | (1) | | (2) | | (3) | | (4) | | (5) | | (6) | |
|---|---|---|---|---|---|---|---|---|---|---|---|---|
| | **All women** | | **White women** | | **Black women** | | **All men** | | **White men** | | **Black men** | |
| | **Mean** | **SE** | **Mean** | **SE** | **Mean** | **SE** | **Mean** | **SE** | **Mean** | **SE** | **Mean** | **SE** |
| Chores, all days | 2.10 | (2.12) | 2.13 | (2.12) | 1.86 | (2.12) | 0.62 | (1.14) | 0.61 | (1.12) | 0.72 | (1.37) |
| Chores, weekdays | 1.99 | (2.05) | 2.01 | (2.04) | 1.73 | (2.08) | 0.50 | (0.99) | 0.49 | (0.95) | 0.68 | (1.33) |
| Chores, weekend | 2.40 | (2.27) | 2.42 | (2.27) | 2.20 | (2.18) | 0.91 | (1.43) | 0.92 | (1.43) | 0.83 | (1.48) |
| Chores, if married | 2.13 | (2.13) | 2.15 | (2.12) | 1.87 | (2.16) | 0.61 | (1.14) | 0.60 | (1.12) | 0.71 | (1.38) |
| Chores, if unwed | 1.81 | (2.00) | 1.82 | (2.03) | 1.75 | (1.78) | 0.66 | (1.14) | 0.64 | (1.09) | 0.77 | (1.37) |
| Chores, if LLFP | 2.93 | (2.34) | 2.96 | (2.33) | 2.59 | (2.49) | 0.96 | (1.52) | 0.96 | (1.52) | 0.97 | (1.54) |
| Chores, if non-LLFP | 1.79 | (1.94) | 1.81 | (1.94) | 1.60 | (1.90) | 0.58 | (1.10) | 0.58 | (1.07) | 0.67 | (1.33) |
| Total housework | 3.41 | (2.78) | 3.46 | (2.78) | 2.82 | (2.66) | 1.82 | (2.35) | 1.84 | (2.36) | 1.71 | (2.22) |
| Age, respondent | 41.35 | (10.42) | 41.35 | (10.45) | 41.38 | (10.06) | 43.27 | (10.59) | 43.26 | (10.62) | 43.35 | (10.27) |
| Age difference | 2.35 | (4.78) | 2.32 | (4.73) | 2.65 | (5.32) | 0.19 | (0.40) | 0.19 | (0.39) | 0.24 | (0.43) |
| Respondent LLFP | 0.27 | (0.45) | 0.27 | (0.45) | 0.27 | (0.44) | 0.09 | (0.28) | 0.08 | (0.27) | 0.17 | (0.38) |
| Partner, employed | 0.88 | (0.32) | 0.89 | (0.31) | 0.78 | (0.41) | 0.71 | (0.45) | 0.71 | (0.46) | 0.73 | (0.45) |
| Respondent's education | 13.90 | (2.90) | 13.91 | (2.94) | 13.79 | (2.47) | 13.76 | (3.02) | 13.78 | (3.06) | 13.46 | (2.50) |
| Educational difference | −0.08 | (2.56) | −0.05 | (2.57) | −0.35 | (2.41) | −0.14 | (2.57) | −0.12 | (2.58) | −0.34 | (2.46) |

**Table 9.1** (continued)

| | (1) | | (2) | | (3) | | (4) | | (5) | | (6) | |
|---|---|---|---|---|---|---|---|---|---|---|---|---|
| | **All women** | | **White women** | | **Black women** | | **All men** | | **White men** | | **Black men** | |
| | **Mean** | **SE** | **Mean** | **SE** | **Mean** | **SE** | **Mean** | **SE** | **Mean** | **SE** | **Mean** | **SE** |
| Respondent (disabled) | 0.03 | (0.18) | 0.03 | (0.17) | 0.07 | (0.25) | 0.03 | (0.18) | 0.03 | (0.17) | 0.07 | (0.25) |
| Respondent (foreign) | 0.13 | (0.34) | 0.13 | (0.34) | 0.14 | (0.34) | 0.14 | (0.35) | 0.14 | (0.35) | 0.13 | (0.34) |
| Partner (foreign) | 0.14 | (0.34) | 0.14 | (0.34) | 0.14 | (0.35) | 0.14 | (0.35) | 0.14 | (0.35) | 0.14 | (0.34) |
| Nb of children <5 | 0.33 | (0.63) | 0.32 | (0.63) | 0.36 | (0.69) | 0.32 | (0.63) | 0.32 | (0.63) | 0.33 | (0.62) |
| Nb of children 5–11 | 0.45 | (0.76) | 0.45 | (0.76) | 0.48 | (0.81) | 0.46 | (0.77) | 0.45 | (0.77) | 0.54 | (0.84) |
| Nb of children 12–17 | 0.36 | (0.67) | 0.35 | (0.67) | 0.39 | (0.67) | 0.37 | (0.69) | 0.36 | (0.68) | 0.46 | (0.79) |
| Hh nonlabor income | 58.32 | (43.16) | 59.50 | (43.42) | 44.15 | (37.09) | 49.69 | (42.00) | 50.39 | (42.33) | 42.27 | (37.55) |
| Urban (versus rural) residence | 0.80 | (0.40) | 0.80 | (0.40) | 0.86 | (0.34) | 0.80 | (0.40) | 0.80 | (0.40) | 0.86 | (0.34) |
| Northeast | 0.18 | (0.38) | 0.18 | (0.39) | 0.14 | (0.34) | 0.19 | (0.39) | 0.19 | (0.39) | 0.15 | (0.36) |
| Midwest | 0.26 | (0.44) | 0.27 | (0.45) | 0.17 | (0.37) | 0.26 | (0.44) | 0.27 | (0.44) | 0.19 | (0.39) |
| South | 0.35 | (0.48) | 0.33 | (0.47) | 0.62 | (0.49) | 0.35 | (0.48) | 0.33 | (0.47) | 0.57 | (0.50) |
| *N* interracial couples | 213 | | 160 | | 53 | | 197 | | 50 | | 147 | |
| % interracial couples | 0.011 | | 0.009 | | 0.041 | | 0.012 | | 0.003 | | 0.116 | |
| *N* observations | 18,836 | | 17,531 | | 1305 | | 16,897 | | 15,627 | | 1270 | |

See Table 9.10 for a description of all the variables

than 1% of white women have a black husband or partner, while the percentage of intermarriage (including unmarried cohabitation) is much larger for black women (4%). White and black men in our sample devote 1.84 and 1.71 h/day, respectively, to *total housework*. The percentage intermarried is about 40 times higher for black men than for white men: 12% versus 3 per 1000. Black men are more than twice as likely to be intermarried than black women, which is consistent with other studies (Kalmijn 1993, 1998; Blackwell and Lichter 2000; Crowder and Tolnay 2000).

*Empirical Strategy* We begin with regressions of *chores* performed by women. We first run Ordinary Least Squares (OLS) regressions of time in chores as a function of intermarriage and of a number of characteristics of respondents and their spouses, as well as characteristics of the household. Black is defined as "black only" and "white–black." Since, we observe a high proportion of "zeros" in the time devoted to chores by women and housework by men, it may be preferable to use alternative models, such as those of Tobin (1958) or Poisson, or a Negative Binomial model. According to Frazis and Stewart (2012), OLS models are preferred in the analysis of time allocation decisions, since estimation techniques for limited dependent variables that assume a nonlinear functional form, such as the Tobit model, will be inconsistent if we want to estimate means of long-run time use from a sample of daily observations. Gershuny (2012) argues that estimations derived from single-day diaries have the problem of too many zeros, but traditional diary studies can still produce accurate estimates of mean times in activities for samples and subgroups. Under this framework, Foster and Kalenkoski (2013) compare the use of Tobit and OLS models in the analysis of time devoted to childcare activities, and find that the qualitative conclusions are similar for the two estimation methods. We have also estimated Tobit, Poisson, and Negative Binomial models and also obtain very similar results (available upon request) and solely report OLS results here. We estimate the following equation:

$$\mathrm{Chores}_{ijt} = \alpha_3 + \mathrm{Intermarried}_{ijt}\delta_1 + \mathrm{X}_{ijt}\delta_2 + \mathrm{Day}_{ijt}\delta_3 + \mathrm{Year}_{ij}\delta_4 + \varepsilon_{ijt}, \qquad (9.2)$$

where Chores is the time devoted to chores by woman *i* in state *j*, and year *t*, measured in hours per day, and *Intermarried* is a dummy variable indicating whether a respondent *i* in state *j*, and year *t* is "married" to a partner who is black, in the case of white respondents, or white in the case of black respondents. We expect to find $\delta_1 < 0$ in the case of white respondents, and $\delta_1 > 0$ in the case of black respondents. Initially it is assumed that whether a person is "intermarried" or not is given exogenously.

Vector *X* includes a number of demographic and economic characteristics of wives and husbands, as well as household characteristics (see Appendix Table 9.10 for a summary of all variable definitions). It includes age of the respondent (and its square), age difference, spouse's age squared, the interaction between respondent's age and age difference, wife's education, educational difference, wife foreign-born, and husband foreign-born. In addition, it includes a dummy variable for respondent's disability, and a dummy variable to control for participation of the spouse in the labor market.

Vector *X* in Eq. 9.2 also includes household nonlabor income defined as the total family income of all family members during the last 12 months, minus husband's and wife's annual earnings. This includes business income, rental income, pensions, dividends, interest, social security payments, and any other nonlabor income received by family members who are 15 or older. Total family income ranges from less than $ 5000 to $ 150,000, where each value of the variable represents the midpoint of the income interval. Nonlabor income is set at zero when annual earnings exceed total family income. A negative relationship between income and time allocated to home production has previously been reported (Robinson and Godbey 1997; Hamermesh 2007; Aguiar and Hurst 2007), possibly the result of outsourcing of home production. Restricting chores to activities with negative income and education elasticities is expected to limit income effects.

The age difference and educational difference between spouses are included as they may affect individual relative bargaining power within a marriage. Square of age is expected to capture particularly large age differences between spouses, which may be associated with compensating differentials taking the form of lower work load in the household (fewer chores) or extra monetary transfers from husbands to wives and therefore lower labor force participation by married women (see Grossbard-Shechtman and Neuman 1988).

Education may be positively related to a person's human capital that enhances productivity in household production and more educated people may be in higher demand in markets for spouses. For both of these reasons more educated people may perform fewer chores. The more educated the spouse relative to the respondent, the less it is likely that the spouse performs chores and the more the spouse may have a demand for the respondent's chores (Grossbard-Shechtman 1993); so, to the extent that husband's chores and wife's chores are substitutes it is expected that the higher the spouse's relative education, the more the respondent performs chores. This result may be facilitated through mate selection or through bargaining within the household after a couple is formed. However, to the extent that partners like to perform chores together, and their time in chores is complementary, higher relative education of the spouse may be associated with fewer chores by the respondent.

Household characteristics also include number of children in the household aged 0–4, 5–12, and 13–17. We expect a positive correlation between number of children and time devoted to chores, with this correlation being higher for younger children. In addition, vector *X* includes urban residence and region (the reference being West).

We also include day of the week dummies, to control for changes in time allocation decisions depending on the day of the week (reference day is Friday), and year dummies (reference is 2009) to control for changes in survey methodology or the possible impact of the economic crisis of 2008.

The preferred models that we report do not include own and spouse's wage, even though Becker's (1965) prediction that the opportunity cost of time as measured by the wage, influences time devoted to household production has often been tested and a large empirical literature on time use has examined the impact of wages on time allocation (including Hamermesh 1990; Kalenkoski et al. 2005, 2007; Friedberg and Webb 2006; Connelly and Kimmel 2009; Bloemen et al. 2010; Bloemen and Stancanelli 2014; Stancanelli and Stratton 2014). However, the inclusion of hourly wages of individuals poses an empirical challenge, as individuals who do not participate in the labor market do not have a real value for their hourly wages. We also estimated all our models, including wages (predicted for those who do not participate in the labor market) and results (available upon request) are similar to the results reported here.

Also omitted from $X$ are married status (married or not) and respondent's labor force participation. These are endogenous to the decision on how much time to devote to chores. We took account of these factors by estimating separate regressions by married status and labor force status. In the case of labor force status we distinguished between respondents with no or low labor force participation (working less than 10 h a week, LLFP) and those working 10 h a week or more. We also estimated separate equations for weekdays and weekends and for married and unmarried couples.

We test for robustness to alternative definitions of black and investigate whether our estimates differ for intermarriages between blacks who reported they are "black only" and those we labeled "mixedblack" based on their responses to this survey question. We also examine interactions between various categories of black and variables possibly capturing prevalence of antiblack discrimination in marriage markets. We also test for robustness of our estimates for women by reestimating our models using *total housework* instead of *chores.*

*Household Chores and Selection in Interracial Couples* Out of concern for the nonrandomness of matching in interracial couples, and to separate this nonrandomness in matching from the nonrandomness in the allocation of time, we follow an approach similar to that used by Meng and Gregory (2005). They estimated simultaneously economic success and intermarriage between immigrants and natives. In our case, we provide a simultaneous estimation of intermarriage and white women's time in chores (sample size is not sufficiently large to allow us to estimate the two equations for the sample of black women). We estimate this model for all white women. The two equations are:

$$\text{Chores}_{\text{ijt}} = \alpha_1 + \text{Husband Black}_{\text{ijt}}\delta_1 + \text{X}_{\text{ijt}}\delta_2 + \text{CH}_{\text{ijt}}\delta_3 + \varepsilon_{\text{ijt}}, \tag{9.3}$$

$$\text{Husband Black}_{\text{ijt}} = \alpha_2 + \text{X}_{\text{ijt}}\beta_1 + \text{HB}_{\text{ijt}}\beta_2 + \varepsilon_{\text{ijt}}, \tag{9.4}$$

where $\text{Chores}_{ijt}$ is the time devoted to chores by woman $i$ in state $j$, and year $t$, measured in hours per day and $\text{Husband Black}_{ijt}$ is a dummy variable indicating whether a woman $i$ in state $j$, and year $t$ is "married" to a partner who is black. We estimate the two equations simultaneously as well as the disturbance covariance matrix using an OLS degrees-of-freedom adjustment. That way we allow for correlation between the error terms of the equations, while taking into account that decisions regarding time devoted to household chores and partner selection are made simultaneously.[5] Vector $X$ in Eqs. 9.3 and 9.4 includes a common set of explanatory variables: Age of the respondent (and its square), the age difference between the couple, spouse's age squared, the interaction between respondent's age and age difference, wife's education, educational difference of the couple, wife foreign-born, husband foreign-born, a dummy variable for respondent's disability, a dummy variable for the husband's labor force participation, household nonlabor income, number of children in the household aged 0–4, 5–12, and 13–17, urban residence, and region.[6]

To identify this system of equations we include variables that are unique to each equation and therefore serve as instruments. To identify the time devoted to *chores*, we use the variables that refer to the day of the week the respondent filled in a diary in the ATUS survey (vector $CH_{ijt}$). Day of week is expected to influence time devoted to *chores* (e.g., more time during weekdays, Connelly and Kimmel 2009) but not the probability that the reference woman has a black husband.

The variables used to identify the intermarriage Eq. 9.4 are in vector $HB_{ijt}$. They include state availability, "Loving" dummies related to state laws regarding miscegenation, regional averages on an attitudinal question about opposition to marriages between blacks and whites obtained from the General Social Survey, the (log of) population density of the state, and interactions between density and some of the other variables. The *availability* is defined as $P_{jt} = \frac{n_{jt}}{N_{jt}}$, where $n$ is the number of white men available for a woman in state $j$ and year $t$, and $N$ is the total number of all men of marriageable age observed in state of residence $j$ and year $t$. Respondent's age is defined in 5-year age groups. Given that the difference in mean age at marriage in the USA is close to 2 years, we use men who are 2 years older than the women (see chap. 6).

The "Loving" dummies aim at controlling for whether the state of residence has had antimiscegenation laws, i.e., laws that forbade marrying across racial lines, and whether states with such laws were forced to repeal them as a result of the 1967 US Supreme Court decision "Loving v. Virginia" (388 US 1). This is based on Fryer (2007) who considers four groups of states: (i) states that never had laws against black–white marital unions; (ii) states that repealed such laws before 1900; (iii) states that repealed such laws after 1900, but before 1967; (iv) states that repealed their laws only after the Supreme Court ruling. We combined the states that voluntarily repealed their antimiscegenation laws, and only use two dummies for states that *never* had antimiscegenation laws and states that voluntarily repealed such laws before the Supreme Court ruling. We expect white women to be less likely to intermarry in states that repealed antimiscegenation laws only after the Supreme Court decision.

---

[5] The REG3 command in STATA is used for the estimations. To allow for clustering at the state level, and the computation of the disturbance correlation matrix, we use the SUEST command, which yields results identical to those obtained with the REG3 command.

[6] Alternative estimates using predicted wages for respondents and their spouses yield similar results (available upon request).

Inspired by Charles and Guryan (2008) we also use information based on an attitudinal question in the GSS, namely "Do you think there should be laws against marriages between blacks and whites?" From here we estimate regional averages on degree of opposition to marriages between blacks and whites. We have calculated the mean value of this variable for white women for each region in the year 1982.[7] The responses of interest to this question are "yes" (1) or "no" (2), where we have recoded "no" to value 0. Consequently a higher value for this variable indicates a stronger opposition to interracial marriages among white women in this region. The last instrument is the (log of) population density, obtained as the population in the state divided by the size of the state in squared kilometers. A higher population density may imply better functioning marriage markets and decrease the probability of racial intermarriage for white women who prefer to marry white men. However, regional population density may also be positively correlated with more open economic, political, and social institutions and a larger proportion of white women who do not discriminate against blacks. In either case population density reflects characteristics of regional marriage markets that may mitigate the effects of laws or mate availability. We, therefore, use the interaction among the availability, the "loving" variables, and attitude toward interracial marriage with the state's population density.

We test for the validity of the estimated model as follows. First, we compute the Spearman's correlation coefficient between the residuals of the two equations, and look at the significance of the correlation. A coefficient that is statistically significant at standard levels would imply that the residuals are not independent and that endogenization of the interracial marriage decision is needed. Second, we look at the instruments' relevance by looking at whether they are statistically significant. For a correct specification of the model, some instruments in each equation must be statistically significant. Third, we compute the Spearman's correlation coefficients between the residuals of the two equations and the instruments included in the other equation, and look at the significance of the coefficients. If we obtain that none of the instruments in one of the equations has a statistically significant correlation with the residuals of the other equation, we can assume that instruments are exogenous to the dependent variable of the other equation.

[7] The nine regions defined in the GSS data are: New England (Maine, Vermont, New Hampshire, Massachusetts, Connecticut, Rhode Island), Middle Atlantic (New York, New Jersey, Pennsylvania), East North Central (Wisconsin, Illinois, Indiana, Michigan, Ohio), West North Central (Minnesota, Iowa, Missouri, North Dakota, South Dakota, Nebraska, Kansas), South Atlantic (Delaware, Maryland, West Virginia, Virginia, North Carolina, South Carolina, Georgia, Florida, District of Columbia), East South Central (Kentucky, Tennessee, Alabama, Mississippi), West South Central (Arkansas, Oklahoma, Louisiana, Texas), Mountain (Montana, Idaho, Wyoming, Nevada, Utah, Colorado, Arizona, New Mexico) and Pacific (Washington, Oregon, California, Alaska, Hawaii).

## Results

### *Women*

Table 9.2 shows the results of estimating time devoted to *chores* by *white women* using Eq. 9.2, OLS, and defining black as "black only" + "white–black." The reference category in column 1 is a childless white woman living in the West and observed on Friday. It can be seen from that column that relative to endogamous white women, intermarried white women devoted 0.38 fewer h/day to *Chores*: $\delta_1\delta_1 < 0$ as predicted. This result, based on a comparison of 160 intermarried and more than 17,000 endogamous women, is significant at the 5 % level. The effect is quite large: In absolute value the effect of presence of a black partner is similar to that of number of children under age 5 (0.39).

We also find that $\delta_1 < 0$ only holds for weekdays, with racial intermarriage being associated with a reduction of almost an hour of chores per day. While based on a smaller sample of 8694 women interviewed on weekdays, of whom 78 were intermarried, this result is significant at the 1 % level. This makes sense, for on weekends activities such as shopping or cooking are more likely to be considered as leisure and less likely to be inversely related to intramarriage distribution.

A comparison of columns 4 and 5 reveals that our finding of a negative delta holds only for married women. For them, the effect of intermarriage is a reduction of 0.47 of an hour of chores per day, which is larger than the effect of number of children under age 5 (in absolute terms). This result is significant at the 1 % level and based on more than 100 intermarried white women out of a total of more than 16,000. A stronger effect was predicted for married than for unmarried women, given that they are more likely to "work" in chores while their husbands work in the labor force. We also estimated chore regressions for women with limited labor force participation, a group likely to include "housewives" (LLFP; column 6). While this result is based on only 33 intermarried couples, it suggests a larger effect of intermarriage on chores by housewives than by women employed in the labor force: Column 7 indicates no effect of intermarriage for white women who work at least 10 h a week in the labor force. This difference in the effect of intermarriage by women's employment status also makes sense within our conceptual framework.

A comparison of columns 8 and 9 reveals that our finding of a negative delta holds especially for married women with employed spouses. The effect of intermarriage on chores is 0.38 of an hour per day for married women with employed spouses, with this result being significant at the 1 % level and based on more than 100 intermarried white women out of a total of more than 14,000. In contrast, the result for white married women with nonemployed spouses is based on only 22 intermarried couples and suggests a very large effect of intermarriage on chores by white married women with nonemployed husbands.

Table 9.3 presents sensitivity analyses of these results to various definitions of black and interactions between "black husband" and variables that may affect the degree of antiblack discrimination in marriage markets. Column 1 reproduces the

**Table 9.2** OLS regressions of chores for white women. (Source: ATUS 2003–2009)

| | (1) All women | (2) Weekend | (3) Weekday | (4) Married | (5) Unmarried | (6) Married with LLF | (7) Married with non-LLF | (8) Husband in LF | (9) Husband not in LF |
|---|---|---|---|---|---|---|---|---|---|
| Husband (black) | −0.38*** | 0.11 | −0.55*** | −0.47*** | −0.11 | −0.69*** | −0.24* | −0.38*** | −0.65** |
| | (0.12) | (0.25) | (0.13) | (0.11) | (0.27) | (0.24) | (0.13) | (0.13) | (0.29) |
| Age (wife) | 0.06*** | 0.11*** | 0.05** | 0.05*** | 0.22*** | 0.08** | 0.05*** | 0.05*** | −0.01 |
| | (0.01) | (0.02) | (0.02) | (0.02) | (0.07) | (0.04) | (0.02) | (0.02) | (0.06) |
| Age of wife (squared) | −0.01 | −0.06 | 0.01 | −0.01 | −0.15 | −0.02 | −0.04 | −0.01 | 0.00 |
| | (0.04) | (0.04) | (0.07) | (0.05) | (0.10) | (0.10) | (0.05) | (0.04) | (0.16) |
| Age difference | 0.03 | 0.02 | 0.03 | 0.03 | 0.04 | 0.03 | 0.02 | 0.04 | −0.11* |
| | (0.02) | (0.02) | (0.03) | (0.03) | (0.06) | (0.04) | (0.03) | (0.03) | (0.06) |
| Husband's age (squared) | −0.04 | −0.03 | −0.05 | −0.02 | −0.10 | −0.04 | 0.00 | −0.01 | 0.02 |
| | (0.05) | (0.03) | (0.07) | (0.05) | (0.09) | (0.09) | (0.05) | (0.04) | (0.16) |
| Age wife*age difference | 0.00 | 0.00 | 0.00 | 0.00 | 0.00 | 0.00 | 0.00 | 0.00 | 0.00 |
| | (0.00) | (0.00) | (0.00) | (0.00) | (0.00) | (0.00) | (0.00) | (0.00) | (0.00) |
| Wife's education | −0.09*** | −0.08*** | −0.10*** | −0.10*** | −0.04* | −0.07*** | −0.08*** | −0.09*** | −0.12*** |
| | (0.01) | (0.01) | (0.01) | (0.01) | (0.03) | (0.02) | (0.01) | (0.01) | (0.03) |
| Educational difference | −0.01 | −0.04** | 0.01 | 0.00 | −0.01 | −0.02 | −0.01 | 0.00 | −0.03 |
| | (0.01) | (0.02) | (0.01) | (0.01) | (0.03) | (0.02) | (0.01) | (0.01) | (0.03) |
| Husband (employed) | 0.20*** | 0.14 | 0.22*** | 0.24*** | −0.16 | 0.20 | 0.26*** | – | – |
| | (0.06) | (0.09) | (0.07) | (0.06) | (0.17) | (0.12) | (0.08) | – | – |
| Wife (disabled) | 0.13 | −0.67*** | 0.40** | 0.05 | 0.89** | −0.59*** | – | 0.05 | −0.15 |
| | (0.14) | (0.21) | (0.18) | (0.15) | (0.37) | (0.16) | – | (0.17) | (0.25) |
| Wife (foreign) | 0.61*** | 0.30** | 0.75*** | 0.61*** | 0.53* | 0.82*** | 0.32*** | 0.59*** | 0.85** |
| | (0.10) | (0.14) | (0.10) | (0.11) | (0.29) | (0.12) | (0.12) | (0.13) | (0.35) |
| Husband foreign | 0.36*** | 0.39*** | 0.32*** | 0.36*** | 0.31 | 0.44** | 0.21** | 0.38*** | 0.07 |
| | (0.08) | (0.12) | (0.11) | (0.08) | (0.21) | (0.18) | (0.09) | (0.12) | (0.40) |
| Number of children <5 | 0.39*** | 0.25*** | 0.45*** | 0.39*** | 0.41*** | 0.34*** | 0.24*** | 0.42*** | 0.12 |
| | (0.04) | (0.04) | (0.05) | (0.04) | (0.09) | (0.06) | (0.04) | (0.04) | (0.15) |

**Table 9.2** (continued)

| | (1) All women | (2) Weekend | (3) Weekday | (4) Married | (5) Unmarried | (6) Married with LLF | (7) Married with non-LLF | (8) Husband in LF | (9) Husband not in LF |
|---|---|---|---|---|---|---|---|---|---|
| Number of children 5–11 | 0.32*** | 0.26*** | 0.36*** | 0.33*** | 0.30*** | 0.29*** | 0.24*** | 0.34*** | 0.26*** |
| | (0.03) | (0.04) | (0.04) | (0.04) | (0.09) | (0.06) | (0.04) | (0.03) | (0.08) |
| Number of children 12–17 | 0.29*** | 0.22*** | 0.31*** | 0.30*** | 0.22 | 0.35*** | 0.23*** | 0.32*** | 0.16** |
| | (0.03) | (0.04) | (0.04) | (0.03) | (0.14) | (0.05) | (0.04) | (0.04) | (0.07) |
| Hh nonlabor income | −0.01* | 0.00 | −0.01* | −0.01* | −0.03 | −0.01 | −0.01* | −0.01* | −0.01 |
| | (0.01) | (0.01) | (0.01) | (0.01) | (0.02) | (0.01) | (0.01) | (0.01) | (0.02) |
| Urban (versus rural) residence | −0.07 | 0.02 | −0.10 | −0.08 | 0.08 | −0.10 | −0.11* | −0.07 | −0.24 |
| | (0.06) | (0.08) | (0.07) | (0.06) | (0.24) | (0.11) | (0.06) | (0.07) | (0.16) |
| Northeast | 0.13** | 0.11 | 0.13 | 0.14** | −0.06 | 0.15* | 0.21*** | 0.14** | 0.12 |
| | (0.06) | (0.09) | (0.08) | (0.07) | (0.11) | (0.09) | (0.08) | (0.07) | (0.19) |
| Midwest | −0.02 | −0.04 | −0.02 | 0.00 | −0.17 | 0.01 | 0.06 | −0.03 | 0.23 |
| | (0.06) | (0.07) | (0.08) | (0.07) | (0.12) | (0.11) | (0.08) | (0.07) | (0.15) |
| South | 0.01 | −0.08 | 0.05 | 0.00 | 0.19 | 0.10 | −0.03 | −0.02 | 0.17 |
| | (0.06) | (0.07) | (0.08) | (0.06) | (0.20) | (0.09) | (0.06) | (0.05) | (0.17) |
| Constant | 0.84*** | 0.19 | 1.20*** | 1.27*** | −2.33* | 0.75 | 0.80* | 1.29*** | 3.78*** |
| | (0.28) | (0.46) | (0.36) | (0.33) | (1.19) | (0.63) | (0.42) | (0.33) | (1.20) |
| *R*-squared | 0.11 | 0.06 | 0.13 | 0.10 | 0.16 | 0.15 | 0.08 | 0.11 | 0.10 |
| *N* observations | 17,531 | 8837 | 8694 | 16,531 | 1000 | 4715 | 11,816 | 14,772 | 1759 |

Standard errors clustered at the state level in parentheses. Age range: women 21–65. *Chores* is measured in hours per day, see Table 9.9 for a description of the activities included in *Chores*. All estimations include day of the week (ref.: Friday) and year of the survey (ref.: 2009) as controls

*$p<0.1$; **$p<0.05$; ***$p<0.01$

**Table 9.3** Sensitivity analysis of results for white women to various definitions of black and intervening variables. (Source: ATUS 2003–2009)

| | (1) | (2) | (3) | (4) | (5) | (6) | (7) |
|---|---|---|---|---|---|---|---|
| Husband black only or white/black | −0.38*** | – | – | – | – | – | – |
| | (0.12) | – | – | – | – | – | – |
| Husband black only | – | −0.35*** | −0.35*** | – | – | −0.34** | – |
| | – | (0.13) | (0.13) | – | – | (0.13) | – |
| Husband mixedblack[a] | – | – | −0.48* | – | – | −0.49* | – |
| | – | – | (0.26) | – | – | (0.27) | – |
| Husband all black (black only + mixedblack) | – | – | – | −0.36*** | – | – | – |
| | – | – | – | (0.11) | – | – | – |
| Husband all black * antimisc. laws abolished in 1967 | – | – | – | – | −0.48*** | – | – |
| | – | – | – | – | (0.13) | – | – |
| Husband all black * antimisc. laws not abolished in 1967 | – | – | – | – | −0.28* | – | – |
| | – | – | – | – | (0.16) | – | – |
| Husband black only * wife foreign born | – | – | – | – | – | −0.14 | – |
| | – | – | – | – | – | (0.44) | – |
| Husband mixedblack * wife foreign born | – | – | – | – | – | 0.65* | – |
| | – | – | – | – | – | (0.36) | – |
| Husband all black * husband Africa born | – | – | – | – | – | – | −0.08 |
| | – | – | – | – | – | – | (0.35) |
| Husband all black * husband not Africa born | – | – | – | – | – | – | −0.36*** |
| | – | – | – | – | – | – | (0.11) |
| Husband Africa born | – | – | – | – | – | – | −0.26 |
| | – | – | – | – | – | – | (0.25) |
| Constant | 0.84*** | 0.84*** | 0.83*** | 0.88*** | 0.88*** | 0.88*** | 0.88*** |
| | (0.28) | (0.28) | (0.28) | (0.28) | (0.28) | (0.28) | (0.28) |
| *R*-squared | 0.11 | 0.11 | 0.11 | 0.11 | 0.11 | 0.11 | 0.11 |
| *N* observations | 17,531 | 17,516 | 17,535 | 17,535 | 17,535 | 17,535 | 17,535 |

Standard errors clustered at the state level in parentheses. Age range: women 21–65. *Chores* is measured in hours per day, see Table 9.9 for a description of the activities included in *Chores*. All estimations include all the other variables in Table 9.2, day of the week (ref.: Friday) and year of the survey (ref.: 2009) as controls

*$p<0.1$; **$p<0.05$; ***$p<0.01$

[a] Mixedblack is defined as "white–black," "white–black–American Indian," "white–black–Asian," or "white–black–American Indian–Asian"

results of column 1 in Table 9.2, where husband black is defined as husband "black only" or white/black. Column 2 separates black only from white/black and excludes all "mixedblack" cases. There are 15 cases of white women married to "mixed-blacks" defined as white/black or "white–black–American Indian," "white–black–Asian," and "white–black–American Indian–Asian." Column 3 includes two categories: Husband black only and husband "mixed black." The total number of observations rises to 17,535. In both columns 2 and 3 women with husbands who are "black only" work 0.35 of an hour less in chores than endogamous white women, not a significant difference from the coefficient of "black" in column 1. According to column 3 if the husband is "mixedblack" a woman works 0.48 of an hour less in chores. However, statistically the difference between the effect of "husband black only" and "husband mixed black" is not significant. If it were significant, it would indicate more discrimination where there has been more of a mix between black and other races than where black men are "black only." This would be inconsistent with the existing literature that has documented that black women with darker shades of skin are less likely to be married (Hamilton et al. 2009).

Column 4 combines all categories of black husbands. In column 5, we use the regression of column 4 and add interaction terms *Husband black * anti-misc. laws abolished in 1967* and *Husband black * anti-misc. laws not abolished in 1967*. It can be seen that if the husband is black and the couples lives in a state where the Supreme Court had to intervene to abolish antiracial marriage white women are doing 0.48 of an hour fewer chores a day, but where the Supreme Court did not have to intervene white women only work 0.28 of an hour less. This is consistent with larger racial intermarriage differentials in states with more pervasive discrimination against white marriages to blacks. However, the difference between the coefficients of these two interaction terms is not statistically significant. In turn, this could be due to the small numbers of interracial couples with white women: 68 in states that abolished antimiscegenation laws in 1967 and 100 in other states.

In column 6, we investigate whether the effect of "husband black" depends on whether the wife is foreign-born or not. It can be seen that to the extent that women married to husbands who are "mixedblack" work fewer hours in chores, this is entirely limited to women born in the USA. If they are foreign-born, women whose husbands are "mixedblack" work slightly more, not less, in chores than endogamous white women (the total partial effect of husband mixedblack is 0.16 (0.65–0.49)). The effect of "black only" does not depend on whether wife is born in the USA or abroad. The last column in Table 9.3 focuses on whether the husband was born in Africa. Interracial marriage differentials may be more prevalent in marriage markets involving American-born whites and blacks given that bans on interracial marriage are related to the history of slavery in the USA. We observe that all African-born husbands chose the category "black" and not "mixedblack." It appears that white women married to black men work less in chores only if the men are not born in Africa. Again, this supports the argument that interracial marriage differentials have a cultural content and may be related to the legacy of slavery in the USA.

Table 9.4 shows parallel results for black women. These results are solely of a suggestive nature, as they are based on slightly more than 1000 women. In columns

**Table 9.4** OLS regressions of chores for black women defined as black only or white/black (column 1–3) or mixed black (column 4–6). (Source: ATUS 2003–2009)

| | (1) | (2) | (3) | (4) | (5) | (6) |
|---|---|---|---|---|---|---|
| | All days | Weekend | Weekday | All days | Weekend | Weekday |
| Husband (white) | 0.47 | −1.18*** | 1.21* | 0.45 | −1.23*** | 1.14* |
| | (0.47) | (0.38) | (0.64) | (0.45) | (0.37) | (0.61) |
| Age (wife) | 0.15** | 0.09 | 0.16* | 0.16** | 0.09 | 0.17** |
| | (0.07) | (0.08) | (0.08) | (0.07) | (0.08) | (0.08) |
| Age of wife (squared) | −0.05 | −0.02 | −0.06 | −0.05 | −0.02 | −0.06 |
| | (0.12) | (0.21) | (0.14) | (0.12) | (0.21) | (0.13) |
| Age difference | 0.16** | 0.11 | 0.17** | 0.17*** | 0.11 | 0.19** |
| | (0.06) | (0.07) | (0.08) | (0.06) | (0.07) | (0.08) |
| Husband's age (squared) | −0.10 | −0.07 | −0.11 | −0.11 | −0.07 | −0.12 |
| | (0.09) | (0.18) | (0.12) | (0.09) | (0.18) | (0.12) |
| Age wife*age difference | 0.00 | 0.00 | 0.00 | 0.00 | 0.00 | 0.00 |
| | (0.00) | (0.00) | (0.00) | (0.00) | (0.00) | (0.00) |
| Wife's education | −0.11*** | 0.00 | −0.14*** | −0.11*** | 0.00 | −0.15*** |
| | (0.03) | (0.05) | (0.04) | (0.03) | (0.05) | (0.04) |
| Educational difference | −0.02 | 0.02 | −0.05 | −0.02 | 0.02 | −0.05 |
| | (0.03) | (0.07) | (0.05) | (0.03) | (0.07) | (0.05) |
| Husband (employed) | −0.03 | −0.07 | 0.04 | −0.03 | −0.07 | 0.04 |
| | (0.18) | (0.34) | (0.20) | (0.18) | (0.34) | (0.20) |
| Wife (disabled) | 0.14 | −0.16 | 0.17 | 0.14 | −0.16 | 0.17 |
| | (0.32) | (0.66) | (0.39) | (0.32) | (0.66) | (0.39) |
| Wife (foreign) | −0.19 | 0.02 | −0.31 | −0.11 | −0.01 | −0.19 |
| | (0.26) | (0.38) | (0.30) | (0.27) | (0.37) | (0.31) |
| Husband (foreign) | 0.26 | 0.04 | 0.36 | 0.19 | 0.07 | 0.25 |
| | (0.25) | (0.29) | (0.34) | (0.26) | (0.28) | (0.35) |
| Number of children <5 | 0.41** | 0.28 | 0.47** | 0.40** | 0.27 | 0.47** |
| | (0.18) | (0.18) | (0.22) | (0.18) | (0.18) | (0.22) |

**Table 9.4** (continued)

| | (1) | (2) | (3) | (4) | (5) | (6) |
|---|---|---|---|---|---|---|
| | All days | Weekend | Weekday | All days | Weekend | Weekday |
| Number of children 5–11 | 0.21** | 0.09 | 0.24* | 0.21** | 0.09 | 0.24** |
| | (0.10) | (0.13) | (0.12) | (0.10) | (0.13) | (0.12) |
| Number of children 12–17 | −0.03 | 0.25 | −0.17 | −0.03 | 0.24 | −0.16 |
| | (0.09) | (0.16) | (0.13) | (0.09) | (0.16) | (0.13) |
| Hh nonlabor income | −0.02 | 0.04 | −0.04 | −0.01 | 0.03 | −0.04 |
| | (0.02) | (0.03) | (0.03) | (0.02) | (0.03) | (0.03) |
| Urban (versus rural) residence | −0.08 | 0.34 | −0.27 | −0.07 | 0.35 | −0.26 |
| | (0.13) | (0.27) | (0.22) | (0.13) | (0.27) | (0.23) |
| Northeast | −0.07 | −0.55 | −0.07 | −0.09 | −0.52 | −0.11 |
| | (0.33) | (0.33) | (0.45) | (0.31) | (0.31) | (0.43) |
| Midwest | −0.32 | −0.95*** | −0.20 | −0.36 | −0.92*** | −0.28 |
| | (0.34) | (0.34) | (0.40) | (0.32) | (0.32) | (0.39) |
| South | −0.40 | −0.63* | −0.40 | −0.40 | −0.60* | −0.42 |
| | (0.31) | (0.35) | (0.37) | (0.29) | (0.34) | (0.36) |
| Constant | −0.46 | 0.03 | −0.12 | −0.59 | −0.51 | −0.21 |
| | (1.34) | (1.66) | (1.70) | (1.34) | (1.60) | (1.73) |
| *R*-squared | 0.08 | 0.07 | 0.12 | 0.082 | 0.07 | 0.125 |
| *N* observations | 1305 | 638 | 667 | 1313 | 641 | 672 |

Standard errors clustered at the state level in parentheses. Age range: women 21–65. *Chores* is measured in hours per day, see Table 9.9 for a description of the activities included in *Chores*. All estimations include day of the week (ref.: Friday) and year of the survey (ref.: 2009) as controls. Mixedblack is defined in Table 9.3

$^{*}p<0.1$; $^{**}p<0.05$; $^{***}p<0.01$

1–3 black is defined as "black only" or "white/black." In columns 4–6 black is defined in terms of all Census categories, including black. In the more restricted sample, 53 were intermarried; in the slightly larger sample, 57 were intermarried. We had predicted $\delta_1 \delta_1 > 0$. Columns 1 and 4 show the results for all days (weekdays or weekends). It can be seen that even though the coefficients of intermarriage are positive and in absolute value slightly larger than the corresponding coefficient for white women, they are not statistically significant. This lack of statistical significance is related to the small sample size. However, positive and significant (at the 10 % level) coefficients of intermarriage are found for weekdays, but based on only 667 observations, including 27 intermarried women. Consistent with the predictions, we thus find a negative effect of intermarriage for white women and (tentatively) a positive effect for black women. This contrast is not due to black women performing more chores in general: Overall black women spend less time on chores than white women. In contrast to the positive $\delta_1$ that we find on weekdays, black women seem to perform fewer chores on weekends when intermarried than when endogamous. Sample size does not permit a further breakdown between married and unmarried, or LLFP and non-LLFP in the case of black women.

Table 9.5 shows the results of estimating Eq. 9.2 for both white and black women when we use a broader definition of time devoted to household production: *Total Housework* as defined above. Results for women are thus robust to alternative definitions of time devoted to household production. As in the regressions of Table 9.2 using the more restricted "chores" measure of housework, we observe in columns 1–4 of Table 9.5 that intermarried white women devote less time to total housework than endogamous white women, and that this effect appears to be larger on weekdays (column 2), for married women (column 3), and for women with limited labor force participation (column 4). We also reestimated a regression for black women interviewed on weekdays (column 5) and found a result very similar to that obtained using "chores" as the dependent variable (Table 9.3).

We also tested whether our results are robust to a further expansion of the definition of chores, including time devoted to basic childcare (e.g., physical care for children, organization and planning for children, looking after children, care for children not specified, use paid childcare). Regressions including basic childcare in the definition of chores (available upon request) yield results similar to those in Tables 9.2 and 9.4, although the coefficients of "husband black" (in the case of white women) and of "husband white" (in the case of black women) are lower in absolute value when chores include basic childcare than when that is not the case. We find that in the case of married white women with low labor force participation—for whom we found large intermarriage effects using our restricted definition of chores—when basic childcare is added to the definition of chores the coefficient of "husband black" is negative but not significant.

**Table 9.5** OLS regressions of total housework, white, and black women. (Source: ATUS 2003–2009)

| | (1) | (2) | (3) | (4) | (5) |
|---|---|---|---|---|---|
| | White women | White women weekday | Married white women | Married white women with LLFP | Black women (weekday) |
| Husband (black) | −0.64*** | −0.91*** | −0.78*** | −1.77*** | – |
| | (0.15) | (0.18) | (0.16) | (0.36) | – |
| Husband (white) | – | – | – | – | 1.23* |
| | – | – | – | – | (0.66) |
| Age (wife) | 0.06** | 0.05* | 0.04 | 0.08* | 0.13 |
| | (0.02) | (0.03) | (0.03) | (0.05) | (0.10) |
| Age of wife (squared) | 0.06 | 0.08 | 0.08 | 0.04 | 0.15 |
| | (0.05) | (0.07) | (0.05) | (0.11) | (0.15) |
| Age difference | 0.03 | 0.03 | 0.03 | 0.04 | 0.21** |
| | (0.03) | (0.04) | (0.03) | (0.06) | (0.09) |
| Husband's age (squared) | −0.09** | −0.10 | −0.08* | −0.09 | −0.28** |
| | (0.04) | (0.07) | (0.05) | (0.11) | (0.13) |
| Age wife*age difference | 0.00* | 0.00 | 0.00 | 0.00 | 0.00 |
| | (0.00) | (0.00) | (0.00) | (0.00) | (0.00) |
| Wife's education | −0.08*** | −0.09*** | −0.08*** | −0.03 | −0.10 |
| | (0.01) | (0.01) | (0.01) | (0.03) | (0.07) |
| Educational difference | 0.00 | 0.01 | 0.00 | −0.01 | −0.02 |
| | (0.01) | (0.02) | (0.01) | (0.03) | (0.07) |
| Husband (employed) | 0.19* | 0.14 | 0.19* | 0.35* | 0.25 |
| | (0.10) | (0.13) | (0.10) | (0.17) | (0.28) |
| Wife (disabled) | 0.06 | 0.46 | 0.01 | −1.04*** | 0.09 |
| | (0.23) | (0.30) | (0.24) | (0.25) | (0.49) |
| Wife (foreign) | 0.46*** | 0.63*** | 0.45*** | 0.64*** | 0.22 |
| | (0.12) | (0.13) | (0.13) | (0.22) | (0.41) |
| Husband (foreign) | 0.15 | 0.08 | 0.20* | 0.21 | −0.18 |
| | (0.10) | (0.14) | (0.11) | (0.24) | (0.39) |
| Number of children <5 | 0.37*** | 0.48*** | 0.35*** | 0.18** | 0.56** |
| | (0.05) | (0.07) | (0.06) | (0.07) | (0.26) |

**Table 9.5** (continued)

| | (1) White women | (2) White women weekday | (3) Married white women | (4) Married white women with LLFP | (5) Black women (weekday) |
|---|---|---|---|---|---|
| Number of children 5–11 | 0.30*** | 0.37*** | 0.31*** | 0.21*** | 0.20 |
| | (0.04) | (0.04) | (0.04) | (0.06) | (0.13) |
| Number of children 12–17 | 0.33*** | 0.36*** | 0.33*** | 0.34*** | −0.23 |
| | (0.04) | (0.05) | (0.04) | (0.07) | (0.16) |
| Hh nonlabor income | 0.01 | 0.01 | 0.01 | 0.01 | −0.04 |
| | (0.01) | (0.01) | (0.01) | (0.01) | (0.03) |
| Urban (versus rural) residence | −0.08 | −0.12 | −0.10 | −0.20 | −0.43 |
| | (0.08) | (0.10) | (0.08) | (0.16) | (0.50) |
| Northeast | 0.11 | 0.10 | 0.12* | 0.11 | −0.28 |
| | (0.07) | (0.09) | (0.07) | (0.10) | (0.45) |
| Midwest | −0.11 | −0.15 | −0.09 | −0.05 | 0.01 |
| | (0.09) | (0.12) | (0.09) | (0.14) | (0.45) |
| South | 0.05 | 0.09 | 0.04 | 0.22* | −0.38 |
| | (0.07) | (0.10) | (0.07) | (0.12) | (0.39) |
| Constant | 1.76*** | 2.10*** | 2.32*** | 1.73** | 0.67 |
| | (0.43) | (0.55) | (0.45) | (0.85) | (1.94) |
| *R*-squared | 0.073 | 0.073 | 0.071 | 0.085 | 0.092 |
| *N* observations | 17,531 | 8694 | 16,531 | 4715 | 667 |

Standard errors clustered at the state level in parentheses. Age range: women 21–65. *Total Housework* is measured in hours per day and is defined following Burda et al. (2008), see Table 9.9 for a description of the activities included in *Total Housework*. All estimations include day of the week (ref.: Friday) and year of the survey (ref.: 2009) as controls

*$p<0.1$; **$p<0.05$; ***$p<0.01$

## *White Women, Controlling for Selection into Intermarriage*

Next, we deal with the question of whether the statistically significant coefficients of intermarriage that we reported for white women indicate effects of intermarriage on chores or originate from *selection into intermarriage* by women less prone to perform chores. Alternatively, an unaccounted variable could simultaneously cause intermarriage and lower levels of chores among white women. Columns 1 and 2 in Table 9.6 show the results of estimating Eqs. 9.3 and 9.4 on the time devoted to *Chores* by white women, considering selection into intermarriage.

It can be seen that after we take account of selection into intermarriage, white women in couple with black men devote 0.38 of an hour less per day to chores. That result is identical to the coefficient of chores in the simple model reported in Table 9.2 (column 1). Furthermore, the rest of regression 3 in Table 9.6 is very similar to regression 1 in Table 9.2. It thus appears that selection into intermarriage do not help explain the association between chores and intermarriage.

Regarding the identification of the two equations, some of the variables that are used as instruments are statistically significantly in the two equations. In the case of the *Chores* equation, day dummies for Monday, Saturday, and Sunday are positive and statistically significant: Women in the USA devote 0.187, 0.59, and 0.35 more hours to *Chores*, respectively, on Monday, Saturday, and Sunday. In the case of the equation for selection into interracial marriage, the following instruments are significant: Availability, opposition to black–white marriages, population density and interactions between population density and availability and between population density, and opposition to black–white marriage.

The Spearman's correlation coefficient between the residuals of the two equations is 0.0017 and is not statistically significant at standard levels. This helps explain why we get identical results with simultaneous equations and separate equations: Selection into interracial marriage does not account for the effect of "husband black" in regressions of time that white women devote to *Chores*. Additionally, the spearman's correlation coefficients between the instruments used in each equation and the residuals from the other equation are low and statistically insignificant, meaning that we can consider instruments in each of the equations as independent from the residuals in the other equation.

## *Men*

Table 9.7 shows the results of estimating Eq. 9.2 for time devoted to *Total Housework* by white men. Only 50 white men out of 15,625 were married to black women so these results are only suggestive. The reference category in column 1 is a childless white man living in the West and observed on Friday. We find a negative delta, as predicted: Relative to their endogamous counterparts, intermarried white men devote 0.6 of an hour less to total housework per day. Given that on average they

**Table 9.6** Simultaneous estimation of chores and husband (black), white women. (Source: ATUS 2003–2009)

| | Chores | Husband (black) |
|---|---|---|
| Husband (black) | −0.38*** | – |
| | (0.12) | – |
| Age (wife) | 0.06*** | 0.00 |
| | (0.01) | (0.00) |
| Age of wife (squared) | −0.01 | 0.00 |
| | (0.04) | (0.00) |
| Age difference | 0.03 | 0.00 |
| | (0.02) | (0.00) |
| Husband's age (squared) | −0.04 | 0.00 |
| | (0.05) | (0.00) |
| Age wife*age difference | 0.00 | −0.00** |
| | (0.00) | (0.00) |
| Wife's education | −0.09*** | −0.00* |
| | (0.01) | (0.00) |
| Educational difference | −0.01 | 0.00 |
| | (0.01) | (0.00) |
| Husband (working) | 0.20*** | 0.00 |
| | (0.06) | (0.00) |
| Wife (disabled) | 0.13 | 0.00 |
| | (0.14) | (0.01) |
| Wife (foreign) | 0.61*** | −0.01** |
| | (0.10) | (0.00) |
| Husband (foreign) | 0.36*** | −0.01*** |
| | (0.08) | (0.00) |
| Number of children <5 | 0.39*** | 0.00 |
| | (0.04) | (0.00) |
| Number of children 5–11 | 0.32*** | 0.00 |
| | (0.03) | (0.00) |
| Number of children 12–17 | 0.29*** | 0.00 |
| | (0.03) | (0.00) |
| Hh nonlabor income | −0.01* | −0.00*** |
| | (0.01) | (0.00) |
| Urban (versus rural) residence | −0.07 | 0.01*** |
| | (0.06) | (0.00) |
| Northeast | 0.13** | 0.00 |
| | (0.06) | (0.00) |
| Midwest | 0.01 | −0.01* |
| | (0.06) | (0.00) |
| South | −0.02 | −0.01** |
| | (0.06) | (0.00) |
| Monday | 0.18** | – |
| | (0.08) | – |
| Tuesday | 0.03 | – |
| | (0.08) | – |
| Wednesday | 0.01 | – |
| | (0.07) | – |

**Table 9.6** (continued)

| | Chores | Husband (black) |
|---|---|---|
| Thursday | 0.09 | – |
| | (0.07) | – |
| Saturday | 0.58*** | – |
| | (0.07) | – |
| Sunday | 0.35*** | – |
| | (0.06) | – |
| Voluntary | – | 0.00 |
| | – | (0.02) |
| Never | – | −0.01 |
| | – | (0.02) |
| Availability ratio | – | −0.01* |
| | – | (0.01) |
| Opposition RacMar | – | 0.14*** |
| | – | (0.05) |
| (Log) density | – | 0.04*** |
| | – | (0.01) |
| Never*(Log) density | – | 0.00 |
| | – | (0.00) |
| Voluntary*(Log) density | – | 0.00 |
| | – | (0.00) |
| Opposition RacMar*(Log) density | – | −0.03*** |
| | – | (0.01) |
| Availability ratio*(Log) density | – | 0.00** |
| | – | (0.00) |
| Constant | 0.84*** | −0.15** |
| | (0.28) | (0.07) |
| Observations | 17,531 | 17,531 |

Standard errors clustered at the state level in parentheses. Age range: women 21–65. *Chores* is measured in hours per day, see Table 9.9 for a description of the activities included in *Chores*. Dummies for year of survey (ref.: 2009) included as controls
*$p<0.1$; **$p<0.05$; ***$p<0.01$

work 1.8 h in housework, 0.6 is a large coefficient. As was the case for women, effects of intermarriage only appear on weekdays. This effect is only found for married men (column 4).

Even though there are fewer black men than white men in our data, the number of black men in interracial couples is substantially larger than the number of white men in such couples. Table 9.8 shows the results of estimating Eq. 9.2 for time devoted to *Total Housework* by black men. Most coefficients of "intermarried" are statistically insignificant. The only positive coefficients that are statistically significant (at the 5% level) are for very small samples of men with limited labor force participation (columns 5 and 6).

**Table 9.7** OLS regressions of total housework for white men. (Source: ATUS 2003–2009)

| | (1) | (2) | (3) | (4) |
|---|---|---|---|---|
| | All men | Weekday | Weekend | Married men |
| Wife (black) | −0.60** | −0.60** | −0.59 | −0.58** |
| | (0.24) | (0.23) | (0.40) | (0.24) |
| Age (husband) | 0.04 | 0.01 | 0.10*** | 0.03 |
| | (0.03) | (0.04) | (0.03) | (0.03) |
| Age husband (squared) | −0.08* | −0.09 | −0.09 | −0.08* |
| | (0.04) | (0.06) | (0.07) | (0.04) |
| Age difference | 0.01 | 0.01 | −0.01 | 0.00 |
| | (0.03) | (0.04) | (0.04) | (0.03) |
| Wife age (squared) | 0.05 | 0.08 | −0.01 | 0.05 |
| | (0.04) | (0.06) | (0.07) | (0.04) |
| Age husband*age difference | 0.00 | 0.00 | 0.00 | 0.00 |
| | (0.00) | (0.00) | (0.00) | (0.00) |
| Husband's education | 0.01 | 0.00 | 0.04*** | 0.01 |
| | (0.01) | (0.01) | (0.01) | (0.01) |
| Educational difference | 0.00 | −0.01 | 0.03* | 0.00 |
| | (0.01) | (0.01) | (0.01) | (0.01) |
| Wife (employed) | 0.19*** | 0.18** | 0.21** | 0.19*** |
| | (0.05) | (0.07) | (0.09) | (0.06) |
| Husband (disabled) | 0.05 | 0.34*** | −0.71*** | 0.01 |
| | (0.10) | (0.12) | (0.16) | (0.11) |
| Husband (foreign) | −0.11 | −0.12 | −0.06 | −0.13 |
| | (0.10) | (0.13) | (0.19) | (0.11) |
| Wife (foreign) | −0.05 | −0.10 | 0.06 | −0.05 |
| | (0.09) | (0.11) | (0.16) | (0.08) |
| Nb of children <5 | 0.00 | 0.00 | −0.01 | 0.00 |
| | (0.04) | (0.06) | (0.07) | (0.05) |

**Table 9.7** (continued)

| | (1) | (2) | (3) | (4) |
|---|---|---|---|---|
| | All men | Weekday | Weekend | Married men |
| Nb of children 5–11 | 0.00 | 0.00 | 0.01 | 0.00 |
| | (0.02) | (0.03) | (0.04) | (0.03) |
| Nb of children 12–17 | 0.03 | 0.05 | −0.03 | 0.03 |
| | (0.05) | (0.05) | (0.07) | (0.05) |
| Hh nonlabor income | 0.00 | 0.00 | 0.01 | 0.00 |
| | (0.01) | (0.01) | (0.01) | (0.01) |
| Urban (versus rural) residence | 0.12** | 0.14* | 0.07 | 0.15** |
| | (0.06) | (0.08) | (0.11) | (0.07) |
| Northeast | −0.15** | −0.28*** | 0.18 | −0.13* |
| | (0.07) | (0.07) | (0.13) | (0.07) |
| Midwest | −0.01 | −0.04 | 0.07 | 0.00 |
| | (0.06) | (0.08) | (0.10) | (0.06) |
| South | −0.22*** | −0.27*** | −0.12 | −0.20*** |
| | (0.06) | (0.07) | (0.12) | (0.07) |
| Constant | 0.48 | 1.18 | −0.12 | 0.65 |
| | (0.61) | (0.84) | (0.53) | (0.60) |
| *R*-squared | 0.067 | 0.014 | 0.02 | 0.068 |
| *N* observations | 15,625 | 7851 | 7774 | 14,732 |

Standard errors clustered at the state level in parentheses. Age range: women 21–65. *Total Housework* is measured in hours per day and is defined following Burda et al. (2008), see Table 9.9 for a description of the activities included in *Total Housework.* All estimations include day of the week (ref.: Friday) and year of the survey (ref.: 2009) as controls

*$p<0.1$; **$p<0.05$; ***$p<0.01$

**Table 9.8** OLS regressions of total housework for black men. (Source: ATUS 2003–2009)

| | (1) | (2) | (3) | (4) | (5) | (6) |
|---|---|---|---|---|---|---|
| | All men | Weekday | Weekend | Married men | Men with LLFP | Married men with LLFP |
| Wife (white) | −0.10 | 0.21 | −0.19 | −0.09 | 1.43*** | 1.78** |
| | (0.25) | (0.29) | (0.33) | (0.26) | (0.51) | (0.72) |
| Age (husband) | −0.03 | 0.08 | −0.09 | 0.04 | 0.19 | 0.21 |
| | (0.08) | (0.11) | (0.10) | (0.07) | (0.18) | (0.17) |
| Age husband (squared) | 0.00 | −0.16 | 0.06 | −0.11 | −0.32 | −0.22 |
| | (0.12) | (0.23) | (0.12) | (0.12) | (0.30) | (0.40) |
| Age difference | 0.03 | 0.08 | 0.03 | 0.03 | −0.16 | −0.11 |
| | (0.08) | (0.14) | (0.10) | (0.08) | (0.21) | (0.24) |
| Wife's age (squared) | 0.05 | 0.09 | 0.06 | 0.09 | 0.19 | 0.07 |
| | (0.10) | (0.25) | (0.10) | (0.11) | (0.42) | (0.47) |
| Age of husband*age difference | 0.00 | 0.00 | 0.00 | 0.00 | 0.01 | 0.00 |
| | (0.00) | (0.00) | (0.00) | (0.00) | (0.01) | (0.01) |
| Husband's education | 0.00 | 0.06 | −0.03 | 0.01 | 0.06 | 0.06 |
| | (0.04) | (0.04) | (0.05) | (0.04) | (0.08) | (0.07) |
| Educational difference | −0.03 | 0.01 | −0.04 | 0.00 | −0.15* | −0.09 |
| | (0.03) | (0.05) | (0.04) | (0.03) | (0.09) | (0.08) |
| Wife (employed) | 0.13 | 0.46** | −0.01 | 0.16 | 0.39 | 0.14 |
| | (0.15) | (0.20) | (0.20) | (0.14) | (0.30) | (0.38) |
| Husband (disabled) | −0.10 | −0.63* | 0.11 | −0.30 | −0.76 | −0.78 |
| | (0.24) | (0.33) | (0.35) | (0.26) | (0.47) | (0.57) |
| Husband (foreign) | 0.32 | −0.19 | 0.62** | 0.23 | 1.77*** | 2.32*** |
| | (0.23) | (0.35) | (0.26) | (0.22) | (0.52) | (0.68) |
| Wife (foreign) | −0.28* | −0.08 | −0.33* | −0.26 | −1.09 | −1.32* |
| | (0.14) | (0.39) | (0.18) | (0.17) | (0.65) | (0.77) |
| Number of children <5 | 0.18 | 0.26 | 0.17 | 0.21 | 0.86*** | 0.62** |
| | (0.14) | (0.18) | (0.17) | (0.15) | (0.29) | (0.30) |

**Table 9.8** (continued)

| | (1) | (2) | (3) | (4) | (5) | (6) |
|---|---|---|---|---|---|---|
| | All men | Weekday | Weekend | Married men | Men with LLFP | Married men with LLFP |
| Number of children 5–11 | 0.15 | −0.01 | 0.27 | 0.19* | 0.39** | 0.52* |
| | (0.10) | (0.08) | (0.16) | (0.10) | (0.19) | (0.26) |
| Number of children 12–17 | 0.19** | 0.16 | 0.17 | 0.26** | 0.04 | 0.12 |
| | (0.09) | (0.15) | (0.14) | (0.11) | (0.18) | (0.32) |
| Hh nonlabor income | −0.01 | 0.02 | −0.03 | 0.00 | −0.05 | −0.04 |
| | (0.01) | (0.04) | (0.03) | (0.02) | (0.05) | (0.07) |
| Urban (versus rural) residence | −0.03 | −0.22 | 0.05 | −0.07 | 0.26 | 0.20 |
| | (0.20) | (0.32) | (0.31) | (0.23) | (0.35) | (0.46) |
| Northeast | −0.71*** | −0.33 | −0.99*** | −0.72*** | −1.47* | −1.26* |
| | (0.20) | (0.23) | (0.20) | (0.25) | (0.76) | (0.74) |
| Midwest | −0.39** | −0.55** | −0.32* | −0.52** | −1.70** | −1.28 |
| | (0.17) | (0.23) | (0.18) | (0.23) | (0.78) | (0.81) |
| South | −0.58*** | −0.88*** | −0.47** | −0.58** | −1.17 | −1.11 |
| | (0.19) | (0.22) | (0.21) | (0.22) | (0.80) | (0.81) |
| Constant | 1.73 | −0.92 | 3.33 | 0.01 | −4.21 | −4.90 |
| | (2.08) | (2.22) | (2.53) | (1.74) | (4.15) | (4.08) |
| *R*-squared | 0.039 | 0.064 | 0.05 | 0.046 | 0.263 | 0.267 |
| *N* observations | 1262 | 666 | 596 | 1098 | 203 | 158 |

Standard errors clustered at the state level in parentheses. Age range: women 21–65. *Total housework* is measured in hours per day and is defined following Burda et al. (2008), see Table 9.9 for a description of the activities included in *Total Housework*. All estimations include day of the week (ref.: Friday) and year of the survey (ref.: 2009) as controls

$^{*}p<0.1$; $^{**}p<0.05$; $^{***}p<0.01$

## *Other Findings*

We first discuss other determinants of chores and housework. Then we look at the determinants of selection of a spouse from a different race (Eq. 9.4 in the system of simultaneous equations above).

Wife's education is associated negatively with hours of chores in the case of both white and black women if we use the strict definition of chores (Tables 9.2, 9.3, and 9.4). If we use "housework" (Table 9.5), the negative association is only found for white women. This finding is consistent with education enhancing productivity in household production and consequently higher value in marriage markets. It may also reflect educated women's higher bargaining power in the household, which allows them to negotiate division of labor arrangements with their husbands that involve fewer chores. This finding is restricted to weekdays, which is consistent with the idea that weekend housework, often shared with other family members, is more "fun" and less "work" than weekday housework. Table 9.7 shows that a lower educational difference (implying a wife with relatively more education) is associated with more housework by men. Also, when we enter wife's education instead of educational difference in regressions of men's housework we find that more educated white men do more housework on weekends and if they are married. We also see from Table 9.2 that when the husbands of white women are relatively more educated these women perform fewer chores on weekends (column 2) and if they are employed more than 10 h a week (column 7). Combined, these results suggest that for more educated white couples time spent on chores and on leisure are complements and not substitutes. This helps explain why positive sorting occurs by education even where the roles of education as earning-enhancing and of colleges as meeting grounds are eliminated, as is the case with movie stars (Bruze 2011).

Nonlabor household income has a negative value on the time devoted to *Chores* for white women, as each $ 10,000 increase in nonlabor income is associated with a decrease of 0.013 h/day in *Chores*. A comparison of the coefficients of "husband black" and nonlabor income in Table 9.2 implies that the presence of a black husband is the equivalent of a decrease of $ 270,000 in nonlabor household income. In the case of married white women, the equivalent is a decrease of $ 350,000 in nonlabor household income, and it is $ 260,000 in the case of married white women with employed husbands. Since the average nonlabor income for white women is $ 59,000 it follows that "husband black" has a much larger effect than most realistic changes in nonlabor income.

As for own age, women's age tends to be positively associated with their time in chores and housework. This may indicate a period effect: Time devoted to chores has decreased considerably among US women in the period 1965–2000 (Bianchi et al. 2006, Table 5.1). Age difference is negative and significant in the case of white married women with nonworking spouses, possibly because these older men can afford not to be employed and to replace women's chores with hired help. These women may be translating the value of their relative youth in a more leisurely lifestyle, as one expects from trophy wives (see Bloemen and Stancanelli 2014). However, age difference has a positive sign for black women, suggesting that black women may have fewer opportunities to trade their youth for material benefits in marriage and enjoy the "trophy wife" lifestyle. In the case of white men, the older they are the more they do housework on weekends. We also find a negative sign of the square of husband's age in the case of married men.

In most regressions, the number of children adds significantly to time devoted to chores. In absolute value, the number of children under age 5 does not affect women's allocation of time to chores significantly more than does being intermarried, and the effect of a child aged 12–17 is 0.29 for white women, which is lower than the coefficient of "husband black." Children aged 12–17 add to the chore work of white women across all samples but not always in the case of black women. Children also add to men's housework hours but not as consistently as they do for women. Men do fewer chores in the South than in the West.

Next, we turn to a discussion of the findings regarding the determinants of white women having selected a black husband. It can be seen from column 2 in Table 9.6 that intermarriages are more likely in densely populated states, which possibly reflects a correlation between population density and more open economic, political, and social institutions. These tend to be states on either coast, with larger cities, more influx of immigrants, and more of a tendency to vote for democrats.

The availability has a negative association with white women's probability of being in couple with a white man, where availability measures the number of white men of the right age relative to all men available. This negative sign has to be interpreted in conjunction with that of the interaction between population density and availability. Availability only takes negative values in low-density states, while in high-density states it turns to positive. For instance, (log) density is 9.20 in the District of Columbia where the total effect of availability is positive (0.08). Overall, this variable is positive in the 35 most densely populated states. In the other states even if white men are "available" on paper they may not be actually available given that searching for mates is more difficult in low-density states.

It also appears from the same regression that the stronger white women opposed black–white marriages in 1982, the more a white woman we observe was likely to marry (or live with) a black man. Again, this finding only makes sense in conjunction with population density and the interaction between population density and opposition to black–white marriages, as the net effect of opposition to marriage between blacks and whites is only positive in low-density states, while in high-density states the relationship turns to negative (for instance, in the high-density District of Columbia log density is 9.20 and the net effect is −0.1547. There are 27 states with higher population density where the net effect of opposition to interracial marriage is negative, as we expected.

## *Discussion*

That white women work less at chores if intermarried than if endogamous is consistent with intermarried white women obtaining a higher price for their WiHo, relative to their endogamous counterparts. This can be viewed as compensating differentials in marriage, in line with the analysis in Chaps. 3 and 5. To the extent that our findings for blacks are reliable and black women work more at chores if intermarried than if in an endogamous relationship, this may mean that they obtain lower WiHo prices if intermarried than if endogamous. Suggestive findings for intermarried and endogamous men go in the same direction.

These findings are consistent with a microlevel marriage market analysis in which marriage as a function of demand and supply in multiple marriage markets is defined by the ethnicity of both men and women. Relative to their endogamous counterparts, intermarried whites may get higher distributions in marriage, and intermarried blacks may get lower distributions, resulting in lower workloads for intermarried whites and higher workloads for intermarried blacks. Workloads were translated in terms of hours of chores or housework in the case of women, and hours of housework in the case of men. We call the differentials in workload associated with racial intermarriage "interracial marriage differentials" and presume they are based on interracial marriage differentials in the unobservable value of men and women in marriage markets. These differentials are likely to reflect the persistence of racial discrimination even among those who intermarried. We find that for white women interracial marriage differentials are larger in states that abolished antimiscegenation laws only after forced to do so by the Supreme Court, suggesting that racial discrimination is more persistent in those states.

As predicted, we also find more effects of intermarriage on chores performed on weekdays than on weekends, which is consistent with housework being less likely to be considered "work" on weekends (Hamermesh 2002; Connelly and Kimmel 2009).

Stronger findings for married women than for unwed women are consistent with married women being more likely to work at home in return for their husbands' work in the labor force than is the case with unmarried women. If marriage provides some sort of contract that better protects the workers in a couple relative to more informal forms of cohabitation (Grossbard-Shechtman 1993) it follows that interracial mating differentials in the unobservable value of men and women in marriage markets would be larger if the mates are married than if they are not.

A comparison of our results for chores as reported in Tables 9.2 and 9.4 and an alternative dependent variable, including basic childcare in addition to chores is also consistent with our basic interpretation. White women's racial intermarriage differential seems to be larger when home production is less enjoyable (childcare excluded) than when (basic) childcare is included and home production is likely to be more enjoyable. Likewise, married white women with low labor force participation may be getting particularly large interracial marriage differentials when we consider chores. However, when basic childcare is added to chores the coefficient of "husband black" becomes significant.

Alternative models dealing with in-marriage distribution, such as bargaining and collective models, may also explain some of these results. These models also imply racial differentials in distribution of the product of marriage, which can possibly imply differentials in time use. However, an explanation based on bargaining or collective models usually assumes that individuals in intermarried and endogamous couples differ in their remarriage options were they to divorce. In contrast, our predictions apply even if the members of a particular couple do not consider divorce or remarriage as relevant options, as they follow from differences in demand and supply in same-race versus interracial hedonic marriage markets.

The following alternative cultural explanation also accounts for our main finding.[8] It could be that there are black/white differences in culture such that it is well-known that white men expect more chores being performed by women than is the case with black men. Consequently, white women married to black men perform fewer chores and black women married to white men perform more chores relative to the endogamous wives of these men. However, this explanation does not easily explain why this finding would be unique to weekdays and not to weekends. It seems far-fetched to posit that such cultural differences would be unique to weekdays and that they reverse on weekends. In contrast, our proposed explanation accounts for all these findings: That intermarriage has a negative effect on chores for whites, a positive effect on chores for blacks, and that intermarriage effects are stronger on weekdays than on weekends.

We also presented a sensitivity analysis to various definitions of black and to interactions between black and variables likely to influence interracial marriage differentials in price of WiHo. We find that white women work less in chores when married to black men, regardless of how "black" is defined. This is more likely to be the case in states that had to be forced to renounce antimiscegenation laws and are therefore more likely to encourage antiblack discrimination on the part of whites participating in marriage markets. Our findings for white women also seem to apply better to US born women and to black men not born in Africa or Haiti. This suggests that racial intermarriage differentials in price of WiHo—at the root of the differences in access to marriage surplus—are based on cultural definitions of what it means to be black or white in the USA.

## *Conclusions*

Time devoted to household production activities by white and black men and women in the USA was analyzed as a function of whether they were racially intermarried or not. Based on an analysis of Marshallian markets for WiHo it was predicted that at given incomes and relative to their endogamous counterparts, whites in couple with blacks would perform fewer chores and that blacks in couple with whites would perform more chores. It was also predicted that racial intermarriage differentials in chores or housework would be largest where household production is more likely

[8] We thank Aki Matsui from the University of Tokyo for this idea.

to be considered *work* rather than leisure: On weekdays, when couples are married rather than cohabiting, when respondents have low or no participation in the labor force, and when spouses have high levels of labor force participation.

Due to limited sample sizes, robust findings apply mostly to white women. We find that, overall, white women in couple with black partners devote less time to chores (0.38 fewer h/day) and housework (0.6 fewer h/day) than their endogamous counterparts. The "effects" of intermarriage do not seem to be spurious: A two-equation model that endogenizes intermarriage reveals that accounting for selection makes no difference. The racial intermarriage differentials are large in comparison to differentials due to the presence of children or income variation.

The findings are also robust to various definitions of black. Racial intermarriage differentials in time spent doing chores appear to larger for US born blacks and in states that had antimiscegenation laws until the Supreme Court ruled it illegal in 1967.

White men also seem to spend less time on housework if intermarried with black women than if married to whites, but estimated effects are smaller and limited to specific subsamples. Even though results for blacks are less robust than for whites, due to smaller sample size, they also suggest that in the US marriage markets whites are a preferred group: When in couple with whites, black women seem to devote more time to chores and housework than when endogamous. Results for black men seem to go in the same direction but are less conclusive than those for black women. A more in-depth analysis with a larger dataset is needed to support the results for black men and women, and white men.

We also found that the effects of intermarriage seem to be stronger on weekdays than on weekends, for married respondents than for cohabitants, and for respondents with limited labor force participation than for respondents with more hours of work in the labor force. These differentials follow from our model based on presumed differentials in WiHo prices and do not follow from alternative explanations based on cultural differences.

Our study suggests that blacks pay a price when in couple with whites, in the sense that their partners seem to work less at household production relative to what a black partner would do. Racial intermarriage seems to benefit whites in the form of the extra time their black partners spend on household production. Our findings are consistent with the existence of whites' discrimination against blacks in US marriage markets. It is hoped that further studies will provide more accurate tests, allowing verification of this exploratory research.

# Appendix

**Table 9.9** Definition of chores

| | Schooling | | Earnings |
|---|---|---|---|
| *Travel related to housework* | *−0.086* | *Food and drink preparation* | *−0.0352* |
| Travel related to civic obligations and participation | −0.0752 | *Interior cleaning* | *−0.0316* |
| *Food and drink preparation* | *−0.0719* | *Travel to/from the grocery store* | *−0.0315* |
| *Interior cleaning* | *−0.0716* | *Grocery shopping* | *−0.0312* |
| Using social services | −0.0703 | Household and personal e-mail and messages | −0.0188 |
| *Travel to/from the grocery store* | *−0.0607* | *Travel related to housework* | *−0.0164* |
| Waiting associated w/civic obligations and participation | −0.0454 | Travel to/from other store | −0.0134 |
| Vehicle repair and maintenance (by self) | −0.0448 | *Laundry* | *−0.0133* |
| *Laundry* | *−0.0397* | Travel related to using home main./repair/décor. svcs | −0.013 |
| *Grocery shopping* | *−0.0287* | Picking up/dropping off household adult | −0.0122 |
| Helping household adults | −0.0283 | *Kitchen and food clean-up* | *−0.0117* |
| Socializing and communicating | −0.0237 | Waiting associated with caring for household adults | −0.0112 |
| Providing medical care to household adult | −0.0221 | Physical care for household adults | −0.0108 |
| *Kitchen and food clean-up* | *−0.0205* | Using home maint/repair/décor/construction svcs | −0.01 |

Sample consists of married or cohabiting women aged 21–65 who responded to the ATUS in 2003–2009. *Schooling* is measured in years of education, *Earnings* is measured in hourly-wage. Activities included from group 2 (*Household Activities*) and group 7 (*Consumer Purchases*) in the ATUS, and their corresponding travelling activities. Selected activities in italics; activities with a correlation lower than −0.01 are not included in the table

**Table 9.10** Variables and definitions

| Variables | Definitions |
|---|---|
| Chores | Hours per day respondent devoted to *chores* |
| Total housework | Hours per day respondent devoted to *total housework* |
| Spouse (black) | Dummy variable equal to 1 if the respondent's partner classified as "black only" or "white–black" |
| Mixedblack | Black or "white–black," "white–black–American Indian," "white–black–Asian," or "white–black–American Indian–Asian according to census categories |
| All black | Black or mixedblack |
| Spouse (white) | Dummy variable equal to 1 if the partner classified as "white only" |
| Age of respondent | Respondent's age in years |
| Age difference | Husband' age minus wife's age |
| Respondent's education | Years of educational attainment of the respondent |

**Table 9.10** (continued)

| Variables | Definitions |
|---|---|
| Educational difference | Years of educational attainment of the husband minus years of educational attainment of the wife |
| Respondent 's hourly wage | Log of the respondent's hourly wage, predicted when no LFP |
| Partner's hourly wage | Log of the respondent's partner hourly wage, predicted when no LFP |
| LLFP | Low or limited labor force participation (LFP) of the respondent (less than 10 h a week), only for women |
| Spouse (working) | Dummy variable equal to 1 if the respondent's spouse does not participate in the labor market |
| Respondent (disabled) | Dummy variable equal to 1 if the respondent is disabled |
| Respondent (foreign) | Dummy variable equal to 1 if the respondent was born outside of the USA |
| Spouse (foreign) | Dummy variable equal to 1 if the respondent's spouse was born outside of the USA |
| Number of children <5 | Number of children younger than 5 in the household |
| Number of children 5–11 | Number of children between 5 and 11 years old in the household |
| Number of children 12–17 | Number of children between 12 and 17 years old in the household |
| Hh nonlabor income | Yearly nonlabor income (divided by 1000) |
| Urban (versus rural) residence | Dummy variable equal to 1 if the couple lives in an urban area |
| Northeast | Dummy variable equal to 1 if the couple lives in the Northeast |
| Midwest | Dummy variable equal to 1 if the couple lives in the Midwest |
| South | Dummy variable equal to 1 if the couple lives in the South |
| Availability ratio | The number of white men available for a woman out of the total number of all men of marriageable age |
| Population density | Log of density of population, information obtained from the Bureau of Labor Statistics |
| Never had antimisceg. law | Dummy variable equal to 1 if the state never had antimiscegenation laws |
| Voluntary repealed antimisceg. law | Dummy variable equal to 1 if the state voluntarily repealed antimiscegenation laws |
| Opposition to black–white couples | GSS question formulated as "Do you think there should be laws against marriages between blacks and whites?" |

Spouses include unmarried cohabiting heterosexual partners

# References

Aguiar, M., and E. Hurst. 2007. Measuring trends in leisure: The allocation of time over five decades. *Quarterly Journal of Economics* 122:969–1007.

Altonji, J. G., and R. Blank. 1999. Race and gender in the labor market. In *Handbook of labor economics,* ed. O. Ashenfelter and D. Card, 3C vol, 3143–3260. Amsterdam: Elsevier.

Arrow, K. J. 1998. What has economics to say about racial discrimination? *Journal of Economic Perspectives* 12:91–100.

Becker, G. S. 1957. *The economics of discrimination.* 2nd ed. Chicago: University of Chicago Press.

Becker, G. S. 1965. A theory of the allocation of time. *Economic Journal* 75:493–515.

Bergmann, B. 1971. The effects on white income of discrimination in employment. *Journal of Political Economy* 79:294–313.

Bianchi, S. M. 2000. Maternal employment and time with children: Dramatic change or surprising continuity. *Demography* 37:401–414.

Bittman, M., P. England, L. Sayer, N. Folbre, and G. Matheson. 2003. When does gender trump money? Bargaining and time in household work. *American Journal of Sociology* 109:186–214.

Blackwell, D. L., and D. T. Lichter. 2000. Mate selection among married and cohabiting couples. *Journal of Family Issues* 21:275–302.

Bloemen, H., and E. Stancanelli. 2014. Market hours, household work, child care, and wage rates of partners: An empirical analysis. *Review of the Economics of the Household* 12:51–81.

Bloemen, H., S. Pasqua, and E. Stancanelli. 2010. An empirical analysis of the time allocation of Italian couples: Are Italian men irresponsive? *Review of Economics of the Household* 8:345–369.

Bruze, G. 2011. Marriage choices of movie stars: Does spouse's education matter? *Journal of Human Capital* 5:1–28.

Burda, M., D. Hamermesh, and P. Weil. 2008. The distribution of total work in the U.S.A. and EU. In *Working hours and job sharing in the EU and USA: Are Americans crazy? Are Europeans lazy?* ed. T. Boeri, M. C. Burda and F. Kramarz. Oxford: Oxford University Press.

Burke, M. 2008. Colorism. In *International encyclopedia of the social sciences,* ed. W. Darity Jr., 2 vol. Detroit: Thomson Gale.

Charles, K. K., and J. Guryan. 2008. Prejudice and wages: An empirical assessment of Becker's the economics of discrimination. *Journal of Political Economy* 116:773–890.

Chiswick, B. R., and C. Houseworth. 2011. Ethnic intermarriage among immigrants: Human capital and assortative mating. *Review of Economics of the Household* 9:149–180.

Cohen, P. N. 1998. Replacing housework in the service economy. *Gender and Society* 12:219–232.

Connelly, R., and J. Kimmel. 2007. Determinants of mothers' time choices in the United States: Caregiving, leisure, home production, and paid work. *Journal of Human Resources* 42:643–681.

Connelly, R., and J. Kimmel. 2009. Spousal influences on parents' non-market time choices. *Review of Economics of the Household* 7:361–394.

Crowder, K. D., and S. E. Tolnay. 2000. A new marriage squeeze for black women: The role of racial intermarriage by black men. *Journal of Marriage and Family* 62:792–807.

Darity, W. A., J. Dietrich, and D. K. Guilkey. 2001. Persistent advantage or disadvantage? Evidence in support of the intergenerational drag hypothesis. *American Journal of Economics and Sociology* 60:435–470.

Foster, G., and C. Kalenkoski. 2013. Tobit or OLS? An empirical evaluation under different diary window lengths. *Applied Economics* 45:2994–3010.

Frazis, H., and J. Stewart. 2012. How to think about time-use data: What inferences can we make about long- and short-run time use from time use diaries? *Annals of Economics and Statistics* 105/106:231–245.

Friedberg, L., and A. Webb. 2006. The chore wars: Household bargaining and leisure time. The Selected Works of Anthony Webb. http://works.bepress.com/anthony_webb/subject_areas.html.

Fryer, R. G. Jr. 2007. Guess who's coming to dinner? Trends in interracial marriages over the 20th century. *Journal of Economic Perspectives* 21 (1): 71–90.

Gershuny, J. 2012. Too many zeros: A method for estimating long-term time-use from short diaries. *Annals of Economics and Statistics* 105/106:247–270.

Gershuny, J. I., and J. P. Robinson. 1988. Historical changes in the household division of labor. *Demography* 25:537–552.

Goldsmith, A., D. Hamilton, and W. Darity Jr. 2007. From dark to light: Skin color and wages among African Americans. *Journal of Human Resources* 42:701–738.

Grossbard-Shechtman, Amyra. 1984. A theory of allocation of time in markets for labor and marriage. *Economic Journal* 94:863–882.

Grossbard-Shechtman, Shoshana. 1993. *On the economics of marriage*. Boulder: Westview Press.

Grossbard-Shechtman, S. A., and X. Fu. 2002. Women's labor force participation and status exchange in intermarriage: An empirical study in Hawaii. *Journal of Bioeconomics* 4 (3): 241–268.

Grossbard-Shechtman, A. S., and S. Neuman. 1988. Women's labor supply and marital choice. *Journal of Political Economy* 96:1294–1302.
Hamermesh, Dan. 1990. Shirking or productive schmoozing: Wages and the allocation of time at work. *Industrial and Labor Relations Review* 43:121S–133S.
Hamermesh, Dan. 2002. Timing, togetherness and time windfalls. *Journal of Population Economics* 15:601–623.
Hamermesh, Dan. 2007. Time to eat: Household production under increasing income inequality. *American Journal of Agricultural Economics* 89:852–863.
Hamermesh, D., H. Frazis, and J. Stewart. 2005. Data watch: The American time use survey. *Journal of Economic Perspectives* 19:221–232.
Hamilton, D., A. Goldsmith, and W. A. Darity Jr. 2009. Shedding 'light' on marriage: The influence of skin shade on marriage of black females. *Journal of Economic Behavior and Organization* 72:30–50.
Hersch, Joni. 2009. Home production and wages: Evidence from the American time use survey. *Review of Economics of the Household* 7:159–178.
Hersch, J., and L. S. Stratton. 2002. Housework and wages. *Journal of Human Resources* 37:217–229.
Hitsch, G. J., A. Hortaçsu, and D. Ariely. 2010. What makes you click?—Mate preferences and matching outcomes in online dating. *Quantitative Marketing and Economics* 8:393–427.
Jenkins, S. P., and L. Osberg. 2005. Nobody to play with? The implications of leisure coordination. In *The economics of time use,* ed. D. S. Hamermesh and G. A. Pfann, Chap. 5, 113–145. Amsterdam: Elsevier.
John, D., and B. A. Shelton. 1997. The production of gender among black and white women and men: The case of household labor. *Sex Roles: A Journal of Research* 36:171–193.
Juster, F. T., and F. P. Stafford. 1985. *Time, goods, and well-being.* Ann Arbor: Institute for Social Research.
Kahneman, D., and A. B. Krueger. 2006. Developments in the measurement of subjective well-being. *Journal of Economic Perspectives* 20:3–24.
Kahneman, D., A. B. Krueger, D. Schkade, N. Schwarz, and A. Stone. 2004. A survey method for characterizing daily life experience: The day reconstruction method. *Science* 306:1776–1780.
Kalenkoski, C., D. Ribar, and L. S. Stratton. 2005. Parental child care in single-parent, cohabiting, and married couples families: Time-diary evidence from the United Kingdom. *American Economic Review* 95:194–198.
Kalenkoski, C., D. Ribar, and L. S. Stratton. 2007. The effect of family structure on parents' child care time in the United States and the United Kingdom. *Review of Economics of the Household* 5:353–384.
Kalmijn, Matthijs. 1993. Trends in black/white intermarriage. *Social Forces* 72:119–146.
Lafortune, J., P.-A. Chiappori, M. Iyigun, and Y. Weiss. 2012. Changing the rules midway: The impact of granting alimony rights on existing and newly-formed partnerships. Working Paper 424, Instituto de Economia, Universidad Catolica de Chile (March).
Meng, X., and R. G. Gregory. 2005. Intermarriage and the economic assimilation of immigrants. *Journal of Labor Economics* 23:135–174.
Meng, X., and D. Meurs. 2009. Intermarriage, language, and economic assimilation process: A case study of France. *International Journal of Manpower* 30:127–144.
Nottmeyer, O. 2011. Couple's relative labor supply in intermarriage. IZA Discussion Paper No. 5567, March.
Reid, Margaret. 1934. *The economics of household production.* London: Wiley.
Robinson, J. P., and G. Godbey. 1997. *Time for life: The surprising ways Americans use their time.* Pennsylvania: Penn State University Press.
Sandberg, J. F., and S. L. Hofferth. 2001. Changes in children's time with parents: United States, 1981–1997. *Demography* 38:423–436.
Sayer, L. C., and L. Fine. 2011. Racial-ethnic differences in US married women's and men's housework. *Social Indicators Research* 101:259–265.
Semyonov, M., D. R. Hoyt, and R. I. Scott. 1984. Place, race and differential occupational opportunities. *Demography* 21:259–270.

Sevilla-Sanz, A., J. I. Gimenez-Nadal, and C. Fernandez. 2010. Gender roles and the division of unpaid work in Spanish households. *Feminist Economics* 16 (4): 137–184

Sevilla-Sanz, A., J. I. Gimenez-Nadal, and J. Gershuny. 2012. Leisure inequality in the United States: 1965–2003. *Demography* 49:939–964.

Smith, J. P., and F. R. Welch. 1989. Black economic progress after Myrdal. *Journal of Economic Literature* 27:519–564.

Spanier, G. B., and P. C. Glick. 1980. Mate selection differentials between whites and blacks in the United States. *Social Forces* 58:707–725.

Stancanelli, E., and L. Stratton. 2014. Her time, his time, or the maid's time: An analysis of the demand for domestic housework. *Economica*. 81:445-467.

Tobin, James. 1958. Estimation of relationships for limited dependent variables. *Econometrica* 26:24–36.

Wright, R., M. Ellis, and S. Holloway. 2013. Gender and the neighborhood location of mixed-race couples. *Demography* 50:393–420.

# Part III
# Consumption and Savings

The concepts of Work-In-Household (WiHo) and its compensation were defined in Chap. 2. In Chapter 10 dealing with consumption, the concept of WiHo is applied to the study of consumption by individuals who are either part of a couple or plan to be. Chapter 11 deals with savings. It includes an overlapping generations model of savings and intra-marriage transfers and applications linked to the concept of WiHo and theory Chaps. 2 and 3.

# Chapter 10
# A Consumption Theory with Competitive Markets for Work-in-Household

*I dedicate this chapter to the late H. Gregg-Lewis for it uses techniques he taught in a graduate labor economics course I took at the University of Chicago in 1973–1974 (This chapter is adapted from Grossbard-Shechtman Shoshana. 2003. A consumer theory with competitive markets for work in marriage. Journal of Socio-Economics 31(6):609–645. http://www-rohan.sdsu.edu/faculty/sgs/documents/consumption_paper_JSE2003.pdf. I thank Marina Adshade, George Davis, and Joni Hersch for helpful comments).*

The models presented in this part of the book apply to individuals who are either part of a couple—married or not—or plan to be in the future. They apply to consumption of commercial goods and services that substitute for home-produced goods, such as food and childcare produced at home, and are based on the concepts of work-in-household (WiHo) and its price that were defined in Chap. 2: WiHo is a particular type of household production benefiting a spouse. The model is most applicable to situations where one spouse does more of the household production than the other, implying that one spouse is the WiHo worker and the other the WiHo user. As in Chaps. 2 and 3 it is assumed that all consumption by marriage partners is private. At the end of the chapter I consider implications of assuming that some consumption is a public good to the couple.

The model leads to some novel implications. It is predicted that—assuming traditional gender roles—men's demand for consumer products replacing household production will be more price elastic than that of women. Sex ratio effects on consumption are predicted and it is shown how compensating differentials in marriage could affect consumption.

## Comparisons with Other Models of Consumption by Individuals Who Are or Plan to Be Part of a Couple and Related Data Issues

Early consumption models that had considered home production—including those by founders of the New Home Economics (NHE), Mincer (1962), Becker (1965), Lancaster (1966), and Grossman (1972)—examined *household* consumption rather



S. Grossbard, *The Marriage Motive: A Price Theory of Marriage*,
DOI 10.1007/978-1-4614-1623-4_10

than *individual* consumption by household members.[1] Possible conflicts of interest between men and women were ignored. These models are called unitary, as they considered household utility and the household's combined resources. In contrast, the consumption models presented here and in the next chapter compare men and women inside the household. This implies separate utility functions for each spouse and means the model is not unitary.

As for some earlier nonunitary models of individual consumption in couples that have taken account of the different interests of men and women, such as McElroy and Horney (1981) and Chiappori (1988), they did not consider home production. Closest to my model are other nonunitary models of individual consumption that make room for home production. Becker's (1973) demand and supply model of marriage is the first to briefly address the question of how consumption is divided inside a couple and he also recognizes home production of what he calls "commodities." Other nonunitary models of consumption and home production are Lundberg and Pollak (1993), Apps and Rees (1997), Chiappori (1997), and Chen and Woolley (2001).

All nonunitary models, including the ones presented in this book, agree that *when analyzing effects of income on individual consumption one has to consider the effects of the income of each spouse separately,* and not (only) pooled household income as done in unitary models of the household. My model reaches the same insight but following a different reasoning. I posit that even after a couple is formed individuals have their own disposable income, a function of own earnings and transfers from or to the spouse. There is no household income in my model; consumption varies only with disposable income. In contrast, most of the models mentioned above state that couples first pool all their incomes, thereby creating a household income, and then the individuals decide on how to divide access to this household income as a function of individual earnings: the more income they bring into the pool, the more they can get consumption goods out of household income.

A problem in implementing my theory is that there is very limited data on individual disposable income and in-marriage transfers. No national survey has attempted to measure such disposable income. However, a number of economists studying consumption from a nonunitary standpoint have introduced survey questions about income pooling in households. To the extent that complete income pooling truly reflects a complete blending of two people's incomes, with no attention paid to who earned the income, it follows that there is no need to try and approximate individual disposable income. The first country to introduce a question about income pooling into some of its consumer surveys is Denmark (encouraged to do so by Martin Browning, one of the authors of a nonunitary consumption model Browning et al. 1994). Using a unique Danish data set including information about whether couples pool their income, Bonke (2015) found that in most couples the internal income distribution is correlated with individual access to consumption and that this holds even if the household reports completely pooling its earnings. This indicates that when examining consumption by couples and given that individual consumption comes out of individual disposable income, own earnings are more likely to be part of an individual's disposal income than spouse's earnings.

[1] Grossman (1972) is a consumption model to the extent that it models household demand for health care services.

The next obstacle is that most countries tend to collect information on nonwage income and wealth at the household level, without assigning them to one or the other partner in a couple. An exception is South Korea, where it is required that each individual in a couple has his or her own savings account (Lee and Pocock 2007). Countries with individual income taxes for members of married couples may do better on such matters than the USA and other countries encouraging joint income tax filing by married couples. Even if there were ideal data on personal income of couple members, it would still be a problem to estimate disposable personal income, unless individuals reported transfers within their couple.

Nevertheless, the following pages raise useful ideas. Other nonunitary theories of consumption have assumed that individual wage (or earnings) in the labor force and nonlabor income is the source of men and women's bargaining power in the household. In contrast, a fundamental insight from this book's earlier chapters is that value of time and individual bargaining power depend on the price of work-in-household (WiHo) and that this price depends on conditions in markets for marriage modeled as markets for WiHo. Even if the price of WiHo cannot be measured it helps to generate new insights on consumption.

## The Model

In Part A, an individual could simultaneously have a demand and a supply of WiHo. In reality, most spouses typically both supply WiHo. However, here it is assumed—for convenience only—that the individual who consumes and uses WiHo does not work at WiHo for the benefit of the spouse acting as WiHo worker. All consumption is private.

As user of WiHo the problem this consumer faces is:

$$\begin{cases} Max\mathrm{U}_i(Z_i) subject\ to \\ Z_i = Z_i(x_i, s_i, h_j) \\ 1 = l_i + s_i \\ I_i + w_i l_i = y_j h_j + p_i x_i, \end{cases} \tag{10.1}$$

where $Z$ is a vector of privately consumed commodities[2] that can be produced with three inputs: a vector of commercial inputs $x$, leisure time $s$, and $h_j$, which stands for WiHo supplied by a (potential) spouse $j$. For simplicity, only one subscript is used for the WiHo user $i$ and the WiHo worker $j$. This suits a macrolevel model with one representative type of each (men and women in the context of traditional gender roles). In the appendix, I use the notation appropriate for a micromodel with multiple types of WiHo users and WiHo workers.

The production function $Z_i$ is assumed to have constant returns to scale. Total time available to an individual is set to 1. $l$ is work for a firm, $w$ wage, $I$ nonwage income, $y$ the price of a spouse's WiHo, and $p$ the price of commercial inputs. It is assumed that

[2] $Z$ is called a "commodity," following Becker (1965).

prices and wages are given to the individual, including the price of WiHo. The individual is selfish in the sense that (potential) spouse's private consumption does not affect own utility. (At the end of this Chap. 1 look at implications of replacing that assumption with the assumption that some consumption commodities Z—let us say food or a clean home—add to the well being of the WiHo worker.) All couples are heterosexual. Demand problem 10.1 includes individual nonwork income but not the spouse's income. Spouse's income may have an indirect effect if it influences the price of WiHo, $y$.

Using Becker's (1965) definition of full income the time and income constraints can be restated as full income constraint $F_i = I_i + w_i = \pi_i Z_i$, where $I_i$ is the nonwork income and $\pi$ is the implicit price of the composite commodity consumed by the individual.

Appendix A solves Problem 1 and derives Eq. 10.2; an individual $i$'s demand for commercial product $x_i$. From here on I omit the subscript "$i$" in order to make the presentation less cumbersome. However, I keep subscript $j$ for the price of the spouse's WiHo, to make it clear that it is a different individual.

$$\dot{x} = \frac{I}{F}\dot{I} - \left(\alpha_x^Z + \alpha_s^Z \sigma_{xs} + \alpha_h^Z \sigma_{xh}\right)\dot{p} + \left[\frac{w}{F} + (\sigma_{xs} - 1)\,\alpha_s^Z\right]\dot{w} + \left(\sigma_{xh} - 1\right)\alpha_h^Z\,\dot{y}_j. \tag{10.2}$$

This demand is expressed in percentage changes denoted by dotted letters. Each term preceding a dotted change on the right-hand side (RHS) is an elasticity of demand. The first term on the RHS is the own income elasticity as it equals $\dot{x}/\dot{I}$, percentage change in quantity divided by percentage change in income; the second term is the price elasticity, the third is the wage elasticity of demand, and the fourth is the elasticity of demand with respect to the price of WiHo. Each elasticity is now examined in more detail.

## *Income Effect*

The income effect in Eq. 10.2 is the effect of the WiHo user's income on his or her demand for goods. Individual income elasticity of demand for commercial products $x$ is the coefficient of first RHS term, namely, $\frac{I}{F}$, and equals individual (nonwork) income divided by individual full income. The income elasticity is positive given all the assumptions stated above and in the appendix.

Relative income of each spouse also matters. Here, we just look at the effect of one spouse's income, holding the other spouse's income constant. Any redistribution of income within the household that causes changes in personal income will be associated with effects on relative consumption. For example, as reported in Lundberg et al. (1997), the UK government switched from paying child subsidies to fathers towards paying them to mothers. Using my assumptions about income this means that after the switch nonwork personal incomes of mothers rose and nonwork personal incomes of fathers declined. With each individual man or woman maximizing their personal utility (with or without WiHo in the model) women will consume more and men less than before the switch. The policy switch will, thus, lead to a decrease in men's relative private consumption, which is what Lundberg et al. found.

Thomas (1990) finds that if nonwork income is in the hands of mothers, children are more likely to benefit than if it is in the hands of fathers.

## *Price Elasticity of Demand*

The price elasticity of $x_i$ is the coefficient of $\dot{p}_i$, the second term on the RHS of Eq. 10.2:

$$\dot{x} = -(\alpha_x^Z + \alpha_s^Z \sigma_{xs} + \alpha_h^Z \sigma_{xh})\dot{p}.$$

The price elasticity is preceded by a minus sign, which is what we expect: a negative price elasticity of demand. It has three components.

The first component is *a full income* effect that depends on $\alpha_x^Z$, the weight of commercial goods in the cost of producing *Z*. The second term is an effect due to *substitution in production* between commercial products and the individual's own time: $\sigma_{xs}$ is the elasticity of substitution in production between goods *x* and own time *s*, and $\alpha_s^Z$ is the share of own time in cost of producing *Z*. The third term shows the effect of *substitution in production* between commercial products *x* and spouse's WiHo and is equal to the product of that elasticity of substitution, $\sigma_{xh}$, and of the share of WiHo in cost of producing $Z\left(\alpha_h^Z\right)$. Equation 10.2 leads to two new insights regarding the law of demand.

**Prediction C1** *The elasticity of demand for x will be larger (in absolute terms) the higher the elasticity of substitution in production between commercial product x and spouse's WiHo*. This implies that the more consumers can rely on a spouse to satisfy their needs for *Z*, the higher the price elasticity. The elasticity of demand is, therefore, a function of marital status and relationship status (in case live-in partners are not married) since people who live alone do not have the option of using WiHo as an alternative to commercial inputs. For individuals in couples price elasticity of demand depends on the degree to which an individual can rely on a partner or spouse to produce their ultimate consumption needs *Z*.

In turn, the elasticity of demand is likely to influence market conditions in various industries supplying the products being demanded. For example, the lower the elasticity of demand faced by restaurants, the more firms with some monopoly power are likely to raise prices without adverse consequences on sales and to price discriminate. It follows that prices are likely to be higher for products and markets where the demand elasticity is lower due to more limited substitution between that product and WiHo OR due to more limited availability of that WiHo (captured in terms of a low $\alpha_h^Z$).

This helps to explain why one is likely to find more expensive restaurants where more people are single than in places where more people are married. A testable prediction is that, after controlling for income and other factors.

**Prediction C1'** *The demand for restaurant meals will be more inelastic in cities with high proportions of singles (such as Manhattan) than in small towns where most adults are married.* This prediction can easily be tested.

Another testable implication is that *commercial products that can more easily be produced with WiHo will have a more elastic demand than products that cannot be easily produced with WiHo*. For instance, it is easier to get a spouse to produce a well-balanced meal at home than it is to get a spouse to recreate the atmosphere of a bar. It follows that the demand for family-style restaurant meals will be more elastic than the demand for bar services.[3]

*The effect of the elasticity of substitution between commercial products and WiHo on the* price elasticity of demand *for commercial goods is weighted by other factors' share in the costs of production*. According to Eq. 10.2 the effect of $\sigma_{xh}$, the elasticity of substitution in production between commercial products $x$ and WiHo, on the price elasticity of demand depends on $\alpha_h^Z$, the share of WiHo in costs in production. It follows that the more an individual $i$ relies on WiHo in the production of $Z$ the more elastic his demand. For instance, if $Z$ is clean garments, the more laundry-related WiHo the individual has access to, the more her demand for commercial laundry services will be elastic. Also, the higher the share of a (potential) spouse's WiHo in fulfilling one's needs for good nutrition, the more elastic the person's demand for frozen dinners and other commercial products that substitute for spouse's WiHo. Generally, it is predicted that the more people can rely on spouses to perform WiHo benefiting them, the less they will be willing to pay for commercial WiHo substitutes.

Given traditional gender roles, this theory can help to explain gender differentials in demand elasticity. Traditional gender roles continue to be prevalent in every country for which we have time use data. It has been documented that women engage in considerably more domestic chores than men (e.g., by Hersch 2003, 2009; Gimenez-Nadal and Sevilla-Sanz 2012). To the extent that this implies that men rely on women's WiHo more than women rely on men's WiHo, the share of WiHo costs will be lower for women and,

*Prediction C2 Assuming traditional gender roles, relative to men, women will have lower price elasticities of demand for commercial goods that substitute for a spouse's WiHo.*

In turn, this leads to differences in product markets depending on whether the products are principally bought by men or women. The more we observe gender differences in the degree to which men and women can rely on a spouse's WiHo, the more the corresponding industries could discriminate against the gender with a lower price elasticity of demand. For example, men do their wives' laundry much less frequently than women do their husbands' laundry. This must be the case because according to the American Time Use Survey, in 2012, men age 20–55 spent an average of 5.58 min a day on doing laundry, in contrast with 19.37 min for women (this gender gap has decreased a bit since 2003, when the numbers stood at 4.39 min for men and 20.74 min for women).[4]

---

[3] Oana Tocoian points out that restaurants may also price discriminate in terms of spousal WiHo availability when they only issue coupons that cannot be used by single customers (free entree with purchase of another, dinner for two for X dollars, etc.).

[4] I thank Victoria Vernon for calculating these numbers specially for this book.

It has also been observed that dry cleaners and commercial laundries often charge different prices to men and women for similar items (shirts and blouses, for example).[5] These two facts are related according to this theory: dry cleaners often charge more for women's blouses than for men's shirts, even if costs of production are the same, because they act as discriminating local monopolies taking advantage of the fact that women's demand is less elastic than that of men.[6]

Women also spend more time than men in food preparation, often as a form of WiHo. This will affect food-related industries that supply products specifically aimed at men or women. It follows from my analysis that women will be charged higher prices for female-oriented food products relative to what men pay for male-oriented products (because their price elasticity of demand is more limited). Take the example of food-away-from home (FAFH). We know that some providers of FAFH are more popular among men (fast food hamburgers for instance) and others more among women (vegan grill for instance). It follows that *ceteris paribus* men's demand for their kind of FAFH will be more elastic than that for "women's FAFH," which may imply that women will be charged more than men for their favorite type of FAFH, taking account of different costs of production, if firms have some monopoly power.[7] USDA data shows that over the last 30 years FAFH expenditures have increased at a steady rate, relative to food-a-home (FAH) expenditures.[8] These statistics on FAFH are not broken down by kinds of food (such as hamburgers versus vegan). We also know that the overall price index for FAFH reached its peak in about 1978 and then declined slowly until about 1998 and has remained about the same since then (Christian and Rashad 2009).[9,10]

It also follows that if women typically engage in more home cleaning than men, men's demand for commercial maid services will be more elastic than women's and women may need to pay more than men for a given quantity of commercial maid services (this may be very difficult to test for lack of data).

Conversely, since women are more likely to rely on men's car-related WiHo than men to rely on women's WiHo of this kind, if commercial products regarding cars, or perhaps even the cars themselves, are designed separately for men and women, I expect car-related products designed for women (possibly including cars) to have a higher demand elasticity than comparable products geared to men. This would imply higher prices for men-oriented cars such as sports cars than for women-oriented

5 Barbara Bergmann, personal communication. Her observation is based on data she collected with the help of students in the Washington, DC area. Some states, including California, have banned gender-based price differentials in dry-cleaning services (see also Cohen 1999).

6 Women, thus, seem to get penalized twice by men's unwillingness to do their wives' laundry. First, women rarely have the option of relying on that form of help in the home. Second, they may get charged more for commercial services if they go to the cleaners, as a result of their lower elasticity of demand which in turn is partially explained by the low levels of WiHo that men supply.

7 Again, this assumes that sellers can take advantage of buyers' less elastic demand.

8 See Davis (2014) for a review of FAH versus FAFH and the implications for nutrition and Health.

9 Prices may be stable if supply side outpaced the demand side, assuming nothing else on the demand side changed.

10 The demand for frozen dinners aimed at children is expected to be very price-elastic as both mothers and fathers may possibly substitute for their children's cooking activities.

cars, after controlling for costs of production and other relevant factors.[11] The same holds for home maintenance tools. Men do more home maintenance than women (Hersch and Stratton 2000; Sevilla-Sanz et al. 2010) and therefore women-oriented tools are likely to be cheaper than men-oriented tools.

Furthermore, this analysis helps us to understand why women's demand for cigarettes is less elastic than men's: Hersch (2000) finds that when calculating elasticities of consumption of cigarettes for a sample of workers, and thus including personal earnings (rather than household income) in the regressions, women's price elasticity of demand (−0.38) is lower than men's (−0.46; also see Chaloupka and Pacula 1998). When the price of cigarettes increases smoking habits become more costly and people may be more motivated to detoxify from smoking. To succeed in such detoxification you can either use commercial services such as patches or clinics or you can rely on a spouse who either nags or encourages you. If men are less supportive of their wives than women are of their husbands when it comes to helping a spouse kick the smoking habit, women will find it costlier and more difficult to free themselves from smoking after the price of cigarettes rises. Therefore, price increases will cause less change in women's consumption of cigarettes than in men's. It is also expected that women's demand for commercial antismoking products and services will be less elastic than men's.[12] Some of these insights may also apply to singles expecting to become part of a couple. The expectation that in the future there will be WiHo available to quick the habit will influence current consumption.

## *Wage Effects*

Equation 10.2 also includes an elasticity of demand for $x$ with respect to own wage, i.e., the coefficient of $\dot{w} : \frac{w}{F} + (\sigma_{xs} - 1)\,\alpha_s^Z$. This elasticity contains a real income effect $\frac{w}{F}$ and a substitution effect $(\sigma_{xs} - 1)\,\alpha_s^Z$ based on substitution between own household production time (leisure) and goods and the share of such leisure in the cost of production of private consumption commodity $Z$. The higher the wage, the more expensive own time at home production and the more inclined the individual will be to rely on commercial goods instead. The wage effect will definitely be positive if $\sigma_{xs} > 1$. *If* elasticity of substitution $\sigma_{xs}$ is less than 1, then the wage elasticity has a positive component (the real income effect) and a negative component (the substitution effect). That substitution effect depends on $\alpha_s^Z$, the share of own time in the cost of producing $Z$. The wage effect will be positive as long as $\frac{w}{F} > \left|(\sigma_{xs} - 1)\,\alpha_s^Z\right|$.

[11] Testing for this will be very complicated, for there may also be some gender differences in the symbolic value of a car. Also, it has been documented that relative to men women are worse at bargaining prices down.

[12] A spouse's time is likely to be a better substitute for the time of professional services than is the case with own time.

## *Effects of the Price of a Spouse's WiHo*

It also follows from Eq. 10.2 that the demand for commercial products is a function of price $y_j$ that the individual has to pay for a spouse's WiHo. The coefficient of $\dot{y}_j$ is the elasticity of demand with respect to spouse *j*'s WiHo price $y_j$ and it equals $(\sigma_{xh}-1)\,\alpha_h^Z$, where $\alpha_h^Z$ is the share of WiHo in the cost of producing *Z* and $\sigma_{xh}$ is the elasticity of substitution in production between commercial goods and WiHo. The more the individual uses a spouse's WiHo the more his demand for commercial goods is likely to respond to changes in WiHo price. We can also see a negative real income effect and a positive effect of substitution in production between commercial goods and home production.

There are no data on WiHo prices. Nevertheless, this part of the theory is useful for it helps to understand how individual consumption can be affected by marriage market conditions that possibly influence the price of WiHo. Next, I discuss how the following three factors can affect consumption via potential effects on WiHo price: sex ratios, income of potential spouses, and characteristics associated with compensating differentials in marriage. The models underlying the rest of this chapter are those of Chaps. 2 and 3, where demands and supplies of WiHo were derived with assumptions more general than those used in this chapter. For example, household production functions were not as specifically defined (no restriction to constant returns to scale) as in Problem 10.1 and the following appendix. Many assumptions could underlie the derivation downward-sloping demand for WiHo. Here, I also use the upward-sloping supplies of WiHo presented in previous chapters.

### Sex Ratio Effects

Sex ratio effects on labor supply were analyzed in Chaps. 4 (at the macrolevel) and 6 (when there are multiple marriage markets). Now, I examine their potential impact on individual consumption. To the extent that gender roles are traditional, higher sex ratios (when women are scarcer relatively to the men in the same marriage market) imply higher prices for women's WiHo, *y*. In turn, a higher price *y* implies higher disposable income for women and lower disposable income for men. Therefore,

*Prediction C3 The higher the sex ratio the more women will consume relative to men.* This is expected to affect both individual consumption in marriage and consumption by singles preparing themselves for marriage.

This prediction also derives from a number of other theories of marriage, including Becker (1973), McElroy (1990), and Chiappori et al. (1998). Our theories are all in agreement as far as the prediction that sex ratios affect individual bargaining power in marriage, and therefore personal access to consumption goods by men and women living in couples. Some of these other theories may not have explicitly stated that sex ratios will affect the consumption of unmarried men and women.

If WiHo markets exist and set prices, it follows that whoever plans to marry—whether it is a first marriage or a later marriage—anticipates WiHo prices that will affect them, once they are in couple, either as suppliers of WiHo or consumers of WiHo (or both). Consequently, spending habits of singles will be influenced by expected future earnings from WiHo (if WiHo suppliers) or expected future expenses (if WiHo users). For instance, given a traditional division of labor in the home, young single women expecting high prices for WiHo (due to a high ratio of males to females) will spend a higher portion of their current income on private consumption (e.g., expensive clothing and travels abroad) than comparable women expecting lower WiHo prices. In contrast, unmarried men expecting to pay high WiHo prices to their future wife will spend less on themselves and save more if they intend to marry (see Chap. 11).

*Evidence* Using data from mainland China Maria Porter (forthcoming, 2015) reports that as women are scarcer in marriage markets men consume less tobacco and alcohol. Since, most tobacco and alcohol are consumed by men it was easy to determine that such consumption benefits men. Studies of personal consumption in couples have also examined spending on children, even though goods bought for children or children outcomes benefit both husband and wife. However, prior research has shown that increases in female income or greater control of household assets leads to greater investment in children (e.g., Thomas 1990; Brown 2009). Porter also establishes that in China higher sex ratios are associated with healthier sons and she shows that this not fully explained by the characteristics of the parents. She then infers that higher sex ratios give women more access to the couple's resources, which they apparently prefer to spend on their sons' health. This is also indirect evidence that sex ratios are positively associated with married women benefiting more from the household's consumption relative to their husbands.

Griskevicius et al. (2012) report a positive simple correlation between sex ratio and amount of consumer debt held by people across 134 cities in the USA. The sex ratios were calculated as number of unmarried men to unmarried women, which correlates positively with my preferred measure of sex ratio, the total number of men to number of women in age groups likely to form couples. They found that the higher the city's sex ratio the higher the average amount of consumer debt carried by people in that city. Assuming such positive association between average consumer debt and sex ratio is robust to more rigorous tests controlling, e.g., for income, education, size of city, this finding fits with prediction C3 to the extent that the consumption items bought with debt benefit women more than men. The savings model presented in Chap. 11 could also throw some light on this tentative finding.

## Effects of Income of Potential Spouses

Assuming normal income effects on consumption and leisure (defined as own time in household production), it follows that individuals with higher incomes will demand more WiHo and be willing to supply less WiHo (see the market analyses in Chaps. 4 and 6). In light of such market analysis, any change that influences the incomes of large numbers of market participants will affect the price of WiHo. For example, consider the UK policy switch involving lower incomes for men and higher incomes for their female partners. This implies that men's demands for WiHo will decrease due to lower disposable incomes, and women's WiHo supplies will decrease (with more income women's willingness to work will be reduced).

The combined effect of this policy switch on equilibrium WiHo price is not clear and will depend on whether the demand shifts more or less than the supply. However, it is clear that equilibrium amount of WiHo supplied will go down. What that means exactly depends on whether we use the macromodel of Chap. 4 or the micromodel of Chap. 6. With the multiple WiHo markets for various types of men and women of Chap. 6 it means that, on average, women willing to work in WiHo will have fewer opportunities to do so.

To the extent that the price of WiHo decreases and we follow the assumptions of Problem 10.1, Eq. 10.2 implies that after taking account of a drop in the price of WiHo traditional men will not be as hurt by the policy shift as they would otherwise be: with cheaper WiHo available as users of WiHo their real income rises and given possible substitution between WiHo and commercial goods their ultimate utility level will not drop as much as is expected when ignoring markets for WiHo. However, if WiHo price rises at the new equilibrium—due to a shift in supply exceeding the shift in demand—men's loss of well being will be exacerbated.

The implications of a shift in who gets government benefits for consumption by traditional women supplying WiHo are also important. The direct effect of the shift on women's income is positive. However, their disposable income will also decrease to the extent that they work less at WiHo, for their disposable income also includes earnings from WiHo. These earnings will decrease even more if the price of their WiHo went down at the new equilibrium. The more traditional the gender roles and the higher the initial price for women's WiHo the less women stand to benefit from a policy transferring welfare benefits from men to women. In terms of the model presented in Chap. 6.

*Prediction C4 The higher the initial k (the proportion of men's income that is transferred to wives and partners) and assuming traditional gender roles, the more a policy that lowers men's earnings is likely to translate into losses for women.*

Consider a traditional "whole wage" system under which husbands handed over most of their paychecks to their wives. In the past, this arrangement was very common among the British and USA middle class (Pahl 1983; Woolley 2003) and it still prevails in Japan (Kureishi and Wakabayashi 2013). The analysis presented here could help explain political action in support or against such system or related policies. For example, under such system there would be less incentive for women to lobby for a change in who gets welfare benefits than under a system where men keep control of most of their earnings, as drops in men's income translate into relatively large drops in women's disposable income.

More generally, assuming traditional gender roles (but not necessarily a whole wage system)

*Prediction C4' The predicted effects of changes in (potential) spouses' income on men and women are not symmetric.* For women who supply WiHo (or plan to do so) in societies with traditional gender roles higher incomes of (potential) husbands could add to own well being even under the assumptions of this model (no altruism and private consumption): men's higher incomes contribute to a higher demand for WiHo and higher earnings for women who supply WiHo, allowing women to consume more. This income effect for WiHo workers has been overlooked by previous models assuming unitary household utility functions and budget constraints, such as Gronau (1977), and by bargaining theories assuming either unitary marital production (e.g., McElroy and Horney 1981) or no household production at all (e.g., Chiappori 1992).

In contrast, for men with a demand for women's WiHo in societies with traditional gender roles higher incomes for wives are likely to reduce well being: with higher disposable incomes women will reduce their supply of WiHo and thus men will obtain less WiHo and/or pay more for it. In such traditional societies, increases in women's income are likely to translate into fewer gains in men's consumption and well being (and possibly lower well being) relative to how increases in men's incomes are likely to affect women's well being.

This helps to explain why historically men have used collective action to limit women's earnings opportunities via laws preventing them from being employed (or from being employed after marriage, see Goldin 1988, 1990), and passage of such laws faced limited resistance on the part of women. More symmetrical income effects for heterosexual men and women require a role reboot:[13] when men do more WiHo and women earn more it is more likely that women's higher incomes translate into higher disposable income for men; when women do less WiHo increases in men's incomes add less to women's disposable income. To the best of my knowledge, there have never been instances of women using collective action to limit men's earning opportunities (Folbre 1994). This is not only because women were politically weak but also because they were coopted into the system of traditional gender roles giving them easy access to their husbands' earnings: women then had a vested interest in protecting male earnings that were mostly transferred to them.

Another connection between consumption and aggregate income effects is that tensions between income effects on demand and supply of WiHo could lead to higher demand for commercial products that substitute for WiHo and can, thus, ease such tensions. As all incomes rise the demand for most services grows, including demand for WiHo. However, supplies of work move to the left, including the supplies of WiHo. At the new equilibria in WiHo markets there will either be higher WiHo prices or excess demand for WiHo at rigid prices. Increased availability of commercial WiHo substitutes that lower demand for WiHo could alleviate problems arising from excess demand.

One such substitute is paid domestic help. Early in the twentieth century rising incomes in the USA have been associated with rapid increases in employment of servants, implying a high income elasticity of servants' services (Stigler 1946). As

[13] I have borrowed the term "role reboot" from https://www.facebook.com/RoleReboot .

servants became increasingly expensive and new technologies sprung up there has been rapid growth in many other substitutes such as frozen meals and appliances, including microwave ovens (see Greenwood et al. 2005).

Demand for commercial substitutes for WiHo may be more income elastic than captured by Eq. 10.2 if one takes account of possible rigidity in WiHo prices. The need for commercial products eliminating excess demand in markets for WiHo is expected to be especially acute among the higher social classes with more education. However, more educated classes may actually experience less of an excess demand for women's WiHo to the extent that higher education is positively associated with men's willingness to reboot their ideas about gender roles.

## Productivity and Related Characteristics of WiHo Workers

Building on Chap. 3 we now examine the possible effects that various characteristics of men and women could have on personal consumption. Any personal characteristic that increases the value of a WiHo worker to WiHo users is expected to be associated with a higher demand for WiHo. Therefore,

*Prediction C5 WiHo suppliers with higher human capital, and therefore expected to be more productive in household production, are likely to obtain higher prices for their WiHo and therefore to consume relatively more both before and after marriage. In contrast, the higher the WiHo price, the smaller the disposable income left for WiHo users and the lower their expected consumption both before and after marriage.*

Factors associated with higher productivity in home production include most characteristics known to be associated with labor productivity in general, such as knowledge, noncognitive skills, and health. It follows from Becker's theory of marriage that married individuals who are more productive in household production will consume relatively more. This also applies to consumption by singles anticipating marriage.

Higher prices for WiHo workers are also expected to originate from more capital-intensive household technology (this factor may not necessarily fit with the strict assumptions used in the derivation of Eq. 10.2). As the share of household production costs consisting of appliances and commercial services rises this leads to increases in the productivity of WiHo workers. This may be captured in rising prices of WiHo over time, compensating for shrinking $\alpha_h^Z$, portions of total costs of production going to WiHo.

## Compensating Differentials

The price of WiHo helps to explain demand and, therefore, so will compensating differentials in markets for WiHo. Such differentials are also likely to help explain relative consumption by men and women. Chapter 5 analyzed how such differentials are associated with variation in labor supply. The analysis was based on expected differentials in WiHo price due to variation in the willingness of WiHo workers to supply their labor to various types of people: less attractive WiHo users are expected to pay WiHo workers more to get them away from the more attractive WiHo users they compete with (see Grossbard-Shechtman 1984, 1993). For instance, if most people consider good looks, health, and intelligence as attractive traits, then WiHo users lacking these traits will have to pay WiHo prices that exceed the prices paid by good-looking smart WiHo users. Assuming traditional gender roles it follows that men who are substantially older than their wives will pay compensating differentials in WiHo price.

It follows that *ceteris paribus*

*Prediction C6 The personal consumption of women married to substantially older men is expected to be higher than the personal consumption of comparable women married to men closer to their own age*. There is evidence supporting this proposition in Browning et al. (1994) in terms of assignable consumption such as clothing. Also consistent with the prediction is Woolley's (2003) finding that in Ottawa, Canada, women married to substantially older men were more likely to be in charge of withdrawing cash from bank accounts than women married to men closer to their own age. Presumably, whoever is more likely to withdraw cash is also more likely to consume their favorite items relatively to what their spouse prefers. This finding supports the idea that women who are substantially younger than their husbands are in a relatively more advantageous bargaining position in their marriage, relative to women married to men close to their age. Older men may be paying compensating differentials judging from evidence from popular culture such as the Trophy Wives show and from the research on compensating differentials and labor supply mentioned in Chap. 5.

The prediction of compensating differentials in marriage does not follow from matching models of marriage that assume a continuum of individual men and women varying in their characteristics, such as Becker's matching model (1974) and Roth and Oliveira Sotomayor (1990), nor does it follow from household production models where individual producers of household production do not own portable general human capital and therefore cannot move from one marriage to the next.

Likewise, predictions follow regarding consumption and other forms of compensating differentials, such as compensations for overweight, lower education, etc.

## Implications for Singles

The theoretical perspective presented here leads not only to insights regarding married respondents but also regarding unmarried ones. For example, it follows that unmarried young women willing to be WiHo suppliers in marriage can expect large disposable incomes if they are willing to marry older men. Anticipating such future income, they may also consume more even when single. In contrast, relative to men intending to marry women their own age or older, men who intend to use the WiHo work of substantially younger women will have to accumulate larger assets prior to marriage, in order to afford higher WiHo prices. Likewise, men with a demand for WiHo and with facial features considered unattractive may have to pay higher prices for women's WiHo relative to men with pleasant facial features. Anecdotal evidence about less attractive grooms paying higher prices for women's WiHo can be traced back three centuries: in the eighteenth century British novelist Laurence Sterne's wrote about Tristram Shandy's grandparents need to pay an appropriate financial compensation for the deficiency of Mr. Shandy in the nose department (Sterne 1760).[14]

### Empirical Research on Price of WiHo?

The grandparents of Tristram Shandy were paying a form of bride-price, which is likely to be positively associated with the price for women's WiHo. Contemporary data on premarital payments in the Western world is more difficult to obtain. Today premarital financial agreements are uncommon in the West but data have been collected on type of marriage contract in France (Laferrere 2001), for example. They could be collected on prenuptial agreements in the USA. Bride-price payments continue to be common in many other parts of the world, including Sub-Saharan Africa. Examples of economic analyses of bride-price include Bronfenbrenner (1971), Rao (1993), and Bishai and Grossbard (2010).

Availability of data on prices for marriage or WiHo could open the door for interesting further studies of consumption and marriage. This theory would be helpful in guiding such research.

## What if Some Consumption Goods Are Shared?

So far it has been assumed that all consumption is private. Clearly not all consumption commodities $Z$ that are consumed in couples are of a private nature. Much of what makes people happy when they live in couple is shared, including satisfaction from children and sex. Recognizing that there are shared consumption commodities adds considerable complexity to the analysis that is beyond the scope of this book. Here are some directions for further research on that topic.[15]

There are a number of reasons why shared consumption commodities $Z$ add complexity. First, so far we separated between WiHo workers and WiHo users. But if consumption commodities are jointly consumed each spouse is likely to be both a WiHo worker and a WiHo user. Second, whenever WiHo is being performed, WiHo workers are likely to enjoy the fruits of their labor, implying rightward shifts in the supply of WiHo. Third, joint consumption may be accompanied with some

[14] John Treble contributed this citation.

[15] A more ambitious treatment of WiHo and shared consumption commodities is found in my WOC model in Grossbard-Shechtman (2003a).

joint production and possible complementarity between the WiHos of the partners. Fourth, availability of commercial substitutes may be a function of how private the consumption is. For instance, it will be more difficult to hire good substitutes for parenting WiHo involving joint consumption than for food-production WiHo involving private consumption.

The assumption of shared $Z$ is likely to affect the supply of WiHo not only because the WiHo worker enjoys his labor more, leading his supply to lie to the right of his supply of WiHo assuming the spouse's $Z$ is a private commodity.[16] In addition, when $Z$ is a shared commodity, the WiHo worker is likely to obtain some full income from the spouse in the form of contributions of $Z$ or commercial goods. With higher full income the WiHo worker may supply less WiHo. These two effects on supply of WiHo may cancel out and the net effect of shared $Z$ consumption on WiHo workers' supply is not clear. To the extent that supply by many market participants shifts to the left, WiHo prices will be higher; if it shifts to the right, WiHo prices will be lower than when all consumption is private. Assuming shared $Z$ is also likely to affect the demand for WiHo and the functioning of markets for WiHo that depend on the assumption that prices are given.

Had we taken into account that consumption commodities are often shared, we would have reached fewer predictions. For example, in the case of Prediction C4' about asymmetric effects of changes in spouse's income for men and women, if men and women share the same consumption commodities $Z$ there will be less of a conflict of interest between genders and men are less likely to oppose increases in women's income from work or government.

*Cultural Influences and Love* To the extent that culture affects individual preferences for consumption of commodities $Z$—including the degree to which they are private or shared—it could be in the best interest of men and women to convince members of the other gender that they could benefit from performing more WiHo at the same WiHo price. One way for men to get that is to convince women to appreciate more what men like to consume (let us say try to convince women to like action movies better). Women could do the same (for instance, try to get men to go to church more).

In a heterosexual context, by changing the preferences of the other gender, individuals can get more WiHo time, more goods, or more resources from them. In the *Feminine Mystique*, Betty Friedan (1963) argued that the ideology of "good homemaking" would get women to become happier doing laundry or cleaning floors. She mostly saw commercial firms behind this manipulation of preferences. Using the economic terms presented here one can say that perhaps men created the good homemaking ideology that transformed their private consumption commodity "clean socks" into an element of a new $Z$ called "good homemaking" and entering women's utility functions in the 1950s. Thereby men got women to supply more spousal labor, which pushed the price of women's WiHo lower and made it cheaper for husbands to get their socks cleaned.

[16] Another factor affecting the disutility of spousal labor is whether small amounts of WiHo are being supplied. This idea can also be found in Blau et al. (1998, Ch. 3). Also, see Amy Wax (1998).

Likewise, it is in the best interest of WiHo workers to make WiHo users want their services more. The ideology of the "good provider" has traditionally encouraged men to earn more so they will want to consume more *Z* commodities that use WiHo. Higher demand would then lead to higher WiHo prices and thus benefits WiHo workers.

More generally, we can use the big L word, *Love*, so often applied to discourse about the topics covered in this book. Let us define it the way that Becker (1974a, p. S12) defines "caring": "if [man] M cares about [woman] F, M's utility would depend on the commodity consumption of F as well as on his own." In other words, if a woman loves her spouse, the spouse's *Z* enters her utility function. It follows that the bigger WiHo worker F's love for M the more she will be willing to supply the *Z* that M wants. Likewise, the more a man M loves a woman F, and the larger the weight of her *Z* in his utility function, the more he will be willing to do WiHo work for her (his supply shifts to the right with the love he has for her).

More emphasis on love will affect both demand and supply of WiHo. Willingness to supply WiHo will decrease if the WiHo worker expects to be paid more because the partner loves him more. To the extent that men love their partner more, and gender roles are traditional, this would translate into more generous WiHo payments, which implies—in a traditional context—a smaller supply of women's WiHo. So to the extent that men manipulate ideologies to get more WiHo out of women they are better off making them "love" homemaking than making everyone more inclined to love in general.

If the propensity to love one's partner is emphasized by the culture, then even before F or M meets their mates they will be ready to love them in the sense of being willing to include a partner's *Z* in their utility function. This implies rightward shifts in supply of WiHo at the market level, and rightward shifts in demand for WiHo. Therefore, one way for culture or society to encourage household production is to foster the willingness to love a spouse in an abstract way, even before individuals are ready to form couples.

Governments and organized religious groups often try to influence supply of WiHo, its demand, or both. The modernization process has been accompanied by an increased role of governments and a decreased role of religious organizations in markets for WiHo. For example, after World War II the US forced the Japanese to legislate that marriage should be motivated by mutual love rather than determined by parental authority (see Joy Hendry 1985). The intention was to weaken traditional institutions regulating marriage and related to the political system. However, this attempt to legislate love backfired, as it led to widespread opposition to USA legal intervention.

Increasingly the media has been influencing preferences related to consumption and willingness to supply or demand WiHo. Consider romantic movies such as Aladdin or fairy tales such as Cinderella that encourage children to be willing to love a partner they have not yet met. By encouraging larger supply of WiHo and demand for WiHo, such cultural expressions could encourage more home production. However, as I have argued elsewhere, romantic ideology of this kind has its drawbacks when it comes to long-term stability of the marriage institution and ability to pick the right partner (see Grossbard-Shechtman 2003b).

Interestingly, over the period 1967–1991 the emphasis on love in marriage seems to have grown. Women's willingness to marry without love decreased significantly. In the 1960s, sociologist William Kephart (1967) asked thousands of college students this question: "If a man (woman) had all other qualities you desired, would you marry this person if you were not in love with him (her)?" At the time, surprisingly high numbers of women (76 %) and men (35 %) said they would forgo love in favor of other important qualities in a marriage partner. More than 20 years later, Allgeier and Wiederman (1991) asked this same question and only 14 % of men said they would marry without love (9 % of women). Willingness to enter a loveless marriage thus dropped from 76 to 9 % for women and from 35 to 14 % for men.[17] The much larger drop in women's willingness to marry without love (relative to that of men) is remarkable. Could it be related to the drop in the asymmetry of gender roles when it comes to WiHo? Let us not forget that the 1960s were also the years that John Kennedy said to Eleanor Roosevelt: "we want to be sure that women are used as effectively as they can to provide a better life for our people, in addition to meeting their primary responsibility, which is in the home." (Rosen 2014). In some cases for women in the 1960s, the ideological brainwash meant entering marriage out of lack of better ways to make a living; for men, it just meant working harder to pay for more WiHo than they really wanted.

Cultural and ideological factors are not necessarily exogeneous. As argued in Heer and Grossbard-Shechtman (1981) the feminist movement may have benefited from the entry of cohorts of women with low sex ratios into dating and marriage markets. It is also possible that as men need women less because of more widespread availability of commercial substitutes they are less willing to marry without love.[18]

## Conclusion

Integrating the concept of WiHo and its price into a theory of consumption has led to valuable insights. Many of those are testable, including predictions regarding gender and marital status differences in consumption levels and demand elasticities of commercial products. Predictions regarding consumption and sex ratios, and consumption and compensating differentials are also testable. This chapter has only touched the tip of the iceberg of potential implications of the concept of WiHo for the study of consumption. Much further work is needed. At the theoretical level, the basic model I have used, assuming private consumption commodities, can benefit from further work such as examining the effect of dropping some of the assumptions (dropping the assumption of constant returns to scale, for example). More importantly, there is a need for further modeling of consumption, WiHo and its price, and shared consumption commodities. It would also be useful to adapt some

[17] I thank Marina Adshade (who can be followed @dollarsandsex) for this insight.

[18] I thank Marina Adshade for this insight.

of the insights presented here assuming competitive conditions to the circumstances characterizing a typical marriage. After marriage, ties between husband and wife are likely to develop, each spouse developing somewhat of a monopoly with respect to the other. One expects that after marriage, marriage market conditions will continue to be influential as they influence remarriage options and therefore internal bargaining. However, after marriage a theory assuming competitive markets for spousal labor becomes less applicable.

Finally, all the predictions presented here are testable. It is my hope that the ideas presented here will inspire some much needed empirical tests.

## Derivation of a Demand for Goods

The demand for input $x$ is derived from the following consumer optimization problem.[19] The subscript used for the WiHo user is $i$ and for the WiHo worker $j$.

$$\begin{cases} Max\mathrm{U}_i\left(Z_i\right) subject\ to \\ Z_i = Z_i\left(x_i, s_i, h_j\right) \\ 1 = l_i + s_i \\ I_i + w_i l_i = y_j h_j + p_i x_i, \end{cases} \qquad (10.3)$$

where $Z$ is a vector of privately consumed goods that individual $i$ can produce with three inputs: a vector of commercial inputs $x$, leisure time $s$, and $h_j$, which stands for WiHo supplied by a (potential) spouse $j$. Leisure is own time in household production. It is assumed that the production function has constant returns to scale.

In the context of a micromodel with many types of WiHo users $i$ and many types of WiHo workers $j$ the problem becomes:

$$\begin{aligned} &\mathrm{Max}\, U_i\left(Z_{ij}\right) \\ &\text{subject to } Z_{ij} = Z_{ij}\left(x_{ij}, s_{ij}, h_{ij}\right) \\ &1 = l_{ij} + s_{ij}, \\ &\text{and } I_{ij} + w_{ij} l_{ij} = y_{ji} h_{ji} + p_i x_i. \end{aligned} \qquad (10.4)$$

Using the definition of full income found in Becker (1965), the time and income constraints can be restated as full income constraint $F_{ij} = I_{ij} + w_{ij} = \Pi_{ij} Z_{ij}$, where $\Pi$ is the implicit price of the composite good consumed by the individual. From here on I omit the subscript "$i$" or "$ij$" in order to make the presentation less cumbersome. The following are all personal functions of an individual $i$. I still use subscript $j$ for the spouse.

[19] The model also leads to a demand for WiHo contributed by a spouse, $hj$, and a supply of labor $li$. The model could be extended to include the derivation of a supply of own WiHo, $hj$.

*Step 1: the real full income effect on the demand for the product. Assume* $F(\Pi) = \Pi Z$. We take the differential, which gives

$$dF = \Pi\, dZ + Z\, d\Pi .$$

We now divide each side by F, which gives $\frac{dF}{F} = \frac{\Pi\, dZ}{\Pi Z} + \frac{Z\, d\Pi}{\Pi Z}$. Denoting percentage changes with dots above the letters, we obtain

$$\dot{F} = \dot{Z} + \dot{\Pi}. \tag{10.5}$$

*Step 2: separating the full income effect into an effect of income and wage.* There are two sources of income: nonwork income $I$ and earnings from wages. Given that this is full income and total time = 1 we obtain $F = I + w$. We differentiate: $dF = dI + dw$ and divide both sides by $F$, which gives:

$$\frac{dF}{F} = \frac{I\, dI}{FI} + \frac{w\, dw}{Fw} \quad \text{or} \quad \dot{F} = \dot{I}\frac{I}{F} + \dot{w}\frac{w}{F}. \tag{10.6}$$

*Step 3: decomposing the implicit price effect.* We assume that the price of household production, Π, is the average cost, an assumption that is fitting when the production function exhibits constant returns to scale and the marginal cost equals the average c.ost. Then

$AC = \Pi = \frac{TC}{Z} = \frac{ws + px + yh_j}{Z}$. We take the differential: $d\Pi = \frac{s.dw}{Z} + \frac{x.dp}{Z} + \frac{h.dy_j}{Z}$, and then divide by Π, which gives $\frac{d\Pi}{\Pi} = \frac{s.dw}{\Pi Z} + \frac{x.dp}{\Pi Z} + \frac{h.dy_j}{\Pi Z}$.

Now, $\Pi Z = C$. We also divide and multiply *dw* by *w, dp* by *p, and* $dy_j$ by $y_j$. Consequently, $\frac{d\Pi}{\Pi} = \frac{sw}{C}\frac{dw}{w} + \frac{px}{C}\frac{dp}{p} + \frac{hy_j}{C}\frac{dy_j}{y_j}$, which can be denoted as

$$\dot{\Pi} = \alpha_s \dot{w} + \alpha_x \dot{p} + \alpha_h \dot{y}_j, \tag{10.7}$$

where $\alpha_k$ is the share of input $k$ in the costs of production. We now replace Π in Eq. 10.3 with 10.7 and replace $F$ with Eq. 10.4. This gives:

$$\dot{Z} = \frac{I}{F}\dot{I} + \frac{w}{F}\dot{w} - \alpha_s \dot{w} - \alpha_x \dot{p} - \alpha_h \dot{y}_j . \tag{10.8}$$

*Step 4: derived demand for input x.* Given that the production function has constant returns to scale the scale effect is separable from an effect of substitution in production. An elasticity of substitution is defined for every two factors of production: for substitution between $x$ and $h_j$ we define elasticity of substitution $\sigma_{xh}$, and for substitution between $x$ and $s$ we define $\sigma_{xs}$. These elasticities are based on technical substitution in production.

It can be shown that when the production function has constant returns to scale the following is the case:

$$\dot{x} = \dot{Z} - (\alpha_s\sigma_{xs} + \alpha_h\sigma_{xh})\dot{p} + \alpha_s\sigma_{xs}\dot{w} + \alpha_h\sigma_{xh}\dot{y}_j. \tag{10.9}$$

*Step 5: combining steps 3 and 4.* We now replace the percentage change in production, $\dot{Z}$, with Eq. 10.8, and combine terms. This gives Eq. 10.4, reproduced below:

$$\dot{x} = \frac{I}{F}\dot{I} - (\alpha_x^Z + \alpha_s^Z\sigma_{xs} + \alpha_h^Z\sigma_{xh})\dot{p} + \left[\frac{w}{F} + (\sigma_{xs} - 1)\alpha_s^Z\right]\dot{w} + (\sigma_{xh} - 1)\alpha_h^Z\dot{y}_j.$$

## References

Allgeier, E. R., and M. W. Wiederman. 1991. Love and mate selection in the 1990s. *Free Inquiry* 11:25–27.

Apps, P., and R. Rees. 1997. Collective labor supply and household production. *Journal of Political Economy* 105:178–190.

Becker, G. S. 1965. A theory of the allocation of time. *Economic Journal* 75:493–515.

Becker, G. S. 1973. A theory of marriage: Part I. *Journal of Political Economy* 81:813–846.

Becker, G. S. 1974a. A theory of marriage: Part II. *Journal of Political Economy* 82:S11–S26.

Becker, G. S. 1974b. A theory of social interactions. *Journal of Political Economy* 82 (6):1063–1093.

Bishai, D., and S. Grossbard. 2010. Far above rubies: The association between bride price and extramarital sexual relations in Uganda. *Journal of Population Economics* 23 (4): 1177–1188.

Blau, F. D., M. A. Ferber, and A. E. Winkler. 1998. *The economics of women, men, and work*. 3rd ed. Englewood Cliffs: Prentice Hall.

Bonke, J. 2015. Pooling of income and sharing of consumption within households. *Review of Economics of the Household* 13 (1). (Forthcoming)

Bronfenbrenner, M. 1971. A note on the economics of the marriage market. *Journal of Political Economy* 79:1424–1425.

Brown, P. H. 2009. Dowry and intrahousehold bargaining: Evidence from China. *Journal of Human Resources* 44 (1): 25–46.

Browning, M., F. Bourguignon, C. Pierre-Andre, and V. Lechene. 1994. Incomes and outcomes: A structural model of intra-household allocation. *Journal of Political Economy* 102 (6): 1067–1096.

Chaloupka, F. J., and R. L. Pacula. 1998. An examination of gender and race differences in youth smoking responsiveness to price and tobacco control policies. National Bureau of Economic Research, Working Paper 6541, April.

Chen, Z., and F. Woolley. 2001. A Cournot – Nash model of family decision making. *The Economic Journal* 111 (474):722–748.

Chiappori, P.-A. 1988. Rational household labor supply. *Econometrica* 56:63–90.

Chiappori, P.-A. 1992. Collective labor supply and welfare. *Journal of Political Economy* 100:437–467.

Chiappori, P.-A. 1997. Introducing household production in collective models of labor supply. *Journal of Political Economy* 105:191–209.

Chiappori, P.-A, B. Fortin and G. Lacroix 1998. Household labor supply, sharing rule and the marriage market. Ms., University of Chicago, May.

Christian, T., and I. Rashad. 2009. Trends in US food prices, 1950–2007. *Economics & Human Biology* 7 (1): 113–120.

Cohen, R. 1999. Cut-rate rationale. The Ethicist Column, New York Times Magazine, 18. July, p. 20.

Davis, G. C. 2014. Food at home production and consumption: Implications for nutrition quality and policy. *Review of Economics of the Household* 12 (3): 565–588.

Folbre, Nancy. 1994. *Who pays for the kids? Gender and the structures of constraint*. London: Routledge.

Friedan, Betty. 1963. *The feminine mystique*. New York: W. W. Norton & Company.

Gimenez-Nadal, J. I., and A. Sevilla-Sanz. 2012. Trends in time allocation: A cross-country analysis. *European Economic Review* 56 (6): 1338–1359.

Goldin, Claudia. 1988. Marriage bars: Discrimination against married women workers, 1920's to 1950's. NBER Paper 2747, Oct.

Goldin, Claudia. 1990. *Understanding the gender gap*. Oxford: Oxford University Press.

Greenwood, J., A. Seshadri, and M. Yorukoglu. 2005. Engines of liberation. *Review of Economic Studies* 72 (1): 109–133.

Griskevicius, V., J. M. Tybur, J. M. Ackerman, A. W. Delton, T. E. Robertson, and A. E. White. 2012. The financial consequences of too many men: Sex ratio effects on saving, borrowing, and spending. *Journal of Personality and Social Psychology* 102 (1): 69.

Gronau, Reuben. 1977. Leisure, home production, and work—The theory of the allocation of time revisited. *Journal of Political Economy* 85:1099–1124.

Grossbard-Shechtman, Amyra. 1984. A theory of allocation of time in markets for labor and marriage. *Economic Journal* 94:863–882.

Grossbard-Shechtman, Shoshana. 1993. *On the economics of marriage*. Boulder: Westview Press.

Grossbard-Shechtman, Shoshana. 2003a. A consumer theory with competitive markets for work in marriage. *Journal of Socio-Economics* 31 (6): 609–645.

Grossbard-Shechtman, Shoshana. 2003b. Marriage and the economy. In *Marriage and the economy: Theory and evidence from advanced industrial societies,* ed. S Grossbard-Shechtman. New York: Cambridge University Press.

Grossman, Michael. 1972. On the concept of health capital and the demand for health. *Journal of Political Economy* 80 (2): 223–255.

Heer, D. M., and A. Grossbard-Shechtman. 1981. The impact of the female marriage squeeze and the contraceptive revolution on sex roles and the women's liberation movement in the United States, 1960 to 1975. *Journal of Marriage and the Family* 43:49–65.

Hendry, Joy. 1985. Marriage in a recently industrialized society: Japan. In *Contemporary marriage: Comparative perspectives on a changing institution,* ed. K. Davis and A. Grossbard-Shechtman. New York: Russell Sage Publications.

Hersch, Joni. 2003. Marriage and household production. In *Marriage and the economy,* ed. S. Grossbard-Shechtman. Cambridge: Cambridge University Press.

Hersch, Joni. 2009. Home production and wages: Evidence from the American time use survey. *Review of Economics of the Household* 7:159–178.

Hersch, J., and L. S. Stratton. 2000. Household specialization and the male marriage wage premium. *Industrial and Labor Relations Review* 54:78.

Kephart, W. M. 1967. Some correlates of romantic love. *Journal of Marriage and the Family* 29:470–479.

Kureishi, Wataru, and Midori Wakabayashi. 2013. What motivates single women to save? The case of Japan. *Review of Economics of the Household* 11:681–704.

Laferrere, Anne. 2001. Marriage settlements. *Scandinavian Journal of Economics* 103: 485–504.

Lancaster, K. J. 1966. A new approach to consumer theory. *Journal of Political Economy* 74:132–157.

Lee, Jungmin, and Mark Pocock. 2007. Intrahousehold allocation of household finances. *Review of Economics of the Household* 5 (1): 41–58.

Lundberg, S., and R. A. Pollak. 1993. Separate sphere bargaining and the marriage market. *Journal of Political Economy* 101:988–1010.

Lundberg, S., R. A. Pollak, and T. J. Wales. 1997. Do husbands and wives pool their resources? Evidence from the U.K. child benefit. *Journal of Human Resources* 32:463–480.

McElroy, M. B. 1990. The empirical content of Nash-Bargained household behavior. *Journal of Human Resources* 25:559–583.

McElroy, M. B., and M. J. Horney. 1981. Nash bargained household decisions: Toward a generalization of the theory of demand. *International Economic Review* 22:333–349.

Mincer, Jacob. 1962. Labor force participation of married women: A study of labor supply. In *Aspects of labor economics,* ed. H. Gregg Lewis. Princeton: Princeton University Press.

Pahl, Jan. 1983. The allocation of money and the structuring of inequality within marriage. *Sociological Review* 13 (2): 237–262.

Porter, Maria. 2015. How do sex ratios in China influence marriage decisions and intrahousehold resource allocation? Review of Economics of the Household. http://link.springer.com/article/10.1007/s11150-014-9262-9. (Forthcoming)

Rao, V. 1993. The rising price of husbands: A hedonic analysis of dowry increases in rural India. *Journal of Political Economy* 101 (4): 666–677.

Rosen, R. J. 2014. Eleanor Roosevelt talks to John F. Kennedy about the status of women in society. *The Atlantic* Feb 19.

Roth, A. E., and M. A. Oliveira Sotomayor. 1990. *Two-matching: A study in game-theoretic modeling and analysis*. Cambridge: Cambridge University Press.

Sevilla-Sanz, A., J. I. Gimenez-Nadal, and C. Fernandez. 2010. Gender roles and the division of unpaid work in Spanish households. *Feminist Economics* 16 (4): 137–184

Sterne, Laurence. 1760. The life and opinions of Tristram Shandy, Gentleman. U.K.: Ann Ward.

Stigler, George. 1946. Domestic servants in the United States, 1900–1940. Occasional Paper No. 24, National Bureau of Economic Research.

Thomas, Duncan. 1990. Intra-household resource allocation: An inferential approach. *Journal of Human Resources* 25:635–664.

Wax, Amy L. 1998. Bargaining in the shadow of the market: Is there a future for egalitarian marriage? *Virginia Law Review* 84 (4):509–672.

Woolley, Frances. 2003. Marriage and control over money. In *Marriage and the economy,* ed. S. Grossbard-Shechtman. Cambridge: Cambridge University Press.

# Chapter 11
# Savings, Marriage, and Work-in-Household

The conventional economic theory has had some difficulty providing a good understanding of the determinants of savings. For instance, there are currently no good explanations for the considerable decrease in personal savings rates in the USA over the past few decades or for the large differences in personal savings observed among industrialized countries (see, for example, Auerbach and Kotlikoff 1990; Guidolin and La Jeunesse 2007). At the same time, there are growing concerns about the lack of effectiveness of conventional policy instruments, such as tax incentives, in promoting personal savings (see, for example, Tanzi and Zee 1999; Hungerford 2006).

Some of the most common explanations for variations in personal savings are related to demographic characteristics such as the age structure of the population, life expectancy, labor force participation rate of the aged, (see, for example, Horioka 1997; Horioka and Wan 2007; Horioka and Terada-Hagiwara 2010), retirement age, family size, percentage of working age population (see, for example, Smith 1990), and percentage of women in the labor force (see, for example, Apps and Rees 2010).

A number of studies have investigated the focus of this chapter: the association between marriage and personal savings. That marriage and divorce are related to savings has also been established, for example, by Auerbach and Kotlikoff (1990), Lupton and Smith (2003), and Zissimopoulos et al. (forthcoming, 2015). Men preparing for marriage appear to save more (see Horioka 1987 on the effects of marriage-related expenses on savings); women preparing for marriage appear to save less (Kureishi and Wakabayashi 2013).

Section 11.1 in this chapter presents a macro-level model showing some of the ways by which marriage (including cohabitation) and divorce could explain savings. It is an inter-temporal model of individual savings behavior that considers intra-marriage financial distributions and that was developed jointly with Alfredo M. Pereira. In Sect. 11.2 these intra-marriage transfers are linked to the concepts of WiHo, WiHo price, and WiHo market models presented in Chaps. 2 and 3. The primary predictions found in that section deal with the savings effects of sex ratios, WiHo-related productivity indicators, older age, and age differences.



S. Grossbard, *The Marriage Motive: A Price Theory of Marriage*,
DOI 10.1007/978-1-4614-1623-4_11

## A Model of Savings, Marriage and Divorce[1]

We consider three periods $i$: youth/period 1, midlife/period 2, and old-age/period 3. In contrast with the previous models in this book, here we ignore time use. Consumption of commercial goods is the only sources of utility. The agent maximizes an individual inter-temporal utility function (11.1) defined on consumption $c_i$, which satisfies positive and decreasing marginal utility and constant absolute risk aversion. Future utility is discounted by a factor $\delta$ that captures impatience.

$$Max[U(c_1)+\delta U(c_2)+\delta^2 U(c_3)]. \tag{11.1}$$

The agent derives income from two sources: work and interest on savings. It is assumed that the wage $w$ and the return on savings $r$ are constant over time. The agent earns the same wage in each period. In the absence of intergenerational altruism and/or uncertainty as to the time of death, there are no savings in period 3.

We assume that the agent is single in period 1. In periods 2 and 3, the budget constraint depends on marital status. There is a probability $p_2$ that the agent will remain single in period 2 and a probability $p_3$ (for simplicity referred to as the probability of divorce) that the agent will be single, widowed, or divorced in the third period. It is assumed that $p_2$ and $p_3$ are exogenous and independent and that divorce does not entail extra expenses or income.

Consumption and saving decisions are personal, not household based.[2] If the individual is married, consumption is a function of the individual's disposable income defined as $\gamma w$, where $\gamma$ is a net intra-household transfer parameter. If $\gamma > 1$ the agent is a net recipient of intra-marriage transfers and disposable income exceeds earned income. If $\gamma < 1$, the agent is making intra-marriage transfers and disposable income is lower than earned income.

It is very likely that the sign of $\gamma$ depends on whether an agent is a WiHo worker or a WiHo user: the person performing household production on behalf of a spouse is often compensated for this in material terms (see more on WiHo in Chap. 2). The budget constraints for each period are:

$$\begin{aligned}
&w = c_1 + s_1 && \\
&w+(1+r)s_1 = c_2 + s_2 && \text{with probability } p_2 \\
&\gamma w+(1+r)s_1 = c_2 + s_2 && \text{with probability } (1-p_2) \\
&w+(1+r)s_2 = c_3 && \text{with probability } p_3 \\
&\gamma w+(1+r)s_2 = c_3 && \text{with probability } (1-p_3).
\end{aligned} \tag{11.2}$$

[1] The analytical framework in this section, Predictions C7, C8, C9 and C10, and the mathematical derivations are taken from Alfredo Marvão Pereira and Shoshana Grossbard "Savings and Family Values," Working Paper, July 2014. Some additional materials come from Shoshana Grossbard and Alfredo M Pereira "Will Women Save more than Men? A Theoretical Model of Savings and Marriage," CESifo Working Paper No. 3146, August 2010, Predictions C7', C8', C9' and C10' are my own.

[2] In South Korea all savings by married individuals have to be personal (see Lee and Pocock 2007).

The optimal level of savings $(s_1, s_2)$ is obtained by maximizing (11.1) subject to (11.2) and can be presented in general terms as the ArgMax of V:

$$V = U(w-s_1)+\delta\{p_2U[w+(1+r)s_1-s_2]+(1-p_2)U[\gamma w+(1+r)s_1-s_2]\}$$
$$+\delta^2\{p_3U[w+(1+r)s_2]+(1-p_3\}U[\gamma w+(1+r)s_2] \quad (11.3)$$

and $(s_1, s_2)$ are determined by:

$$\frac{\partial V}{\partial s_1} = -U'(w-s)+\delta(1+r)$$
$$\{p_2U'[w+(1+r)s_1-s_2]+(1-p_2)U'[\gamma w+(1+r)s_1-s_2]\}=0, \quad (11.4)$$

$$\frac{\partial V}{\partial s_2} = -\delta\{p_2U'[w+(1+r)s_1-s_2]+(1-p_2)U'[\gamma w+(1+r)s_1-s_2]\}$$
$$+\delta(1+r)\{p_3U'[w+(1+r)s_2]+(1-p_3)U'[\gamma w+(1+r)s_2]\}=0. \quad (11.5)$$

These conditions are denoted in an implicit form by $F_1(s_1, s_2; p_2, p_3)=0$ and $F_2(s_1, s_2; p_2, p_3)=0$, and the effects of the probabilities of marriage and divorce on savings behavior are obtained using the implicit function theorem and the related information in the Appendix.

## *Probability of Marriage and Savings While Young and Single*

Keeping in mind that in the model *p* is the probability of staying single and that in period 1 (youth) everyone is single, it follows from the model that:

*Prediction C7* Savings at youth decrease (increase) with the probability of marriage for agents expecting to be net recipients (contributors) of intra-household transfers.

**Proof:** Using standard techniques we obtain

$$\frac{\partial s_1}{\partial p_2} = \left(-\frac{\partial F_1}{\partial p_2}\frac{\partial F_2}{\partial s_2}+\frac{\partial F_1}{\partial p_2}\frac{\partial F_1}{\partial s_2}\right) \Big/ \det(F_s). \quad (11.6)$$

It can be shown that

$$sign\left(\frac{\partial s_1}{\partial p_2}\right) = sign\left\{\frac{\partial F_1}{\partial p_2}+\frac{\partial F_2}{\partial p_2}\left[\frac{\partial F_1}{\partial s_2}\Big/\left(-\frac{\partial F_1}{\partial s_2}\right)\right]\right\},$$

where the term in the square bracket is positive. The sign of $\frac{\partial s_1}{\partial p_2}$ is ambiguous because $sign\frac{\partial F_1}{\partial p_2} \neq sign\frac{\partial F_1}{\partial p_2}$ regardless of the value of $\gamma$.

Now it can be shown that:

$$sign\frac{\partial F_1}{\partial p_2} = sign\left\{(1+r) - \left[\frac{\partial F_1}{\partial s_2} \Big/ \left(-\frac{\partial F_2}{\partial s_2}\right)\right]\right\} if\, \gamma > 1 and$$

$$sign\frac{\partial s_1}{\partial p_2} \neq sign\left\{(1+r) - \left[\frac{\partial F_1}{\partial s_2} \Big/ \left(-\frac{\partial F_2}{\partial s_2}\right)\right]\right\} if\, \gamma < 1.$$

From the derivatives above and (11.12) it can be seen that $\left[\frac{\partial F_1}{\partial s_2} \Big/ \left(-\frac{\partial F_2}{\partial s_2}\right)\right] = (1+r)B$, where $0 < B < 1$.

Accordingly,

$$\frac{\partial s_1}{\partial p_2} > 0 if\, \gamma > 1.$$

**QED** The intuition behind Prediction C7 is that the probability of marriage has opposite effects on the savings of agents expected to receive intra-household transfers and on those expected to make such transfers. The same earned wage earned in periods 1 and 2 will enable more consumption for those with a $\gamma$ exceeding one but it will translate into less consumption for those whose disposable income decreases if they marry. Those expected to pay transfers in marriage save more in youth to prepare for their extra expenses; those expected to gain income in marriage can afford to save less while single.

*Gender, Probability of Marriage, and Savings While Young and Single* In societies with traditional gender roles women tend to obtain intra-marriage transfers from men, generally in return for supplying more WiHo. This implies that for women $\gamma$ is larger than one while it is smaller than one for men. There may be many other gender differences influencing savings rate, such as different discount rates (see Croson and Gneezy 2009) but ignoring those and assuming that the genders only differ in their $\gamma$ it follows that:

*Prediction C7′* Assuming traditional gender roles, the higher their probability of marriage (i.e., a lower $p_2$) the less young women will save and the more young men will save.

*Evidence* Japan has a traditional culture in which most household production responsibilities fall on women while men are expected to share more of their income with their wives than the other way around (Hendry 1985). It is thus a society where prediction C7′ is likely to apply. Indeed, a recent Japanese study found that single women with a higher likelihood of marriage save less than their counterparts with a lower likelihood of marriage (Kureishi and Wakabayashi 2013). It is also the case that according to Japan's 2008 Family Income and Expenditure Survey (Statistics Bureau, Japan 2008), the savings rate for single male workers aged 34 or younger was 31.9% single, which is considerably more than the savings rate of 22.4% for single women in that age range. This finding is consistent with high proportions of young Japanese planning to marry.

In the USA women's median age at marriage was 21.1 in 1975 and the personal savings rate then stood at around 13.9%. By 2012 the median age at marriage for women was 27.1 and the savings rate had dropped to 7.1% (source for median age at marriage is Census; source for savings rate is Federal Reserve Bank of St. Louis), so we see that savings rate and median age at marriage are inversely related. The median age at marriage and the probability of marriage are also inversely related. Therefore, we see that the higher the prevalence of marriage (lower $p_2$) the higher the overall household savings rate. This is consistent with Prediction C7′ if the national personal savings rate reflects the savings rate of young single men. Further research on this topic would be useful.

One reason people save is to buy housing. Real estate is also one form in which wealth is held, and savings are often measured as changes in wealth over time (see Lupton and Smith 2003). Many cultures following traditional gender roles have encouraged men to acquire housing in order to qualify for marriage. This expectation was historically more prevalent in Italy than in some other Western countries. For instance, in 1990 on average total Italian household savings as a percentage of household disposable income stood at 21.7%, much higher than 8.2% for the USA and most other Western countries. However, by 2010 Italy's household savings rate had dropped to 4.9% while the US savings rate dropped by a much smaller proportion, to 5.9%.[3] During this period there was also a retreat from marriage in both countries but a proportionally larger one in Italy: In Italy in 1991 69.1% of men ages 30–34 had been married at least once. By 2010 that percentage had dropped to 38.8%, i.e., the percentage in 2010 was 56.15% of what it had been in 1991. In the USA the corresponding percentages of men ever married by age 34 were 73.8% in 1990 and 63% in 2010 (i.e., 85.4% of what it had been in 1990).[4]

## *Probability of Marriage and Savings in Midlife*

It also follows from the model that:

*Prediction C8* Midlife savings increase (decrease) with the probability of marriage for agents expecting to be net recipients (contributors) of intra-marriage transfers.

---

[3] OECD (2014), "Household savings" (indicator). DOI: 10.1787/cfc6f499-en.

[4] Data for Italy were not available for 1990. The corresponding percentages ever married by age 34 for women were 82.2 and 57.9% for Italy and 81.8 and 72.8% for the U.S. The data were obtained from UN world marriage data at http://www.un.org/esa/population/publications/WMD2012/MainFrame.html. For the U.S. in 2010 the percent ever married was computed using the US census table creator at http://www.census.gov/cps/data/cpstablecreator.html.

**Proof:**

$$\frac{\partial s_2}{\partial p_2} = \left( -\frac{\partial F_1}{\partial s_1} \cdot \frac{\partial F_2}{\partial p_2} + \frac{\partial F_1}{\partial p_2} \cdot \frac{\partial F_2}{\partial s_1} \right) / \det(F_s). \tag{11.7}$$

It can be shown that

$$sign\left(\frac{\partial s_2}{\partial p_2}\right) = sign\left\{\frac{\partial F_1}{\partial p_2} + \frac{\partial F_2}{\partial p_2}\left[\left(-\frac{\partial F_1}{\partial s_1}\right) \Big/ \left(-\frac{\partial F_2}{\partial s_2}\right)\right]\right\},$$

where the term in the square bracket is positive.

It can also be shown that

$$sign\left(\frac{\partial F_2}{\partial s_2}\right) = sign\left\{(1+r) - \left[\left(-\frac{\partial F_1}{\partial s_1}\right) \Big/ \left(\frac{\partial F_2}{\partial s_1}\right)\right]\right\} if\, \gamma > 1,$$

$$sign\left(\frac{\partial F_2}{\partial s_2}\right) \neq sign\left\{(1+r) - \left[\left(\frac{\partial F_1}{\partial s_1}\right) \Big/ \frac{\partial F_2}{\partial s_1}\right]\right\} if\, \gamma < 1.$$

From the derivatives above and (11.16) it can be seen that $\left[\left(-\frac{\partial F_1}{\partial s_1}\right) \Big/ \frac{\partial F_2}{\partial s_1}\right] = (1+r) + C$, where $C > 0$. Accordingly,

$$\frac{\partial s_2}{\partial p_2} < 0 if\, \gamma > 1,$$

$$\frac{\partial s_2}{\partial p_2} > 0 if\, \gamma < 1.$$

**QED** The impact of a change in the probability of marriage on individual savings in midlife is the opposite of its impact on savings in youth.

*Gender, Probability of Marriage, and Savings in Midlife* In societies with traditional gender roles men are the ones expected to make intra-marriage financial transfers to women. Therefore:

*Prediction C8′* Assuming traditional gender roles the more women save in midlife the higher their probability of marriage (i.e., a lower $p_2$) and the less men save less in midlife the higher their probability of marriage.

## *Probability of Marriage and Lifetime Savings*

*Prediction C9* Consider an economy with significant rates of divorce and incidence of intra-marriage transfers. Consider an agent with a relatively high rate of impatience. Then, an increase in the probability of marriage increases (decreases) the present value of lifetime savings for agents expecting to be net recipients (contributors) of intra-marriage transfers. The net effect of an increase in the probability of marriage on all personal savings is not clear: It will depend on whether or not effects on recipients of transfers exceed effects on contributors of such transfers.

**Proof:**

From (11.6), (11.7), (11.13), and (11.19)

$$sign\left[\frac{\partial s_1}{\partial p_2}+\frac{1}{1+r}\frac{\partial s_2}{\partial p_2}\right]=sign\left[\frac{\partial F_1}{\partial s_2}-(1+r)^2\frac{\partial F_2}{\partial s_2}\right] if\, \gamma>1, (\neq if\, \gamma<1).$$

In turn, using (11.10) and (11.18)

$$sign\left[\frac{\partial F_1}{\partial s_1}-(1+r)^2\frac{\partial F_2}{\partial s_2}\right]=sign[U''(w-s_1)$$
$$-\delta^2(1+r)^4\left\{p_3U''[w+(1+r)s_2]+(1-p_3)U''[\gamma w+(1+r)s_2]\right\}].$$

Suppose now that the rate of time impatience is such that $\delta^2(1+r)^4=1$ and as assumed that $U(\cdot)$ displays constant relative risk aversion *c*, such that $\frac{U''(\cdot)}{U'}=-c$.

In this case

$$sign\left[\frac{\partial F_1}{\partial s_1}(1+r)^2\frac{\partial F_2}{\partial s_2}\right]=sign[p_3U'[w+(1+r)s_2]$$
$$+(1-p_3)U'[\gamma w+(1+r)s_2]-U'(w-s_1)].$$

Notice that $w-s_1<w+(1+r)s_2$, and from the concavity of $U(\cdot)$, for a sufficiently high $p_3$, the sign of the above expression is negative. Moreover, if $\gamma>1$, then the sign of the above equation is unambiguously negative since the first two terms are a convex combination of two terms each of which is lower than the third term in absolute value. In this case the magnitude of the probability of divorce does not matter. On the other hand, if $\gamma<1$, the sign of the equation will also be negative unless both $\gamma$ and $p_3$ are very low.

It should be noted that in reality one should expect $\delta^2(1+r)^4>1$. For this proposition to hold it is sufficient that the discount rate is relatively low (corresponding to a relatively high rate of time impatience) such that this expression is not much larger than one. **QED**

*Gender, Probability of Marriage, and Lifetime Savings* In societies with traditional gender roles men are the ones expected to make intra-marriage financial transfers to women. Therefore:

*Prediction C9′* Assume traditional gender roles, significant rates of divorce and incidence of intra-marriage transfers, and a relatively high rate of impatience. Then, an increase in the probability of marriage increases women's present value of lifetime savings and decreases men's present value of lifetime savings.

*Evidence* We have not found direct evidence for this proposition which requires data on marriage probability and on individual savings of men and women and there are very few data sets that include separate savings for husbands and wives. An exception is the South Korean data analyzed by Lee and Pocock (2007): In South Korea the government requires that each individual in a couple has his/her own savings account. However, they do not connect savings rate with marriage probability prior to marriage.

To the extent that most individuals marry, i.e., the probability of marriage is high, one expects that the individual savings rate of married women (out of their own earnings) will be higher than the individual savings rate of married men (out of their own earnings). Kim (1997) and Lee and Pocock (2007) found that married women save more than married men in South Korea. This is also the case in Kenya (Anderson and Baland 2002). Lee and Pocock also found that higher earnings of women relative to men are associated with higher savings rate.

Hungerford's (1999) analysis of individual contributions to 401(K) pension plans in the USA showed that participating women had significantly higher contribution rates to their plans than participating men. Likewise, Seguino and Floro (2003) analyzed a panel data set for semi-industrialized countries and showed that the higher women's income relative to men's the higher the country's gross domestic savings rate. However, when Phipps and Woolley (2008) examined contributions of married men and women to a "Registered Retirement Savings Plan" in Ottawa, Canada,[5] they found that an increase in male earnings had a much larger effect on a couple's total savings into this kind of retirement plan than an equivalent increase in female earnings, implying that husbands' propensity to save in this way was higher than wives. One way to reconcile the various findings is that the semi-industrialized countries examined by Seguino and Floro followed more traditional gender roles than the sample of highly educated Ottawa couples studied by Phipps and Woolley. In North America high education tends to be positively associated with egalitarian gender roles, but that is not as likely to be the case in the countries studied by Seguino and Floro (Brazil, Chile, Colombia, Costa Rica, Cyprus, El Salvador, Greece, Hong Kong, Indonesia, Korea, Malaysia, Mexico, Paraguay, Philippines, Portugal, Singapore, Sri Lanka, Taiwan, Thailand, and Turkey).

[5] This is a Canadian cousin of IRA programs in the USA.

## *Probability of Divorce and Lifetime Savings*

*Prediction C10* Lifetime savings increase (decreases) with the probability of divorce for agents expecting to be net recipients (contributors) of intra-household transfers.

**Proof:**

$$\frac{\partial s_1}{\partial p_3} = \left( \frac{\partial F_1}{\partial s_2} \cdot \frac{\partial F_2}{\partial p_3} \right) \Big/ \det(F_s), \tag{11.8}$$

$$\frac{\partial s_2}{\partial p_3} = \left( -\frac{\partial F_1}{\partial s_1} \cdot \frac{\partial F_2}{\partial p_3} \right) \Big/ \det(F_s). \tag{11.9}$$

Notice that given the results above,

$$sign\left( \frac{\partial s_1}{\partial p_3} \right) = sign\left( \frac{\partial s_2}{\partial p_3} \right) = sign\left( \frac{\partial s_2}{\partial p_3} \right),$$

which is positive if $\gamma > 1$ and negative if $\gamma < 1$.

Notice also that from (11.10) and (11.11), $-\frac{\partial F_1}{\partial s_1} > \frac{\partial F_1}{\partial s_2}$, which implies that $\frac{\partial s_1}{\partial p_3} < \frac{\partial s_2}{\partial p_3}$, i.e., the probability of divorce affecting savings behavior (negatively or positively) more at midlife than in youth. **QED**

*Gender, Probability of Divorce, and Lifetime Savings* In societies with traditional gender roles men are the ones expected to make intra-marriage financial transfers to women. Therefore

*Prediction C10′* Assume traditional gender roles and incidence of intra-marriage transfers. Then women's lifetime savings will increase with the probability of divorce and men's lifetime savings will decrease with probability of divorce.

*Evidence* It follows that if divorce is legalized (an increase in the probability of divorce), and traditional gender roles dominate, on average women will save more and men will save less. Gonzalez and Ozcan (2013) found that after divorce was legalized in Ireland, the propensity to save of married couples increased significantly, relative to singles (and to married couples in other European countries). In terms of our model, assuming traditional gender roles, this would indicate that midlife (mostly married) women's predicted response of increased savings dominated that of reduced savings on the part of midlife married men.

## Savings, Sex Ratios, Compensating Differentials, and the Price of WiHo

All the factors that could possibly shift demand or supply in markets for WiHo will also affect savings. We now examine some of the same factors that were shown to affect labor supply (Part B of this book) and could affect consumption (Chap. 10). In light of the basic model of WiHo markets presented in Chaps. 2 and 3, intra-household transfers are likely to be payments for WiHo that vary positively with the price charged by WiHo workers. In the context of traditional gender roles women tend to be WiHo workers and men the ones who pay for such work. We have examined how the price of WiHo is likely to vary with conditions in marriage markets and thereby affect labor supply (Chaps. 4 and 6), and therefore the higher the sex ratio the less women are expected to participate in the labor force while men are expected to participate more. In Chap. 10 consumption was also linked to marriage market conditions. Assuming traditional gender roles it was argued that the higher the price that men pay women in order to obtain their WiHo in marriage, the more women will be consuming relative to men. Given that the price of women's WiHo is a function of sex ratios it was predicted that when sex ratios are higher women are more likely to consume relative to men. We now apply a similar reasoning to predict sex ratio effects on savings.

### *Macro Analysis: Sex Ratio Effects*

The model used in Chap. 10 on consumption was a one-period model. Given that an analysis of savings has to consider decisions over more than one period I now integrate sex ratios in the Pereira-Grossbard model presented in the previous section. I assume that net intra-household transfer parameter $\gamma$ captures payment for WiHo. Therefore, the higher the price of WiHo the higher $\gamma$ will be. Adding traditional gender roles, it can be assumed that after marriage men pay women for their WiHo more than vice versa, implying that $\gamma$ exceeds 1 for women and is smaller than 1 for men. Therefore in marriage women's spending power exceeds their earned income while the opposite holds for men. Sex ratio effects on savings follow from a demand and supply analysis at both the macro and micro levels.

At the *macro level* it was assumed that $\gamma$, the factor capturing intra-marriage transfers, was given to all agents and the same for all men and for all women. Sex ratios can be integrated using the following steps: (a) $\gamma$ affects the savings rate of men and women at different stages in their lives; (b) $\gamma$ varies positively with the price of women's WiHo; and (c) higher sex ratios are associated with a higher price for women's WiHo. It follows that at every stage in life the contrast between men and women will be more pronounced if sex ratios are higher. Comparing across countries or periods differing in sex ratio it follows that:

*Prediction C11* A higher sex ratio is expected to be associated with a higher savings rate among young single men and a lower savings rate among young single women.

*Prediction C12* A higher sex ratio is expected to be associated with a lower savings rate among married men in midlife and a higher savings rate among married women in midlife.

The effect of sex ratios on net aggregate savings will depend on which of these four effects predominate.

*Evidence* Shang-Jin Wei and Xiaobo Zhang (2011) have investigated recent changes in China's household savings as a function of the increasingly high sex ratio that China has been experiencing since male births have become an increasing proportion of all Chinese births. The sex ratio at birth in China climbed from 1.06 in 1980 (with 106 boys per 100 girls) to 1.27 in 2007, implying men outnumbering women at age 25 or below by at least 30 million. They found that increases in sex ratios account for about half of the observed increase in Chinese household savings in recent years.

With Qingyuan Du, Wei also provided cross-sectional macro evidence based on data for 159 countries for the years 1990–2010 (Du and Wei 2013). They computed sex ratios as the number of boys and men ages 10–24 divided by the number of girls and women in the same age group, and found that the more sex ratios diverge from 1 either positively or negatively the higher the savings rates. In addition, if the sex ratio is smaller than 1, i.e., there is a *shortage* of men in marriage markets, the savings rate is significantly higher. In addition, Wei and Zhang (2011) show that across Chinese provinces there was a strong positive correlation between local savings rates and local sex ratios, controlling for the age structure of local population, per capita income, the share of employment in state-owned firms in the local labor force, and the share of local labor force enrolled in social security. They estimate that 40–60 % of the rise in China's household savings rate from 1990 to 2007 can be attributed to the rise in the sex ratio for the premarital age cohort.

Both the cross-sectional evidence and the comparisons over time support Prediction C11 to the extent that changes in savings by young men (and boys and their families) dominate changes for other gender and age groups. They find support for Prediction C11 if we add "or their parents" after young men and young women in Prediction C11. In addition, Du and Wei find that in countries where the sex ratio is unusually low, savings rates are also higher, a finding that they cannot explain.

Wei and Zhang (2011) and Du and Wei (2013) interpret their own findings of a positive relationship between savings rates and sex ratios as evidence that there is a competitive savings motive. What they call "the competitive savings motive" overlaps to a large extent with the basic arguments presented in this book, since marriage-related prices are established as a result of competition. Wei, his coauthors, and I all predict that when there is an excess number of men in the marriage market, young men (or their parents) will have to compete more to find a wife and that this will lead men and their parents to save more. We all have the following steps in our reasoning: excess men in marriage market ➔ more competition among men (+ their relatives) ➔ men (+ their relatives) save more. We all recognize that prices in marriage markets play a role: the funds that men save are meant to pay for a wife. However, there also is a fundamental difference in our interpretations.

To Wei and coauthors prices are paid before marriage, and mostly by parents. In contrast, Pereira and I model preparation for marriage (in period 1 in the model presented in the previous section) by young people themselves. For example, comparing two Chinese regions with different sex ratios Wei and Zhang (2011, p. 525) write: "The expectation for how much the parents (or the sons) need to contribute to their son's new household, given costs of housing, cars, furniture, or honeymoons, would differ in the two regions. The types of furniture, cars, and honeymoons, and local housing prices may reflect the degree of competition in a local marriage market and thus affect the savings required of parents with a son." Anthropologists call prices paid prior to marriage "brideprice" (when men or their families pay) and "dowry" (when women or their families pay).[6] Brideprice tends to be paid in societies that restrict women's access to resources after marriage.[7]

The models by Wei and coauthors and those presented here all give a primary role to competition in marriage markets. They mostly view competition by parents outbidding each other in the form of expensive premarital promises. In contrast, in the model presented here, competition occurs in WiHo markets. Men need to save so they can afford future payments $(1-\gamma)$ $w$ to their wives. Women and their families save less because they know that after marriage women can capture their market value in the form of intra-marriage transfers in return for the WiHo they supply. The higher the sex ratio in a marriage market, the higher the price for women's WiHo, the more net intra-household transfers women can expect after marriage and the less they and their families need to save in youth. Would I test my predictions on sex ratio and savings I would not calculate sex ratios for ages 10–24, placing the emphasis on parental savings but for ages at which young adults usually form couples. The sex ratio predictions regarding labor supply that were tested and discussed in Part B of this book included individuals in their 20s. When calculating sex ratios to estimate their effects on labor supply I also assumed that men were slightly older than women. This indicates that who competes and how is a question that has important empirical ramifications.

Furthermore, the emphasis that Wei and coauthors place on premarital payments appears to be more applicable in the context of China and other societies that place enormous restrictions on women's freedom to deal with financial matters than in the context of Western European or North American societies that lifted such restrictions decades ago. For instance, according to Leta Hong Fincher (2014) overwhelming social and regulatory obstacles to women's property ownership in China created stark new gender inequalities in wealth. Although the shortage of women in

[6] A useful survey of the economic literature on this topic was published by Siwan Anderson (2007).

[7] Wei and Zhang (2011) also assert that the parents of daughters may save more, not less, even if the sex ratio is greater than one. The reason is that, although such parents may not need to save as much for their child's marriage, they need to save more for old age because daughters are less likely than sons to help their parents during old age, especially if they have to move away after marriage to live with her husband's family (see pp. 528–529).

China theoretically ought to give them the upper hand in the marriage market, deeply entrenched patriarchal norms combined with intense pressure to marry and buy a home have caused many women to believe that they have little bargaining power in marriage. For many reasons, university-educated women in their 20s are often so anxious to marry that they succumb to pressure from the man's family to leave their names off the marital property deed, even when the women have contributed their life savings to finance the purchase of the home. In addition, Chinese parents tend to buy homes for their sons rather than their daughters. As a result, most residential property in China belongs solely to men.

The institution of brideprice in China and elsewhere is rooted in restrictions on women's control over their own lives after they marry. Based on Becker (1981), I have written this on brideprice and dowry payments: "Such transfer payments at marriage originate from rigid rules regarding compensation levels for WiHo [spousal labor] after marriage. If elements of the price for women's WiHo [women's compensations for spousal labor] are fixed by law or tradition, individual variations in payments for that WiHo [spousal compensations] after marriage will be limited. Consequently, one may find transfers negotiated prior to marriage that capture some of the positive or negative differences between the net compensation for women's WiHo [spousal labor] set by law and the value of such compensation, had market-clearing WiHo prices been allowed to operate." (Grossbard-Shechtman 1993).

Within the context of three Asian societies, China, Korea, and India, Horioka and Terada-Hagiwara (2014) find that the premarriage-age sex ratio has a positive impact on the household saving rate in Korea where (as in China) the custom is for the groom's side to pay a brideprice to the bride's side. However, they find that in India, where the dominant custom is for the bride's side to pay a dowry to the groom's side, the premarriage-age sex ratio has a negative impact on the household saving rate.[8] This suggests that in India the larger the excess number of women and girls in a particular marriage market (and therefore the lower the sex ratio) the more parents save. Overall there is a shortage of women in India, as is the case in Korea and China, but within the higher social classes practising dowry there often is a shortage of grooms given that women in higher classes are strongly discouraged from marrying men from lower social classes while the same restriction does not apply to the same degree to men. The higher the overall sex ratio the less competition there will be for grooms for higher class women and the less there is need for the parents of girls to save for dowries.

For a competitive marriage market theory of savings to be more inclusive it has to be adapted to Western countries where women typically capture the value of their WiHo as well as to countries such as China that have institutional restrictions preventing women from obtaining intra-marriage transfers in line with their value in WiHo markets.

[8] See Bronfenbrenner (1971) on the co-existence of brideprice and dowry in India and Grossbard-Shechtman (1993) on how asymmetric marriage rules in India and pre-revolutionary France can help explain the existence of dowries in higher classes.

*Competitive Savings Motive?* As pointed out in Chap. 1 the term "competitive savings motive" is problematic as it does not specify that the competition is in marriage markets. It is more logical to call this savings motive a "marriage motive." Parental savings for the sake of marrying children have been analyzed at least since Horioka (1987, 1997). Horioka found that a substantial proportion of Japanese households save for their children's marriage expenses, especially as their children reach marriageable age. Horioka et al. (2000) found that that saving for (one's children's) marriage is far more important in Japan than in the USA.

## *Micro Analysis of Savings and Markets for WiHo*

I now return to the micro-level model of Chap. 3 considering multiple types of men and women who may marry each other. Accordingly, there are multiple markets for WiHo defined by individual characteristics of men and women and in each market an equilibrium price of WiHo, $y_{ij}$, and quantity of WiHo, $h_{ij}$, is established. In turn, price $y_{ij}$ and quantity $h_{ij}$ are associated with the typical WiHo worker's earnings in that market, amounting to transfer $\gamma_{ij} w_{ij}$ in light of the Pereira-Grossbard model presented earlier in this chapter. The value of that $\gamma_{ij}$ will vary over time and across marriage submarkets depending on individual male and female characteristics. If both men and women engage in WiHo the analysis is more complex, so for simplicity I return to the old-fashioned assumption that only women get paid for WiHo.

The higher $\gamma_{ij}$ paid after marriage the less single women will save and the more single men will save (Prediction C7″), and the more midlife women will save and the less midlife men will save (Prediction C8″). In line with previous analyses of the determinants of the market price of WiHo presented in the chapters on labor supply and consumption, WiHo prices and savings rates will also be affected by the following factors: factors influencing WiHo productivity (such as age) and compensating differentials in marriage (related to characteristics of men in societies following traditional gender roles).

*Factors Associated with the Productivity of WiHo Workers* As discussed in previous Chaps. 4, 6, and 10, individuals with higher human capital are likely to get paid more for their WiHo work. They will therefore benefit from a higher net intra-household transfer parameter $\gamma$. Assuming traditional gender roles and that women's reproductive capacity is valued, it follows that young women with a healthier appearance—often associated with higher fecundity—will obtain a higher price for their WiHo and therefore get a higher $\gamma$ relative to women with a more sickly appearance. It follows that:

*Prediction C13* Healthy-looking single women will save less than women with a more sickly appearance. Men who intend to marry healthy-looking women will need to save more. After marriage it is predicted that healthy-looking women will save more than their less attractive counterparts and the men who marry them will save less.

Kureishi and Wakabayashi (2013) did not have information on healthy looks but they could estimate probability that a single woman marries, and this is likely to be positively related to unmeasured looks. They found that the more a woman was likely to marry, the less she saved.

Any characteristic affecting productivity in WiHo is expected to also affect the savings rate of men and women due to their effect on $\gamma$. More educated women may also be more productive at WiHo but they may also earn more in labor markets. Therefore, the net predicted effect of women's education on their savings rate while young and unmarried is not clear. I also expect that women without previous marriages will get paid more for their WiHo and therefore will save less while unmarried relative to women with previous marriages. Furthermore, in societies with racial or religious prejudices women belonging to the higher status communities may get a higher price for their WiHo and therefore a higher net intra-household transfer parameter $\gamma$. If light-skinned women are more in demand in markets for women's WiHo relative to women with dark skin (see Hamilton et al. 2009 for a study of shade of black effects on likelihood of marriage) *ceteris paribus* the savings rates of young light-skinned women will be lower than those of darker-skinned women. Conversely, men preparing themselves to marry light-skinned women will have to save more than men interested in marrying dark-skinned women.

*Compensating Differentials* Compensating differentials in marriage markets were associated with labor supply (Chap. 5) and consumption of married men and women (Chap. 10). If certain types of men with a demand for WiHo are considered less attractive by women, marriage market analysis implies that they will have to pay higher prices to get women's WiHo. This will lead to a higher $\gamma$ and consequently more savings by men preparing for marriage and by women in midlife as well as fewer savings by married men (at midlife) and young single women. Applying this to the example of older men who, competing with younger men in the same marriage markets, have to compensate for being substantially older than the women they would like to marry (see Chaps. 5 and 10) it follows that:

*Prediction C14* Relative to men and women of similar age, men who are substantially older than the women they court or marry will save more prior to marriage (as they compete with large numbers of younger men) and they will save less after marriage (as they need to continue to pay large compensations for their wife's WiHo). In contrast, women willing to marry older men (or married to them) will save less before marriage and more after marriage

*Some Institutional Considerations* Furthermore, at a macro level, age differences at marriage vary widely across the globe (see Grossbard-Shechtman 1993). The more common it is that older men compete with younger men for the same women, the more this is likely to cause competition among men seeking mates (including wives, mistresses, and girlfriends). The more competition, the more men will save to be more successful in courting and keeping the women they want to form couples with. However, to the extent that (1) men exit the marriage market and stay in the couples they formed and (2) women in couples have access to their value in marriage markets after marriage, individual women will save more and individual men, including older men, will save less.

Following the same reasoning, asymmetric *polygamy,* allowing men to take multiple wives but not allowing women to marry more than one husband, is also expected to lead to higher WiHo prices and higher $\gamma$. Therefore, compared to monogamy, polygamy is likely to be associated with higher savings rates among men preparing for marriage (which in this case would include most men) and lower savings rates among women preparing for marriage.

In Grossbard-Shechtman (1993) and Grossbard (2014), I elaborated on an idea first developed by Guttentag and Secord (1983), namely that men in polygamous societies have more reasons to reduce women's rights and freedom so that women are less likely to capture their high value in markets for WiHo. Using the same argument, older wealthy men in monogamous societies with high levels of wealth concentration will also try to find ways to reduce young women's access to wealth and their opportunities of capturing their market value in marriage, a value likely to be high if men of all ages compete for the same young women.

A marriage market analysis of savings could also include discussions of other factors that were mentioned in Chaps. 5 and 10, such as the income of potential spouses participating in the same marriage markets and technology influencing home production.

## Conclusions

First, this chapter presents an inter-temporal model of personal savings with uncertainty about marriage and divorce and intra-marriage financial transfers. We find that the likelihood of marriage and of divorce and the expectation of being a net contributor or recipient of intra-marriage transfers may be important determinants of individual savings behavior. The predicted effect of marriage or divorce is conditional to whether agents expect to receive or pay intra-marriage financial distributions. As a result and given gender differences on who does the WiHo work in couples, we get different predictions for men and women depending on whether they are at the premarital stage or already in couple.

Second, this chapter ties in with previous chapters on labor supply and consumption. Sex ratio effects on savings are derived based on the market analyses of marriage that were presented in previous chapters. They help interpret interesting recent findings on sex ratio effects on savings. Predictions regarding WiHo productivity effects on savings and compensating differentials in marriage effects have also been derived.

# Appendix

The determinant of the Jacobian matrix of the first-order conditions with respect to $s_1$ and $s_2$ is positive, i.e., $Det(F_s) > 0$. This is a direct requirement of the optimization problem in that it relates to the strict concavity of the objective function with respect to the decision variables and satisfies the conditions of the implicit function theorem. To obtain the necessary information for the identification of the effects on savings behavior we totally differentiate $F_1$ and $F_2$ to obtain:

$$\frac{\partial F_1}{\partial s_1} = U''(w - s_1) + \delta(1+r)^2 \{p_2 U''[w+(1+r)s_1 - s_2] + (1-p_2)U''[\gamma w + (1+r)s_1 - s_2]\} < 0, \tag{11.10}$$

$$\frac{\partial F_1}{\partial s_2} = -\delta(1+r)\{p_2 U''[w+1(1+r)s_1 - s_2] + (1-p_2)U''[\gamma w + (1+r)s_1 - s_2]\} > 0, \tag{11.11}$$

or using (11.10)

$$-\frac{\partial F_1}{\partial s_1} = -U''(w - s_1) + (1+r)\frac{\partial F_1}{\partial s_2} > \frac{\partial F_1}{\partial s_2}, \tag{11.12}$$

$$\frac{\partial F_1}{\partial p_2} = \delta(1+r)\{U'[w+(1+r)s_1 - s_2] - U'[\gamma w + (1+r)s_1 - s_2]\} > 0 \; if \, \gamma > 1 (< 0 \; if \, \gamma < 1), \tag{11.13}$$

$$\frac{\partial F_1}{\partial p_3} = 0, \tag{11.14}$$

$$\frac{\partial F_2}{\partial S_1} = \frac{\partial F_1}{\partial S_2} = -\delta(1+r) \{p_2 U''[w+(1+r)s_1 - s_2] + (1-p_2)U''[\gamma w + (1+r)s_1 - s_2]\} > 0, \tag{11.15}$$

$$\frac{\partial F_2}{\partial S_2} = \delta\{p_2 U''[w+(1+r)s_1 - s_2] + (1-p_2)U''[\gamma w + (1+r)s_1 - s_2]\} + \delta^2(1+r)^2 \{p_3 U''[w+(1+r)s_2] + (1-p_3)U''[\gamma w + (1+r)s_2]\} = -\frac{1}{1+r}\cdot\frac{\partial F_1}{\partial S_2} + \delta^2(1+r)^2 \{p_3 U''[w+(1+r)s_2] + (1-p_3)U''[\gamma w + (1+r)s_2]\} < 0, \tag{11.16}$$

or using (11.10), (11.11), and (11.16)

$$\frac{\partial F_2}{\partial S_2} = -\frac{1}{(1+r)^2} \cdot \left[ U''(w-s_1) - \frac{\partial F_2}{\partial S_2} \right] + \delta^2 (1+r)^2 \left\{ p_3 U''[w+(1+r)s_2] + (1-p_3) U''[\gamma w + (1+r)s_2] \right\} < 0, \quad (11.17)$$

where given (11.10) the first term has a negative sign.

$$\frac{\partial F_2}{\partial p_2} = -\delta \{ U'[w+(1+r)s_1 - s_2] - U'[\gamma w + (1+r)s_1 - s_2] \} < 0 \; if \; \gamma > 1 (> 0 \; if \; \gamma < 1). \quad (11.18)$$

From (11.13) and (11.18) it follows that $\frac{\partial F_1}{\partial p_2} = -(1+r)\frac{\partial F_2}{\partial p_2}$ and these two derivatives will always have the opposite sign regardless of $\gamma$.

$$\frac{\partial F_2}{\partial p_3} = \delta^2 \{ U'[w+(1+r)s_2] - U'[\gamma w + (1+r)s_2] \} > 0 \; if \; \gamma > 1 (< 0 \; if \; \gamma < 1). \quad (11.19)$$

## References


Anderson, Siwan, and Jean-Marie Baland. 2002. The economics of roscas and intrahousehold resource allocation. *Quarterly Journal of Economics* 117 (3):963–995.

Apps, Patricia, and Ray Rees. 2010. Family labor supply, taxation and saving in an imperfect capital market. *Review of Economics of the Household* 8:297–324.

Auerbach, Alan J., and Lawrence J. Kotlikoff. 1990. Demographics, fiscal policy, and U.S. savings in the 1980s and beyond. In *Tax policy and the economy,* ed. Lawrence. H. Summers, 4 vol. Cambridge: MIT Press.

Becker, Gary S. 1981. *A treatise on the family*. Cambridge: Harvard University Press.

Bronfenbrenner, Martin. 1971. A note on the economics of the marriage market. *Journal of Political Economy* 79:1424–1425.

Croson, Rachel, and Gneezy Uri. 2009. Gender differences in preferences. *Journal of Economic literature* 47:448–474.

Du, Qingyuan, and Shang-Jin Wei. 2013. A theory of competitive saving motive. *Journal of International Economics* 91:275–289.

Fincher, Leta Hong. 2014. *Leftover women: The resurgence of gender inequality in China*. London: Zed Books.

Gonzales, Libertad, and Berkay, Ozcan. 2013. The risk of divorce and household saving behavior. *Journal of Human Resources* 48 (2): 404–434.

Grossbard, Shoshana. 2014. Polygamy and the regulation of marriage markets. In *The polygamy question,* ed. J. Bennion and L. F. Joffe. Logan: Utah State University Press.

Grossbard-Shechtman, Shoshana. 1993. *On the economics of marriage*. Boulder: Westview.

Guidolin, Massimo, and Elizabeth A. La Jeunesse. 2007. The decline in the US personal savings rate: Is it real and is it a puzzle? *Federal Reserve Bank of St. Louis Review* 89 (6): 491–514.

Guttentag, Marcia, and Paul F. Secord. 1983. *Too many women: The sex ratio question*. Beverly Hills: Sage.

Hamilton, D, A. Goldsmith, and W. A. Darity Jr. 2009. Shedding 'light' on marriage: The influence of skin shade on marriage of black females. *Journal of Economic Behavior and Organization* 72:30–50.

Hendry, Joy. 1985. Marriage in a recently industrialized society: Japan. In *Contemporary marriage: Comparative perspectives on a changing institution,* ed. K. Davis and A. Grossbard-Shechtman. New York: Russell Sage.
Horioka, Charles Yuji. 1987. The cost of marriages and marriage-related saving in Japan. *Kyoto University Economic Review* 57 (1): 47–58.
Horioka, Charles Yuji. 1997. A cointegration analysis of the impact of the age structure of the population on the household saving rate in Japan. *Review of Economics and Statistics* 79 (3): 511–516.
Horioka, Charles Yuji and Wan. Junmin. 2007. The determinants of household saving in China: A dynamic panel analysis of provincial data. *Journal of Money, Credit and Banking* 39 (8): 2077–2096.
Horioka, Charles Yuji, and Akiko Terada-Hagiwara. 2010. *Sources and prospects for Asia's growth: Saving rate*. Philippines: Mimeo. Asian Development Bank.
Horioka, Charles Yuji, and Akiko Terada-Hagiwara. 2014. *The impact of the gender ratio on the household saving rate in India and Korea*. Philippines: Mimeo. Asian Development Bank.
Horioka, Charle Yuji, Hideki Fujisaki, Wako Watanabe, and Takatsugu Kouno. 2000. Are Americans more altruistic than the Japanese? A U.S.-Japan comparison of saving and bequest motives. *International Economic Journal* 14 (1): 1–31.
Hungerford, T. 1999. Savings for a rainy day: *Does pre-retirement access to retirement savings increase retirement savings?* Mimeo (Washington, DC, Social Security Administration).
Hungerford, T. 2006. Savings incentives: What may work, what may not. Congressional research service report. http://www.policyarchive.org/handle/10207/bitstreams/2867.pdf.
Kim, S.-K. 1997. *Class struggle or family struggle?: The lives of women factory workers in South Korea.* Cambridge: Cambridge University Press.
Kureishi, Wataru, and Midori Wakabayashi. 2013. What motivates single women to save? The case of Japan. *Review of Economics of the Household* 11:681–704.
Lee, Jungmin, and Mark Pocock. 2007. Intrahousehold allocation of household finances. *Review of Economics of the Household* 5 (1): 41–58.
Lupton, Joseph P., and James P. Smith. 2003. Marriage, assets, and savings. In *Marriage and the Economy,* ed. S. Grossbard-Shechtman. New York: Cambridge University Press.
Phipps, Shelley, and Woolley, Frances. 2008. Control over money and the savings decisions of Canadian households. *Journal of Behavioral and Experimental Economics (formerly The Journal of Socio-Economics)* 37 (2): 592–611.
Seguino, Stephanie, and Maria S. Floro. 2003. Does gender have any effect on aggregate savings? An empirical analysis. *International Review of Applied Economics* 17 (2):147–166.
Smith, Roger S. 1990. Factors affecting savings, policy tools, and tax reform: A review. *International Monetary Fund Staff Paper* 37 (1):1–70.
Tanzi, Vito, and Howell Zee. 1999. Taxation and the household savings rate: Evidence from OECD countries, International Monetary Fund. Working Paper 98/36.
Wei, Shan-Jin, and Xiaobo Zhang. 2011. The competitive savings motive: Evidence from rising sex ratios and savings rates in China. *Journal of Political Economy* 119 (3): 511–564.
Zissimopoulos, Julie, Benjamin Karney, and Amy Rauer. 2015. Marriage and economic well-being at older ages. *Review of Economics of the Household* 13(1). (Forthcoming)

MIX
Papier aus verantwortungsvollen Quellen
Paper from responsible sources
FSC® C105338

If you have any concerns about our products, you can contact us on
**ProductSafety@springernature.com**

In case Publisher is established outside the EU, the EU authorized representative is:
**Springer Nature Customer Service Center GmbH**
**Europaplatz 3, 69115 Heidelberg, Germany**

Printed by Libri Plureos GmbH
in Hamburg, Germany